Computer Networking

Computer Networking

Edited by
Paxton Byrne

Larsen & Keller
www.larsen-keller.com

Computer Networking
Edited by Paxton Byrne
ISBN: 978-1-63549-159-3 (Hardback)

© 2017 Larsen & Keller

 Larsen & Keller

Published by Larsen and Keller Education,
5 Penn Plaza,
19th Floor,
New York, NY 10001, USA

Cataloging-in-Publication Data

Computer networking / edited by Paxton Byrne.
   p. cm.
Includes bibliographical references and index.
ISBN 978-1-63549-159-3
   1. Computer networks. 2. Computer network protocols.
3. Computer network resources.
I. Byrne, Paxton.
TK5105.5 .C67 2017
004.6--dc23

The publisher's policy is to use permanent paper from mills that operate a sustainable forestry policy. Furthermore, the publisher ensures that the text paper and cover boards used have met acceptable environmental accreditation standards.

Printed and bound in the United States of America.

For more information regarding Larsen and Keller Education and its products, please visit the publisher's website www.larsen-keller.com

Table of Contents

Preface

This book elucidates the concepts and innovative models around prospective developments with respect to computer networking. It elucidates the various theories and techniques of this field. Computer networking refers to the science that enables computers to share data and information. It is a telecommunications network which uses a data-link system to let computers connect. These networks are used in digital audio and video, printers, World Wide Web, email, fax machines and instant messaging. The topics introduced in this text cover new techniques and the applications of computer networking. It unfolds the innovative aspects of this area, which will be crucial for the holistic understanding of the subject matter. The textbook is appropriate for those seeking detailed information in this field and will serve as a reference to a broad spectrum of readers.

To facilitate a deeper understanding of the contents of this book a short introduction of every chapter is written below:

Chapter 1- The exchange of data that occurs between computers is known as computer networks. The finest computer network is the Internet. Computer networks are used in major parts of the world and help in telecommunication facilities. This chapter provides the reader with a fascinating explanation on computer networking.

Chapter 2- Computer networks are set up with a view to permit transmission of data within a parameter and transmission protocols are created with a view of the same. Some common architectures of computer networks are personal area network, local area network, campus network and wide area network. All these topics as well as others have been included in this chapter.

Chapter 3- There are various elements involved in computer networking, such as network links and network nodes. The arrangement of these elements is termed as network topology. Some of the classifications of network topology are ring network, bus network, star network and mesh networking. This section is an overview of the subject matter incorporating all the major aspects of network topology.

Chapter 4- Packet switching is a technique by which all the data of networking communications are collected and grouped into blocks which are incidentally referred to as packets. The various packet switched networks are ARPANET, CYCLADES and IPSANET. This text provides the reader with an integrated understanding of packet switching.

Chapter 5- The Internet protocol suite or TCP/IP is the abstract model on which the Internet functions. It is mainly used in protocols, and specifies how data should be grouped, directed and then received. Some of the key principles of Internet protocol suite are also elucidated in this chapter, such as End- to- end principle and robustness principle.

Chapter 6- Network nodes are either the sending, receiving or redirecting processes as well as devices of a computer network. The nature of the data and its reception and transmission differs in each aspect of network nodes. This chapter discusses the basic processes related to nodes and the hardware related to them.

Chapter 7- Routing can be defined as the hardware and software that enable the transmission and distribution of data. It is a networking device that allows for the connection of a device to a network by navigating through various existing networks. The themes in this chapter describe the concepts, processes and technology that is used in routing.

Chapter 8- Fast local Internet protocol specifies security transparency and security and routing protocols helps in the communication of routers. The various network protocols discussed in this section are fast local Internet protocol, routing protocol, HTTPS, datagram congestion control protocol and point-to-point protocol.

Chapter 9- Network sockets are endpoints that connect computer networks whereas encapsulation is a process of designing modular communications. Other aspects of computer networking are circuit switching and routing. The following chapter unfolds its crucial aspects in a critical yet systematic manner.

Chapter 10- Computer networking has a history spanning to many decades. It began in the late 1950s and since then has made enormous progress. The history discussed in the following text is of great importance to broaden the existing knowledge on computer networking.

Finally, I would like to thank the entire team involved in the inception of this book for their valuable time and contribution. This book would not have been possible without their efforts. I would also like to thank my friends and family for their constant support.

Editor

Introduction to Computer Networking

The exchange of data that occurs between computers is known as computer networks. The finest computer network is the Internet. Computer networks are used in major parts of the world and help in telecommunication facilities. This chapter provides the reader with a fascinating explanation on computer networking.

A computer network or data network is a telecommunications network which allows computers to exchange data. In computer networks, networked computing devices exchange data with each other using a data link. The connections between nodes are established using either cable media or wireless media. The best-known computer network is the Internet.

Network computer devices that originate, route and terminate the data are called network nodes. Nodes can include hosts such as personal computers, phones, servers as well as networking hardware. Two such devices can be said to be networked together when one device is able to exchange information with the other device, whether or not they have a direct connection to each other.

Computer networks differ in the transmission medium used to carry their signals, communications protocols to organize network traffic, the network's size, topology and organizational intent.

Computer networks support an enormous number of applications and services such as access to the World Wide Web, digital video, digital audio, shared use of application and storage servers, printers, and fax machines, and use of email and instant messaging applications as well as many others. In most cases, application-specific communications protocols are layered (i.e. carried as payload) over other more general communications protocols.

History

The chronology of significant computer-network developments includes:

- In the late 1950s, early networks of computers included the military radar system Semi-Automatic Ground Environment (SAGE).

- In 1959, Anatolii Ivanovich Kitov proposed to the Central Committee of the Communist Party of the Soviet Union a detailed plan for the re-organisation of the control of the Soviet armed forces and of the Soviet economy on the basis of a network of computing centres.

- In 1960, the commercial airline reservation system semi-automatic business research environment (SABRE) went online with two connected mainframes.

- In 1962, J.C.R. Licklider developed a working group he called the "Intergalactic Computer Network", a precursor to the ARPANET, at the Advanced Research Projects Agency (ARPA).

- In 1964, researchers at Dartmouth College developed the Dartmouth Time Sharing System for distributed users of large computer systems. The same year, at Massachusetts Institute of Technology, a research group supported by General Electric and Bell Labs used a computer to route and manage telephone connections.

- Throughout the 1960s, Leonard Kleinrock, Paul Baran, and Donald Davies independently developed network systems that used packets to transfer information between computers over a network.

- In 1965, Thomas Marill and Lawrence G. Roberts created the first wide area network (WAN). This was an immediate precursor to the ARPANET, of which Roberts became program manager.

- Also in 1965, Western Electric introduced the first widely used telephone switch that implemented true computer control.

- In 1969, the University of California at Los Angeles, the Stanford Research Institute, the University of California at Santa Barbara, and the University of Utah became connected as the beginning of the ARPANET network using 50 kbit/s circuits.

- In 1972, commercial services using X.25 were deployed, and later used as an underlying infrastructure for expanding TCP/IP networks.

- In 1973, Robert Metcalfe wrote a formal memo at Xerox PARC describing Ethernet, a networking system that was based on the Aloha network, developed in the 1960s by Norman Abramson and colleagues at the University of Hawaii. In July 1976, Robert Metcalfe and David Boggs published their paper "Ethernet: Distributed Packet Switching for Local Computer Networks" and collaborated on several patents received in 1977 and 1978. In 1979, Robert Metcalfe pursued making Ethernet an open standard.

- In 1976, John Murphy of Datapoint Corporation created ARCNET, a token-passing network first used to share storage devices.

- In 1995, the transmission speed capacity for Ethernet increased from 10 Mbit/s to 100 Mbit/s. By 1998, Ethernet supported transmission speeds of a Gigabit. Subsequently, higher speeds of up to 100 Gbit/s were added (as of 2016). The ability of Ethernet to scale easily (such as quickly adapting to support new fiber optic cable speeds) is a contributing factor to its continued use.

Properties

Computer networking may be considered a branch of electrical engineering, telecommunications, computer science, information technology or computer engineering, since it relies upon the theoretical and practical application of the related disciplines.

A computer network facilitates interpersonal communications allowing users to communicate efficiently and easily via various means: email, instant messaging, chat rooms, telephone, video telephone calls, and video conferencing. Providing access to information on shared storage devices is an important feature of many networks. A network allows sharing of files, data, and other types of information giving authorized users the ability to access information stored on other computers on the network. A network allows sharing of network and computing resources. Users may access and use resources provided by devices on the network, such as printing a document on a shared network printer. Distributed computing uses computing resources across a network to accomplish tasks. A computer network may be used by computer crackers to deploy computer viruses or computer worms on devices connected to the network, or to prevent these devices from accessing the network via a denial of service attack.

Network Packet

Computer communication links that do not support packets, such as traditional point-to-point telecommunication links, simply transmit data as a bit stream. However, most information in computer networks is carried in *packets*. A network packet is a formatted unit of data (a list of bits or bytes, usually a few tens of bytes to a few kilobytes long) carried by a packet-switched network.

In packet networks, the data is formatted into packets that are sent through the network to their destination. Once the packets arrive they are reassembled into their original message. With packets, the bandwidth of the transmission medium can be better shared among users than if the network were circuit switched. When one user is not sending packets, the link can be filled with packets from other users, and so the cost can be shared, with relatively little interference, provided the link isn't overused.

Packets consist of two kinds of data: control information, and user data (payload). The control information provides data the network needs to deliver the user data, for example: source and destination network addresses, error detection codes, and sequencing information. Typically, control information is found in packet headers and trailers, with payload data in between.

Often the route a packet needs to take through a network is not immediately available. In that case the packet is queued and waits until a link is free.

Network Topology

The physical layout of a network is usually less important than the topology that connects network nodes. Most diagrams that describe a physical network are therefore topological, rather than geographic. The symbols on these diagrams usually denote network links and network nodes.

Network Links

The transmission media (often referred to in the literature as the *physical media*) used to link devices to form a computer network include electrical cable (Ethernet, HomePNA, power line communication, G.hn), optical fiber (fiber-optic communication), and radio waves (wireless networking). In the OSI model, these are defined at layers 1 and 2 — the physical layer and the data link layer.

A widely adopted *family* of transmission media used in local area network (LAN) technology is collectively known as Ethernet. The media and protocol standards that enable communication between networked devices over Ethernet are defined by IEEE 802.3. Ethernet transmits data over both copper and fiber cables. Wireless LAN standards (e.g. those defined by IEEE 802.11) use radio waves, or others use infrared signals as a transmission medium. Power line communication uses a building's power cabling to transmit data.

Wired Technologies

Fiber optic cables are used to transmit light from one computer/network node to another

The orders of the following wired technologies are, roughly, from slowest to fastest transmission speed.

- *Coaxial cable* is widely used for cable television systems, office buildings, and other work-sites for local area networks. The cables consist of copper or aluminum wire surrounded by an insulating layer (typically a flexible material with a high dielectric constant), which itself is surrounded by a conductive layer. The insulation helps minimize interference and distortion. Transmission speed ranges from 200 million bits per second to more than 500 million bits per second.

- ITU-T G.hn technology uses existing home wiring (coaxial cable, phone lines and power lines) to create a high-speed (up to 1 Gigabit/s) local area network

- *Twisted pair wire* is the most widely used medium for all telecommunication. Twisted-pair cabling consist of copper wires that are twisted into pairs. Ordinary telephone wires consist of two insulated copper wires twisted into pairs. Computer network cabling (wired Ethernet as defined by IEEE 802.3) consists of 4 pairs of copper cabling that can be utilized for both voice and data transmission. The use of two wires twisted together helps to reduce crosstalk and electromagnetic induction. The transmission speed ranges from 2 million bits per second to 10 billion bits per second. Twisted pair cabling comes in two forms: unshielded twisted pair (UTP) and shielded twisted-pair (STP). Each form comes in several category ratings, designed for use in various scenarios.

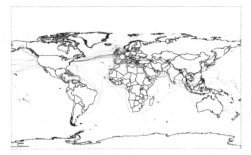

2007 map showing submarine optical fiber telecommunication cables around the world.

- An *optical fiber* is a glass fiber. It carries pulses of light that represent data. Some advantages of optical fibers over metal wires are very low transmission loss and immunity from electrical interference. Optical fibers can simultaneously carry multiple wavelengths of light, which greatly increases the rate that data can be sent, and helps enable data rates of up to trillions of bits per second. Optic fibers can be used for long runs of cable carrying very high data rates, and are used for undersea cables to interconnect continents.

Price is a main factor distinguishing wired- and wireless-technology options in a business. Wireless options command a price premium that can make purchasing wired computers, printers and other devices a financial benefit. Before making the decision to purchase hard-wired technology products, a review of the restrictions and limitations of the selections is necessary. Business and employee needs may override any cost considerations.

Wireless Technologies

Computers are very often connected to networks using wireless links

- *Terrestrial microwave* – Terrestrial microwave communication uses Earth-based transmitters and receivers resembling satellite dishes. Terrestrial microwaves are in the low-gigahertz range, which limits all communications to line-of-sight. Relay stations are spaced approximately 48 km (30 mi) apart.

- *Communications satellites* – Satellites communicate via microwave radio waves, which are not deflected by the Earth›s atmosphere. The satellites are stationed in space, typically in geosynchronous orbit 35,400 km (22,000 mi) above the equator. These Earth-orbiting systems are capable of receiving and relaying voice, data, and TV signals.

- *Cellular and PCS systems* use several radio communications technologies. The systems divide the region covered into multiple geographic areas. Each area has a low-power transmitter or radio relay antenna device to relay calls from one area to the next area.

- *Radio and spread spectrum technologies* – Wireless local area networks use a high-frequency radio technology similar to digital cellular and a low-frequency radio technology. Wireless LANs use spread spectrum technology to enable communication between multiple devices in a limited area. IEEE 802.11 defines a common flavor of open-standards wireless radio-wave technology known as Wifi.

- *Free-space optical communication* uses visible or invisible light for communications. In most cases, line-of-sight propagation is used, which limits the physical positioning of communicating devices.

Exotic Technologies

There have been various attempts at transporting data over exotic media:

- IP over Avian Carriers was a humorous April fool's Request for Comments, issued as RFC 1149. It was implemented in real life in 2001.

- Extending the Internet to interplanetary dimensions via radio waves, the Interplanetary Internet.

Both cases have a large round-trip delay time, which gives slow two-way communication, but doesn't prevent sending large amounts of information.

Network Nodes

Apart from any physical transmission medium there may be, networks comprise additional basic system building blocks, such as network interface controller (NICs), repeaters, hubs, bridges, switches, routers, modems, and firewalls.

Network Interfaces

An ATM network interface in the form of an accessory card. A lot of network interfaces are built-in.

A network interface controller (NIC) is computer hardware that provides a computer with the ability to access the transmission media, and has the ability to process low-level network information. For example, the NIC may have a connector for accepting a cable, or an aerial for wireless transmission and reception, and the associated circuitry.

The NIC responds to traffic addressed to a network address for either the NIC or the computer as a whole.

In Ethernet networks, each network interface controller has a unique Media Access Control (MAC) address—usually stored in the controller's permanent memory. To avoid address conflicts between network devices, the Institute of Electrical and Electronics Engineers (IEEE) maintains and administers MAC address uniqueness. The size of an Ethernet MAC address is six octets. The three most significant octets are reserved to identify NIC manufacturers. These manufacturers, using only their assigned prefixes, uniquely assign the three least-significant octets of every Ethernet interface they produce.

Repeaters and Hubs

A repeater is an electronic device that receives a network signal, cleans it of unnecessary noise and regenerates it. The signal is retransmitted at a higher power level, or to the other side of an obstruction, so that the signal can cover longer distances without degradation. In most twisted pair Ethernet configurations, repeaters are required for cable that runs longer than 100 meters. With fiber optics, repeaters can be tens or even hundreds of kilometers apart.

A repeater with multiple ports is known as a hub. Repeaters work on the physical layer of the OSI model. Repeaters require a small amount of time to regenerate the signal. This can cause a propagation delay that affects network performance. As a result, many network architectures limit the number of repeaters that can be used in a row, e.g., the Ethernet 5-4-3 rule.

Hubs have been mostly obsoleted by modern switches; but repeaters are used for long distance links, notably undersea cabling.

Bridges

A network bridge connects and filters traffic between two network segments at the data link layer (layer 2) of the OSI model to form a single network. This breaks the network's collision domain but maintains a unified broadcast domain. Network segmentation breaks down a large, congested network into an aggregation of smaller, more efficient networks.

Bridges come in three basic types:

- Local bridges: Directly connect LANs

- Remote bridges: Can be used to create a wide area network (WAN) link between LANs. Remote bridges, where the connecting link is slower than the end networks, largely have been replaced with routers.

- Wireless bridges: Can be used to join LANs or connect remote devices to LANs.

Switches

A network switch is a device that forwards and filters OSI layer 2 datagrams (frames) between ports based on the destination MAC address in each frame. A switch is distinct from a hub in that it only forwards the frames to the physical ports involved in the communication rather than all ports connected. It can be thought of as a multi-port bridge. It learns to associate physical ports to MAC addresses by examining the source addresses of received frames. If an unknown destination is targeted, the switch broadcasts to all ports but the source. Switches normally have numerous ports, facilitating a star topology for devices, and cascading additional switches.

Multi-layer switches are capable of routing based on layer 3 addressing or additional logical levels. The term *switch* is often used loosely to include devices such as routers and bridges, as well as devices that may distribute traffic based on load or based on application content (e.g., a Web URL identifier).

Routers

A typical home or small office router showing the ADSL telephone line and Ethernet network cable connections

A router is an internetworking device that forwards packets between networks by processing the routing information included in the packet or datagram (Internet protocol information from layer 3). The routing information is often processed in conjunction with the routing table (or forwarding table). A router uses its routing table to determine where to forward packets. A destination in a routing table can include a "null" interface, also known as the "black hole" interface because data can go into it, however, no further processing is done for said data, i.e. the packets are dropped.

Modems

Modems (MOdulator-DEModulator) are used to connect network nodes via wire not originally designed for digital network traffic, or for wireless. To do this one or more carrier signals are modulated by the digital signal to produce an analog signal that can be tailored to give the required properties for transmission. Modems are commonly used for telephone lines, using a Digital Subscriber Line technology.

Firewalls

A firewall is a network device for controlling network security and access rules. Firewalls are typically configured to reject access requests from unrecognized sources while allowing actions from recognized ones. The vital role firewalls play in network security grows in parallel with the constant increase in cyber attacks.

Network Structure

Network topology is the layout or organizational hierarchy of interconnected nodes of a computer network. Different network topologies can affect throughput, but reliability is often more critical. With many technologies, such as bus networks, a single failure can cause the network to fail entirely. In general the more interconnections there are, the more robust the network is; but the more expensive it is to install.

Common Layouts

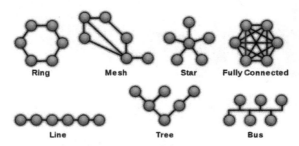

Common network topologies

Common layouts are:

- A bus network: all nodes are connected to a common medium along this medium. This was the layout used in the original Ethernet, called 10BASE5 and 10BASE2.

- A star network: all nodes are connected to a special central node. This is the typical layout found in a Wireless LAN, where each wireless client connects to the central Wireless access point.

- A ring network: each node is connected to its left and right neighbour node, such that all nodes are connected and that each node can reach each other node by traversing nodes left- or rightwards. The Fiber Distributed Data Interface (FDDI) made use of such a topology.

- A mesh network: each node is connected to an arbitrary number of neighbours in such a way that there is at least one traversal from any node to any other.

- A fully connected network: each node is connected to every other node in the network.

- A tree network: nodes are arranged hierarchically.

Note that the physical layout of the nodes in a network may not necessarily reflect the network topology. As an example, with FDDI, the network topology is a ring (actually two counter-rotating rings), but the physical topology is often a star, because all neighboring connections can be routed via a central physical location.

Overlay Network

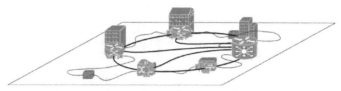

A sample overlay network

An overlay network is a virtual computer network that is built on top of another network. Nodes in the overlay network are connected by virtual or logical links. Each link corresponds to a path, perhaps through many physical links, in the underlying network. The topology of the overlay network may (and often does) differ from that of the underlying one. For example, many peer-to-peer networks are overlay networks. They are organized as nodes of a virtual system of links that run on top of the Internet.

Overlay networks have been around since the invention of networking when computer systems were connected over telephone lines using modems, before any data network existed.

The most striking example of an overlay network is the Internet itself. The Internet itself was initially built as an overlay on the telephone network. Even today, each Internet node can communicate with virtually any other through an underlying mesh of sub-networks of wildly different topologies and technologies. Address resolution and routing are the means that allow mapping of a fully connected IP overlay network to its underlying network.

Another example of an overlay network is a distributed hash table, which maps keys to nodes in the network. In this case, the underlying network is an IP network, and the overlay network is a table (actually a map) indexed by keys.

Overlay networks have also been proposed as a way to improve Internet routing, such as through quality of service guarantees to achieve higher-quality streaming media. Previous proposals such as IntServ, DiffServ, and IP Multicast have not seen wide acceptance largely because they require modification of all routers in the network.On the other hand, an overlay network can be incrementally deployed on end-hosts running the overlay protocol software, without cooperation from Internet service providers. The overlay network has no control over how packets are routed in the underlying network between two overlay nodes, but it can control, for example, the sequence of overlay nodes that a message traverses before it reaches its destination.

For example, Akamai Technologies manages an overlay network that provides reliable, efficient content delivery (a kind of multicast). Academic research includes end system multicast, resilient routing and quality of service studies, among others.

Communications Protocols

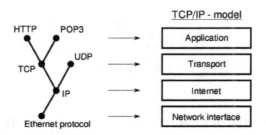

The TCP/IP model or Internet layering scheme and its relation to common protocols often layered on top of it.

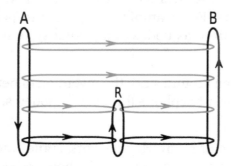

Figure. Message flows (A-B) in the presence of a router (R), red flows are effective communication paths, black paths are the actual paths.

A communications protocol is a set of rules for exchanging information over network links. In a protocol stack, each protocol leverages the services of the protocol below it. An important example of a protocol stack is HTTP (the World Wide Web protocol) running over TCP over IP (the Internet protocols) over IEEE 802.11 (the Wi-Fi protocol). This stack is used between the wireless router and the home user's personal computer when the user is surfing the web.

Whilst the use of protocol layering is today ubiquitous across the field of computer networking, it has been historically criticized by many researchers for two principal reasons. Firstly, abstracting the protocol stack in this way may cause a higher layer to duplicate functionality of a lower layer, a prime example being error recovery on both a per-link basis and an end-to-end basis. Secondly, it is common that a protocol implementation at one layer may require data, state or addressing information that is only present at another layer, thus defeating the point of separating the layers in the first place. For example, TCP uses the ECN field in the IPv4 header as an indication of congestion; IP is a network layer protocol whereas TCP is a transport layer protocol.

Communication protocols have various characteristics. They may be connection-oriented or connectionless, they may use circuit mode or packet switching, and they may use hierarchical addressing or flat addressing.

There are many communication protocols, a few of which are described below.

IEEE 802

IEEE 802 is a family of IEEE standards dealing with local area networks and metropolitan area networks. The complete IEEE 802 protocol suite provides a diverse set of networking capabilities. The protocols have a flat addressing scheme. They operate mostly at levels 1 and 2 of the OSI model.

For example, MAC bridging (IEEE 802.1D) deals with the routing of Ethernet packets using a Spanning Tree Protocol. IEEE 802.1Q describes VLANs, and IEEE 802.1X defines a port-based Network Access Control protocol, which forms the basis for the authentication mechanisms used in VLANs (but it is also found in WLANs) – it is what the home user sees when the user has to enter a "wireless access key".

Ethernet

Ethernet, sometimes simply called *LAN*, is a family of protocols used in wired LANs, described by a set of standards together called IEEE 802.3 published by the Institute of Electrical and Electronics Engineers.

Wireless LAN

Wireless LAN, also widely known as WLAN or WiFi, is probably the most well-known member of the IEEE 802 protocol family for home users today. It is standarized by IEEE 802.11 and shares many properties with wired Ethernet.

Internet Protocol Suite

The Internet Protocol Suite, also called TCP/IP, is the foundation of all modern networking. It offers connection-less as well as connection-oriented services over an inherently unreliable network traversed by data-gram transmission at the Internet protocol (IP) level. At its core, the protocol suite defines the addressing, identification, and routing specifications for Internet Protocol Version 4 (IPv4) and for IPv6, the next generation of the protocol with a much enlarged addressing capability.

SONET/SDH

Synchronous optical networking (SONET) and Synchronous Digital Hierarchy (SDH) are standardized multiplexing protocols that transfer multiple digital bit streams over optical fiber using lasers. They were originally designed to transport circuit mode communications from a variety of different sources, primarily to support real-time, uncompressed, circuit-switched voice encoded in PCM (Pulse-Code Modulation) format. However, due to its protocol neutrality and transport-oriented features, SONET/SDH also was the obvious choice for transporting Asynchronous Transfer Mode (ATM) frames.

Asynchronous Transfer Mode

Asynchronous Transfer Mode (ATM) is a switching technique for telecommunication networks. It uses asynchronous time-division multiplexing and encodes data into small, fixed-sized cells. This differs from other protocols such as the Internet Protocol Suite or Ethernet that use variable sized packets or frames. ATM has similarity with both circuit and packet switched networking. This makes it a good choice for a network that must handle both traditional high-throughput data traffic, and real-time, low-latency content such as voice and video. ATM uses a connection-oriented model in which a virtual circuit must be established between two endpoints before the actual data exchange begins.

While the role of ATM is diminishing in favor of next-generation networks, it still plays a role in the last mile, which is the connection between an Internet service provider and the home user.

Geographic Scale

A network can be characterized by its physical capacity or its organizational purpose. Use of the network, including user authorization and access rights, differ accordingly.

Nanoscale Network

A nanoscale communication network has key components implemented at the nanoscale including message carriers and leverages physical principles that differ from macroscale communication mechanisms. Nanoscale communication extends communication to very small sensors and actuators such as those found in biological systems and also tends to operate in environments that would be too harsh for classical communication.

Personal Area Network

A personal area network (PAN) is a computer network used for communication among computer and different information technological devices close to one person. Some examples of devices that are used in a PAN are personal computers, printers, fax machines, telephones, PDAs, scanners, and even video game consoles. A PAN may include wired and wireless devices. The reach of a PAN typically extends to 10 meters. A wired PAN is usually constructed with USB and FireWire connections while technologies such as Bluetooth and infrared communication typically form a wireless PAN.

Local Area Network

A local area network (LAN) is a network that connects computers and devices in a limited geographical area such as a home, school, office building, or closely positioned group of buildings. Each computer or device on the network is a node. Wired LANs are most likely based on Ethernet technology. Newer standards such as ITU-T G.hn also provide a way to create a wired LAN using existing wiring, such as coaxial cables, telephone lines, and power lines.

The defining characteristics of a LAN, in contrast to a wide area network (WAN), include higher data transfer rates, limited geographic range, and lack of reliance on leased lines to provide connectivity. Current Ethernet or other IEEE 802.3 LAN technologies operate at data transfer rates up to 100 Gbit/s, standarized by IEEE in 2010. Currently, 400 Gbit/s Ethernet is being developed.

A LAN can be connected to a WAN using a router.

Home Area Network

A home area network (HAN) is a residential LAN used for communication between digital devices typically deployed in the home, usually a small number of personal computers and accessories, such as printers and mobile computing devices. An important function is the sharing of Internet access, often a broadband service through a cable TV or digital subscriber line (DSL) provider.

Storage Area Network

A storage area network (SAN) is a dedicated network that provides access to consolidated, block level data storage. SANs are primarily used to make storage devices, such as disk arrays, tape libraries, and optical jukeboxes, accessible to servers so that the devices appear like locally attached devices to the operating system. A SAN typically has its own network of storage devices that are generally not accessible through the local area network by other devices. The cost and complexity of SANs dropped in the early 2000s to levels allowing wider adoption across both enterprise and small to medium-sized business environments.

Campus Area Network

A campus area network (CAN) is made up of an interconnection of LANs within a limited geographical area. The networking equipment (switches, routers) and transmission media (optical fiber, copper plant, Cat5 cabling, etc.) are almost entirely owned by the campus tenant / owner (an enterprise, university, government, etc.).

For example, a university campus network is likely to link a variety of campus buildings to connect academic colleges or departments, the library, and student residence halls.

Backbone Network

A backbone network is part of a computer network infrastructure that provides a path for the exchange of information between different LANs or sub-networks. A backbone can tie together diverse networks within the same building, across different buildings, or over a wide area.

For example, a large company might implement a backbone network to connect departments that are located around the world. The equipment that ties together the departmental networks constitutes the network backbone. When designing a network backbone, network performance and network congestion are critical factors to take into account. Normally, the backbone network's capacity is greater than that of the individual networks connected to it.

Another example of a backbone network is the Internet backbone, which is the set of wide area networks (WANs) and core routers that tie together all networks connected to the Internet.

Metropolitan Area Network

A Metropolitan area network (MAN) is a large computer network that usually spans a city or a large campus.

Wide Area Network

A wide area network (WAN) is a computer network that covers a large geographic area such as a city, country, or spans even intercontinental distances. A WAN uses a communications channel that combines many types of media such as telephone lines, cables, and air waves. A WAN often makes use of transmission facilities provided by common carriers, such as telephone companies. WAN technologies generally function at the lower three layers of the OSI reference model: the physical layer, the data link layer, and the network layer.

Enterprise Private Network

An enterprise private network is a network that a single organization builds to interconnect its office locations (e.g., production sites, head offices, remote offices, shops) so they can share computer resources.

Virtual Private Network

A virtual private network (VPN) is an overlay network in which some of the links between nodes are carried by open connections or virtual circuits in some larger network (e.g., the Internet) instead of by physical wires. The data link layer protocols of the virtual network are said to be tunneled through the larger network when this is the case. One common application is secure communications through the public Internet, but a VPN need not have explicit security features, such as authentication or content encryption. VPNs, for example, can be used to separate the traffic of different user communities over an underlying network with strong security features.

VPN may have best-effort performance, or may have a defined service level agreement (SLA) between the VPN customer and the VPN service provider. Generally, a VPN has a topology more complex than point-to-point.

Global Area Network

A global area network (GAN) is a network used for supporting mobile across an arbitrary number of wireless LANs, satellite coverage areas, etc. The key challenge in mobile communications is handing off user communications from one local coverage area to the next. In IEEE Project 802, this involves a succession of terrestrial wireless LANs.

Organizational Scope

Networks are typically managed by the organizations that own them. Private enterprise networks may use a combination of intranets and extranets. They may also provide network access to the Internet, which has no single owner and permits virtually unlimited global connectivity.

Intranet

An intranet is a set of networks that are under the control of a single administrative entity. The intranet uses the IP protocol and IP-based tools such as web browsers and file transfer applications. The administrative entity limits use of the intranet to its authorized users. Most commonly, an intranet is the internal LAN of an organization. A large intranet typically has at least one web server to provide users with organizational information. An intranet is also anything behind the router on a local area network.

Extranet

An extranet is a network that is also under the administrative control of a single organization, but supports a limited connection to a specific external network. For example, an organization may provide access to some aspects of its intranet to share data with its business partners or customers. These other entities are not necessarily trusted from a security standpoint. Network connection to an extranet is often, but not always, implemented via WAN technology.

Internetwork

An internetwork is the connection of multiple computer networks via a common routing technology using routers.

Internet

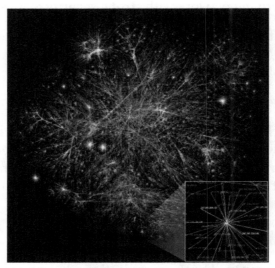

Partial map of the Internet based on the January 15, 2005 data found on opte.org. Each line
is drawn between two nodes, representing two IP addresses. The length of the lines
are indicative of the delay between those two nodes. This graph represents less
than 30% ofthe Class C networks reachable.

The Internet is the largest example of an internetwork. It is a global system of interconnected governmental, academic, corporate, public, and private computer networks.
It is based on the networking technologies of the Internet Protocol Suite. It is the successor of the Advanced Research Projects Agency Network (ARPANET) developed by
DARPA of the United States Department of Defense. The Internet is also the communications backbone underlying the World Wide Web (WWW).

Participants in the Internet use a diverse array of methods of several hundred documented, and often standardized, protocols compatible with the Internet Protocol Suite
and an addressing system (IP addresses) administered by the Internet Assigned Numbers Authority and address registries. Service providers and large enterprises exchange
information about the reachability of their address spaces through the Border Gateway
Protocol (BGP), forming a redundant worldwide mesh of transmission paths.

Darknet

A darknet is an overlay network, typically running on the internet, that is only accessible through specialized software. A darknet is an anonymizing network where connections are made only between trusted peers — sometimes called "friends" (F2F) — using
non-standard protocols and ports.

Darknets are distinct from other distributed peer-to-peer networks as sharing is anonymous (that is, IP addresses are not publicly shared), and therefore users can communicate with little fear of governmental or corporate interference.

Routing

Routing calculates good paths through a network for information to take. For example, from node 1 to node 6 the best routes are likely to be 1-8-7-6 or 1-8-10-6, as this has the thickest routes.

Routing is the process of selecting network paths to carry network traffic. Routing is performed for many kinds of networks, including circuit switching networks and packet switched networks.

In packet switched networks, routing directs packet forwarding (the transit of logically addressed network packets from their source toward their ultimate destination) through intermediate nodes. Intermediate nodes are typically network hardware devices such as routers, bridges, gateways, firewalls, or switches. General-purpose computers can also forward packets and perform routing, though they are not specialized hardware and may suffer from limited performance. The routing process usually directs forwarding on the basis of routing tables, which maintain a record of the routes to various network destinations. Thus, constructing routing tables, which are held in the router's memory, is very important for efficient routing.

There are usually multiple routes that can be taken, and to choose between them, different elements can be considered to decide which routes get installed into the routing table, such as (sorted by priority):

1. *Prefix-Length*: where longer subnet masks are preferred (independent if it is within a routing protocol or over different routing protocol)

2. *Metric*: where a lower metric/cost is preferred (only valid within one and the same routing protocol)

3. *Administrative distance*: where a lower distance is preferred (only valid between different routing protocols)

Most routing algorithms use only one network path at a time. Multipath routing techniques enable the use of multiple alternative paths.

Routing, in a more narrow sense of the term, is often contrasted with bridging in its assumption that network addresses are structured and that similar addresses imply proximity within the network. Structured addresses allow a single routing table entry to represent the route to a group of devices. In large networks, structured addressing (routing, in the narrow sense) outperforms unstructured addressing (bridging). Routing has become the dominant form of addressing on the Internet. Bridging is still widely used within localized environments.

Network Service

Network services are applications hosted by servers on a computer network, to provide some functionality for members or users of the network, or to help the network itself to operate.

The World Wide Web, E-mail, printing and network file sharing are examples of well-known network services. Network services such as DNS (Domain Name System) give names for IP and MAC addresses (people remember names like "nm.lan" better than numbers like "210.121.67.18"), and DHCP to ensure that the equipment on the network has a valid IP address.

Services are usually based on a service protocol that defines the format and sequencing of messages between clients and servers of that network service.

Network Performance

Quality of Service

Depending on the installation requirements, network performance is usually measured by the quality of service of a telecommunications product. The parameters that affect this typically can include throughput, jitter, bit error rate and latency.

The following list gives examples of network performance measures for a circuit-switched network and one type of packet-switched network, viz. ATM:

- Circuit-switched networks: In circuit switched networks, network performance is synonymous with the grade of service. The number of rejected calls is a measure of how well the network is performing under heavy traffic loads. Other types of performance measures can include the level of noise and echo.

- ATM: In an Asynchronous Transfer Mode (ATM) network, performance can be measured by line rate, quality of service (QoS), data throughput, connect time, stability, technology, modulation technique and modem enhancements.

There are many ways to measure the performance of a network, as each network is different in nature and design. Performance can also be modelled instead of measured.

For example, state transition diagrams are often used to model queuing performance in a circuit-switched network. The network planner uses these diagrams to analyze how the network performs in each state, ensuring that the network is optimally designed.

Network Congestion

Network congestion occurs when a link or node is carrying so much data that its quality of service deteriorates. Typical effects include queueing delay, packet loss or the blocking of new connections. A consequence of these latter two is that incremental increases in offered load lead either only to small increase in network throughput, or to an actual reduction in network throughput.

Network protocols that use aggressive retransmissions to compensate for packet loss tend to keep systems in a state of network congestion—even after the initial load is reduced to a level that would not normally induce network congestion. Thus, networks using these protocols can exhibit two stable states under the same level of load. The stable state with low throughput is known as *congestive collapse*.

Modern networks use congestion control and congestion avoidance techniques to try to avoid congestion collapse. These include: exponential backoff in protocols such as 802.11's CSMA/CA and the original Ethernet, window reduction in TCP, and fair queueing in devices such as routers. Another method to avoid the negative effects of network congestion is implementing priority schemes, so that some packets are transmitted with higher priority than others. Priority schemes do not solve network congestion by themselves, but they help to alleviate the effects of congestion for some services. An example of this is 802.1p. A third method to avoid network congestion is the explicit allocation of network resources to specific flows. One example of this is the use of Contention-Free Transmission Opportunities (CFTXOPs) in the ITU-T G.hn standard, which provides high-speed (up to 1 Gbit/s) Local area networking over existing home wires (power lines, phone lines and coaxial cables).

For the Internet RFC 2914 addresses the subject of congestion control in detail.

Network Resilience

Network resilience is "the ability to provide and maintain an acceptable level of service in the face of faults and challenges to normal operation."

Security

Network Security

Network security consists of provisions and policies adopted by the network administrator to prevent and monitor unauthorized access, misuse, modification, or denial of the computer network and its network-accessible resources. Network security is the authorization of access to data in a network, which is controlled by the network administrator. Users are assigned an ID and password that allows them access to information and programs within their authority. Network security is used on a variety of computer networks, both public and private, to secure daily transactions and communications among businesses, government agencies and individuals.

Network Surveillance

Network surveillance is the monitoring of data being transferred over computer networks such as the Internet. The monitoring is often done surreptitiously and may be done by or at the behest of governments, by corporations, criminal organizations, or individuals. It may or may not be legal and may or may not require authorization from a court or other independent agency.

Computer and network surveillance programs are widespread today, and almost all Internet traffic is or could potentially be monitored for clues to illegal activity.

Surveillance is very useful to governments and law enforcement to maintain social control, recognize and monitor threats, and prevent/investigate criminal activity. With the advent of programs such as the Total Information Awareness program, technologies such as high speed surveillance computers and biometrics software, and laws such as the Communications Assistance For Law Enforcement Act, governments now possess an unprecedented ability to monitor the activities of citizens.

However, many civil rights and privacy groups—such as Reporters Without Borders, the Electronic Frontier Foundation, and the American Civil Liberties Union—have expressed concern that increasing surveillance of citizens may lead to a mass surveillance society, with limited political and personal freedoms. Fears such as this have led to numerous lawsuits such as *Hepting v. AT&T*. The hacktivist group Anonymous has hacked into government websites in protest of what it considers "draconian surveillance".

End to End Encryption

End-to-end encryption (E2EE) is a digital communications paradigm of uninterrupted protection of data traveling between two communicating parties. It involves the originating party encrypting data so only the intended recipient can decrypt it, with no dependency on third parties. End-to-end encryption prevents intermediaries, such as Internet providers or application service providers, from discovering or tampering with communications. End-to-end encryption generally protects both confidentiality and integrity.

Examples of end-to-end encryption include PGP for email, OTR for instant messaging, ZRTP for telephony, and TETRA for radio.

Typical server-based communications systems do not include end-to-end encryption. These systems can only guarantee protection of communications between clients and servers, not between the communicating parties themselves. Examples of non-E2EE systems are Google Talk, Yahoo Messenger, Facebook, and Dropbox. Some such systems, for example LavaBit and SecretInk, have even described themselves as offering "end-to-end" encryption when they do not. Some systems that normally offer end-to-end encryption have turned out to contain a back door that subverts negotiation of the encryption key between the communicating parties, for example Skype or Hushmail.

The end-to-end encryption paradigm does not directly address risks at the communications endpoints themselves, such as the technical exploitation of clients, poor quality random number generators, or key escrow. E2EE also does not address traffic analysis, which relates to things such as the identities of the end points and the times and quantities of messages that are sent.

Views of Networks

Users and network administrators typically have different views of their networks. Users can share printers and some servers from a workgroup, which usually means they are in the same geographic location and are on the same LAN, whereas a Network Administrator is responsible to keep that network up and running. A community of interest has less of a connection of being in a local area, and should be thought of as a set of arbitrarily located users who share a set of servers, and possibly also communicate via peer-to-peer technologies.

Network administrators can see networks from both physical and logical perspectives. The physical perspective involves geographic locations, physical cabling, and the network elements (e.g., routers, bridges and application layer gateways) that interconnect via the transmission media. Logical networks, called, in the TCP/IP architecture, subnets, map onto one or more transmission media. For example, a common practice in a campus of buildings is to make a set of LAN cables in each building appear to be a common subnet, using virtual LAN (VLAN) technology.

Both users and administrators are aware, to varying extents, of the trust and scope characteristics of a network. Again using TCP/IP architectural terminology, an intranet is a community of interest under private administration usually by an enterprise, and is only accessible by authorized users (e.g. employees). Intranets do not have to be connected to the Internet, but generally have a limited connection. An extranet is an extension of an intranet that allows secure communications to users outside of the intranet (e.g. business partners, customers).

Unofficially, the Internet is the set of users, enterprises, and content providers that are interconnected by Internet Service Providers (ISP). From an engineering viewpoint, the Internet is the set of subnets, and aggregates of subnets, which share the registered IP address space and exchange information about the reachability of those IP addresses using the Border Gateway Protocol. Typically, the human-readable names of servers are translated to IP addresses, transparently to users, via the directory function of the Domain Name System (DNS).

Over the Internet, there can be business-to-business (B2B), business-to-consumer (B2C) and consumer-to-consumer (C2C) communications. When money or sensitive information is exchanged, the communications are apt to be protected by some form of communications security mechanism. Intranets and extranets can be securely superimposed onto the Internet, without any access by general Internet users and administrators, using secure Virtual Private Network (VPN) technology.

References

- Spurgeon, Charles E. (2000). Ethernet The Definitive Guide. O'Reilly & Associates. ISBN 1-56592-660-9.

- Simmonds, A; Sandilands, P; van Ekert, L (2004). "An Ontology for Network Security Attack". Lecture Notes in Computer Science. Lecture Notes in Computer Science. 3285: 317–323. doi:10.1007/978-3-540-30176-9_41. ISBN 978-3-540-23659-7.

- A. Hooke (September 2000), Interplanetary Internet (PDF), Third Annual International Symposium on Advanced Radio Technologies, archived from the original (PDF) on 2012-01-13, retrieved 2011-11-12

- "Anonymous hacks UK government sites over 'draconian surveillance' ", Emil Protalinski, ZDNet, 7 April 2012, retrieved 12 March 2013

- For an interesting write-up of the technologies involved, including the deep stacking of communications protocols used, see.Martin, Thomas. "Design Principles for DSL-Based Access Solutions" (PDF). Retrieved 18 June 2011.

- D. Andersen; H. Balakrishnan; M. Kaashoek; R. Morris (October 2001), Resilient Overlay Networks, Association for Computing Machinery, retrieved 2011-11-12

- Wood, Jessica (2010). "The Darknet: A Digital Copyright Revolution" (PDF). Richmond Journal of Law and Technology. 16 (4). Retrieved 25 October 2011.

Types of Computer Networks

Computer networks are set up with a view to permit transmission of data within a parameter and transmission protocols are created with a view of the same. Some common architectures of computer networks are personal area network, local area network, campus network and wide area network. All these topics as well as others have been included in this chapter.

IEEE P1906.1

The IEEE P1906.1 - Recommended Practice for Nanoscale and Molecular Communication Framework is a standards working group sponsored by the IEEE Communications Society Standards Development Board whose goal is to develop a common framework for nanoscale and molecular communication. Because this is an emerging technology, the standard is designed to encourage innovation by reaching consensus on a common definition, terminology, framework, goals, metrics, and use-cases that encourage innovation and enable the technology to advance at a faster rate. The draft passed an initial sponsor balloting with comments on January 2, 2015. The comments were addressed by the working group and the resulting draft ballot passed again on August 17, 2015. Finally, additional material regarding SBML was contributed and the final draft passed again on October 15, 2015. The draft standard was approved by IEEE RevCom in the final quarter of 2015.

Membership

Working group membership includes experts in industry and academia with strong backgrounds in mathematical modeling, engineering, physics, economics and biological sciences.

Content

Electronic components such as transistors, or electrical/electromagnetic message carriers whose operation is similar at the macroscale and nanoscale are excluded from the definition. A human-engineered, synthetic component must form part of the system because it is important to avoid standardizing nature or physical processes. The definition of communication, particularly in the area of cell-surface interactions as viewed by biologists versus non-biologists has been a topic of debate. The interface is viewed as a communication channel, whereas the 'receptor-signaling-gene expression' events are the network.

The draft currently comprises: definition, terminology, framework, metrics, use-cases, and reference code (ns-3).

Definition

- A precise definition of nanoscale networking

  - o Academic and industrial researchers have been playing with the concept of nanoscale communication networks, but without a common, well-defined, and precise definition. The IEEE P1906.1 working group has adopted the definitive specification for a nanoscale communication network. The draft standard sets the context of communication within length scales by defining communication length scales ranging from the Planck length scale to relativistic length scales. A focus is upon the progression of physical changes that impact communication as length scale is reduced.

Terminology

- Common terminology for nanoscale networking

  - o Nanoscale communication networking is a highly interdisciplinary endeavor. A clear, common language is required so that interdisciplinary researchers can work smoothly together and minimize cross-discipline misunderstanding due to the common definitions that are defined differently in different fields. The P1906.1 working group has reached consensus on common definitions unique to nanoscale communication networks.

Framework

- A framework for ad hoc nanoscale networking

  - o There is a pressing need for a conceptual model of nanoscale networks. A standardized platform for nanoscale communication network simulation is needed. Researchers are developing simulation models and packages for components related to nanoscale communication networks; however the simulation components are not interoperable, even at a conceptual level. The IEEE P1906.1 working group has adopted a nanoscale communication framework that addresses this need. The result of the framework is known as the *standard model*.

Metrics

- Metrics and analytical model are in development
    - The working group is currently in the process of developing metrics to uniquely characterize nanoscale communication networks. Twenty metrics have been defined:
        - Message Deliverability
        - Message Lifetime
        - Information Density
        - Bandwidth-Delay Product
        - Information and Communication Energy
        - Collision Behavior
        - Mass Displacement
        - Positioning Accuracy of Message Carriers
        - Persistence Length
        - Diffusive Flux
        - Langevin Noise
        - Specificity
        - Affinity
        - Sensitivity
        - Angular (Angle-of-Arrival) Spectrum
        - Delay (Time-of-Arrival) Spectrum
        - Active Network Programmability
        - Perturbation Rate
        - Supersystem Degradation
        - Bandwidth-Volume Ratio

Use-Cases

- Specific example applications of the standard

    o   Specific use-cases of nanoscale communication implemented using the P1906.1 definition and framework are provided. A standard mapping between a use-case, or implementation, and the standard model of the framework allows a brief summary of the information required about a use-case to understand its relevance to a nanoscale communication network.

Reference Model

- Reference code to model the recommended practice is in development

    o   Ns-3 reference code is currently in development that implements the developing IEEE P1906.1 recommended practice. The communication framework conceived by the P1906.1 working group has been implemented. A simple example highlighting the interaction and the role of each component in electromagnetic-based, diffusion-based, and molecular motor-based communication at the nanoscale has been developed.

Applications

Applications are numerous, however, there appears to be strong emphasis on medical and biological use-cases in nanomedicine.

Simulation Software

The IEEE P1906.1 working group is developing ns-3 nanoscale simulation software that implements the IEEE 1906.1 standard and serves as a reference model and base for development of a wide-variety of interoperable small-scale communication physical layer models.

Literature Review

The Best Readings on nanoscale communication networks provides good background information related to the standard. The Topics section breaks down the information using the standard approach.

Personal Area Network

A personal area network (PAN) is a computer network used for data transmission amongst devices such as computers, telephones, tablets and personal digital assistants. PANs can be used for communication amongst the personal devices themselves (interpersonal communication), or for connecting to a higher level network and the Internet (an uplink) where one "master" device takes up the role as internet router.

A wireless personal area network (WPAN) is a low-powered PAN carried over a short-distance wireless network technology such as:

- INSTEON
- IrDA
- Wireless USB
- Bluetooth
- Z-Wave
- ZigBee
- Body Area Network

The reach of a WPAN varies from a few centimeters to a few meters. A PAN may also be carried over wired computer buses such as USB and FireWire.

Although a (secured) Wi-Fi tethering connection could be used by only one single user it is not considered to be a PAN.

Wired PAN connection

The data cable is an example of the above PAN. This is also a Personal Area Network because that connection is for the users personal use. PAN is used for personal use only.

Wireless Personal Area Network

A wireless personal area network (WPAN) is a personal area network—a network for interconnecting devices centered on an individual person's workspace—in which the connections are wireless. Wireless PAN is based on the standard IEEE 802.15. The two kinds of wireless technologies used for WPAN are Bluetooth and Infrared Data Association.

A WPAN could serve to interconnect all the ordinary computing and communicating devices that many people have on their desk or carry with them today; or it could serve a more specialized purpose such as allowing the surgeon and other team members to communicate during an operation.

A key concept in WPAN technology is known as "plugging in". In the ideal scenario, when any two WPAN-equipped devices come into close proximity (within several meters of each other) or within a few kilometers of a central server, they can communicate as if connected by a cable. Another important feature is the ability of each device to lock out other devices selectively, preventing needless interference or unauthorized access to information.

The technology for WPANs is in its infancy and is undergoing rapid development. Proposed operating frequencies are around 2.4 GHz in digital modes. The objective is to facilitate seamless operation among home or business devices and systems. Every device in a WPAN will be able to plug into any other device in the same WPAN, provided they are within physical range of one another. In addition, WPANs worldwide will be interconnected. Thus, for example, an archeologist on site in Greece might use a PDA to directly access databases at the University of Minnesota in Minneapolis, and to transmit findings to that database.

Bluetooth

Bluetooth uses short-range radio waves over distances up to approximately 10 metres. For example, Bluetooth devices such as a keyboards, pointing devices, audio head sets, printers may connect to personal digital assistants (PDAs), cell phones, or computers wirelessly.

A Bluetooth PAN is also called a *piconet* (combination of the prefix "pico," meaning very small or one trillionth, and network), and is composed of up to 8 active devices in a master-slave relationship (a very large number of devices can be connected in "parked" mode). The first Bluetooth device in the piconet is the master, and all other devices are slaves that communicate with the master. A piconet typically has a range of 10 metres (33 ft), although ranges of up to 100 metres (330 ft) can be reached under ideal circumstances.

Infrared Data Association

Infrared Data Association (IrDA) uses infrared light, which has a frequency below the human eye's sensitivity. Infrared in general is used, for instance, in TV remotes. Typical WPAN devices that use IrDA include printers, keyboards, and other serial data interfaces.

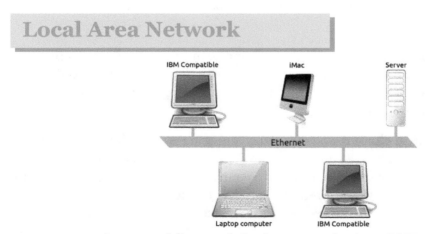

A conceptual diagram of a local area network using 10BASE5 Ethernet

A local area network (LAN) is a computer network that interconnects computers within a limited area such as a residence, school, laboratory, university campus or office building and has its network equipment and interconnects locally managed. By contrast, a wide area network (WAN), not only covers a larger geographic distance, but also generally involves leased telecommunication circuits or Internet links.

Ethernet and Wi-Fi are the two most common transmission technologies in use for local area networks. Historical technologies include ARCNET, Token ring, and AppleTalk.

History

The increasing demand and use of computers in universities and research labs in the late 1960s generated the need to provide high-speed interconnections between computer systems. A 1970 report from the Lawrence Radiation Laboratory detailing the growth of their "Octopus" network gave a good indication of the situation.

A number of experimental and early commercial LAN technologies were developed in the 1970s. Cambridge Ring was developed at Cambridge University starting in 1974. Ethernet was developed at Xerox PARC in 1973–1975, and filed as U.S. Patent 4,063,220. In 1976, after the system was deployed at PARC, Robert Metcalfe and David Boggs published a seminal paper, "Ethernet: Distributed Packet-Switching for Local Computer Networks". ARCNET was developed by Datapoint Corporation in 1976 and announced in 1977. It had the first commercial installation in December 1977 at Chase Manhattan Bank in New York.

The development and proliferation of personal computers using the CP/M operating system in the late 1970s, and later DOS-based systems starting in 1981, meant that many sites grew to dozens or even hundreds of computers. The initial driving force for networking was generally to share storage and printers, which were both expensive at the time. There was much enthusiasm for the concept and for several years, from about 1983 onward, computer industry pundits would regularly declare the coming year to be, "The year of the LAN".

In practice, the concept was marred by proliferation of incompatible physical layer and network protocol implementations, and a plethora of methods of sharing resources. Typically, each vendor would have its own type of network card, cabling, protocol, and network operating system. A solution appeared with the advent of Novell NetWare which provided even-handed support for dozens of competing card/cable types, and a much more sophisticated operating system than most of its competitors. Netware dominated the personal computer LAN business from early after its introduction in 1983 until the mid-1990s when Microsoft introduced Windows NT Advanced Server and Windows for Workgroups.

Of the competitors to NetWare, only Banyan Vines had comparable technical strengths, but Banyan never gained a secure base. Microsoft and 3Com worked together to create a simple network operating system which formed the base of 3Com's 3+Share, Microsoft's LAN Manager and IBM's LAN Server - but none of these was particularly successful.

During the same period, Unix workstations were using TCP/IP based networking. Although this market segment is now much reduced, the technologies developed in this area continue to be influential on the Internet and in both Linux and Apple Mac OS X networking—and the TCP/IP protocol has now almost completely replaced IPX, Apple-Talk, NBF, and other protocols used by the early PC LANs.

Cabling

Early LAN cabling had generally been based on various grades of coaxial cable. Shielded twisted pair was used in IBM's Token Ring LAN implementation, but in 1984, StarLAN showed the potential of simple *unshielded* twisted pair by using Cat3 cable—the same simple cable used for telephone systems. This led to the development of 10BASE-T (and its successors) and structured cabling which is still the basis of most commercial LANs today.

While fiber-optic cabling is common for links between switches, use of fiber to the desktop is rare.

Wireless Media

Many LANs are now based partly or wholly on wireless technologies. Smartphones, tablet computers and laptops typically have wireless networking support built-in. In a wireless local area network, users may move unrestricted in the coverage area. Wireless networks have become popular in residences and small businesses, because of their ease of installation. Guests are often offered Internet access via a hotspot service.

Technical Aspects

Network topology describes the layout of interconnections between devices and network segments. At the Data Link Layer and Physical Layer, a wide variety of LAN topologies have been used, including ring, bus, mesh and star, but the most common LAN topology in use today is switched Ethernet. At the higher layers, NetBEUI, IPX/SPX, AppleTalk and others were once common, but the Internet Protocol Suite (TCP/IP) is now the standard.

Simple LANs generally consist of cabling and one or more switches. A switch can be connected to a router, cable modem, or ADSL modem for Internet access. A LAN can include a wide variety of other network devices such as firewalls, load balancers, and sensors; and more complex LANs are characterized by their use of redundant links with switches using the spanning tree protocol to prevent loops, their ability to manage differing traffic types via quality of service (QoS), and to segregate traffic with VLANs.

LANs can maintain connections with other LANs via leased lines, leased services, or across the Internet using virtual private network technologies. Depending on how the connections are established and secured, and the distance involved, such linked LANs may also be classified as a metropolitan area network (MAN) or a wide area network (WAN).

Home Network

A home network or home area network (HAN) is a type of computer network that facilitates communication among devices within the close vicinity of a home. Devices capable of participating in this network, for example, smart devices such as network printers and handheld mobile computers, often gain enhanced emergent capabilities through their ability to interact. These additional capabilities can be used to increase the quality of life inside the home in a variety of ways, such as automation of repetitious tasks, increased personal productivity, enhanced home security, and easier access to entertainment.

Origins

Establishing this kind of network is often necessary when there is need to distribute residential Internet access to all internet capable devices in the home. Due to the effect of IPv4 address exhaustion, most Internet service providers provide only a single WAN-facing IP address for each residential subscription. Therefore, most homes require a device capable of network address translation that can route packets between a single public address visible to the outside world and the multiple private addresses within the home network.

Infrastructure

An example of a simple home network

A home network usually relies on one or more of the following equipment to establish physical layer, data link layer, and network layer connectivity both internally amongst devices and externally with outside networks:

- A modem exposes an Ethernet interface to a service provider's native telecommunications infrastructure. In homes these usually come in the form of a DSL modem or cable modem.

- A router manages network layer connectivity between a WAN and the HAN. Most home networks feature a particular class of small, passively cooled, table-top device with an integrated wireless access point and 4 port Ethernet switch. These devices aim to make the installation, configuration, and management of a home network as automated, user friendly, and "plug-and-play" as possible.

- A network switch is used to allow devices on the home network to talk to one another via Ethernet. While the needs of most home networks are satisfied with the built-in wireless and/or switching capabilities of their router, certain situations require the introduction of a distinct switch. For example:

  o When the router's switching capacity is exceeded. Most home routers expose only 4 to 6 Ethernet ports.

  o When a non-standard port feature such as power over Ethernet is required by devices such as IP cameras and IP phones

  o When distant rooms have a large amount of wired devices in close proximity

- A wireless access point is required for connecting wireless devices to a network. Most home networks rely on one wireless router combination device to fill this role.

- A home automation controller is used to enable low-power wireless communications with simple, non-data-intensive devices such as light bulbs and locks.

- A network bridge connecting two network interfaces to each other, often in order to grant a wired-only device, e.g. Xbox, access to a wireless network medium.

Transmission Media

Home networks can use either wired or wireless technologies to connect endpoints. Wireless is the predominant option in homes due to the ease of installation, lack of unsightly cables, and network performance characteristics sufficient for residential activities.

Wireless

IEEE 802.11 (WLAN)

One of the most common ways of creating a home network is by using wireless radio signal technology; the 802.11 network as certified by the IEEE. Most wireless-capable residential devices operate at a frequency of 2.4 GHz under 802.11b and 802.11g or 5 GHz under 802.11a. Some home networking devices operate in both radio-band signals and fall within the 802.11n or 802.11ac standards. Wi-Fi is a marketing and compliance certification for IEEE 802.11 technologies. The Wi-Fi Alliance has tested compliant products, and certifies them for interoperability.

IEEE 802.15 (WPAN)

Low power, close range communication based on IEEE 802.15 standards has a strong presence in homes. Bluetooth continues to be the technology of choice for most wireless accessories such as keyboards, mice, headsets, and game controllers. These connections are often established in a transient, ad-hoc manner and are not thought of as permanent residents of a home network.

IEEE 802.15.4 (LR-WPAN)

A "low-rate" version of the original WPAN protocol was used as the basis of ZigBee. Despite originally being conceived as a standard for low power machine-to-machine communication in industrial environments, the technology has been found to be well suited for integration into embedded "Smart Home" offerings that are expected to run on battery for extended periods of time. ZigBee utilizes mesh networking to overcome the distance limitations associated with traditional WPAN in order to establish a single network of addressable devices spread across the entire building. Z-Wave is an additional standard also built on 802.15.4, that was developed specifically with the needs of home automation device makers in mind.

Wired

Twisted Pair Cables

Most wired network infrastructures found in homes utilize Category 5 or Category 6 twisted pair cabling with RJ45 compatible terminations. This medium provides physical connectivity between the Ethernet interfaces present on a large number of residential IP-aware devices. Depending on the grade of cable and quality of installation, speeds of up to 10 Mbit/s, 100 Mbit/s, 1 Gbit/s, or 10Gbit/s are supported.

Fiber Optics

Newer upscale neighborhoods can feature fiber optic cables running directly into the homes. This enables service providers to offer internet services with much higher bandwidth and/or lower latency characteristics associated with end-to-end optical signaling.

Telephone Wires

- VDSL and VDSL2

- HomePNA support up to 160 Mbit/s

Coaxial Cables

The following standards allow devices to communicate over coaxial cables, which are frequently installed to support multiple television sets throughout homes.

- DOCSIS

- The Multimedia over Coax Alliance (MoCA) standard can achieve up to 270 Mbit/s

- CWave

- HomePNA support up to 320 Mbit/s

Power Lines

The ITU-T G.hn and IEEE Powerline standard, which provide high-speed (up to 1 Gbit/s) local area networking over existing home wiring, are examples of home networking technology designed specifically for IPTV delivery. Recently, the IEEE passed proposal P1901 which grounded a standard within the Market for wireline products produced and sold by companies that are part of the HomePlug Alliance. The IEEE is continuously working to push for P1901 to be completely recognized worldwide as the sole standard for all future products that are produced for Home Networking.

- HomePlug and HomePNA are associated standards

- Universal Powerline Association

Endpoint Devices and Services

Traditionally, data-centric equipment such as computers and media players have been the primary tenants of a home network. However, due to the lowering cost of computing and the ubiquity of smartphone usage, many traditionally non-networked home equipment categories now include new variants capable of control or remote monitoring through an app on a smartphone. Newer startups and established home equipment manufacturers alike have begun to offer these products as part of a "Smart" or "Intelligent" or "Connected Home" portfolio. The control and/or monitoring interfaces for these products can be accessed through proprietary smartphone applications specific to that product line.

General Purpose

- Personal computers such as desktops, laptops, netbooks, and tablets

- A network attached storage (NAS) device can be easily accessed via the CIFS or NFS protocols for general storage or for backup purposes.

- A print server can be used to share any directly connected printers with other computers on the network.

- IP phones or smartphones (when connected via Wi-Fi) utilizing VoIP technologies

Entertainment

- Television: Some new TVs and DVRs include integrated WiFi connectivity which allows the user to access services such as Netflix and YouTube

- Home audio: Digital audio players, and stereo systems with network connectivity can allow a user to easily access their music library, often using Bonjour to discover and interface with an instance of iTunes running on a remote PC.

- Gaming: video game consoles rely on connectivity to the home network to enable a significant portion of their overall features, such as the multiplayer in games, social network integration, ability to purchase or demo new games, and receive software updates. Recent consoles have begun more aggressively pursuing the role of the sole entertainment and media hub of the home.

- DLNA is a common protocol used for interoperability between networked media-centric devices in the home

Some older entertainment devices may not feature the appropriate network interfaces required for home network connectivity. In some situations, USB dongles and PCI Network Interface Cards are available as accessories that enable this functionality.

Lighting

- "Connected" light bulbs such as Lifx, Phillips Hue, Samsung Smart Bulb, GE Link

- ZigBee Light Link is the open standards protocol used by current major "Connected" light bulb vendors

Security and Access Control

- Security alarms: iSmartAlarm

- Garage door and gate openers: Liftmaster MyQ, GoGogate

Environmental Monitoring and Conditioning

- HVAC: Nest Learning Thermostat

- Smoke/CO detectors: Nest Protect

Network Management

Embedded Devices

Small standalone embedded home network devices typically require remote configuration from a PC on the same network. For example, broadband modems are often configured through a web browser running on a PC in the same network. These devices usually use a minimal Linux distribution with a lightweight HTTP server running in the background to allow the user to conveniently modify system variables from a GUI rendered in their browser. These pages use HTML forms extensively and make attempts to offer styled, visually appealing views that are also descriptive and easy to use.

Apple Ecosystem Devices

Apple devices aim to make networking as hidden and automatic as possible, utilizing a zero-configuration networking protocol called Bonjour embedded within their otherwise proprietary line of software and hardware products.

Microsoft Ecosystem Devices

Microsoft offers simple access control features built into their Windows operating system. Homegroup is a feature that allows shared disk access, shared printer access and shared scanner access among all computers and users (typically family members) in a home, in a similar fashion as in a small office workgroup, e.g., by means of distributed peer-to-peer networking (without a central server). Additionally, a home server may be added for increased functionality. The *Windows HomeGroup* feature was introduced with Microsoft Windows 7 in order to simplify file sharing in residences. All users (typically all family members), except guest accounts, may access any shared library on any computer that is connected to the home group. Passwords are not required from the family members during logon. Instead, secure file sharing is possible by means of a temporary password that is used when adding a computer to the HomeGroup.

Common Infrastructure Issues

Wireless Signal Loss

The wireless signal strength of the standard residential wireless router may not be powerful enough to cover the entire house or may not be able to get through to all floors of multiple floor residences. In such situations, the installation of one or more wireless repeaters may be necessary.

"Leaky" Wi-Fi

WiFi often extends beyond the boundaries of a home and can create coverage where it is least wanted, offering a channel through which non-residents could compromise a system and retrieve personal data. To prevent this it is usually sufficient to enforce the use of authentication, encryption, or VPN that requires a password for network connectivity.

However new Wi-Fi standards working at 60 GHz, such as 802.11ad, enable confidence that the LAN will not trespass physical barriers, as at such frequencies a simple wall would attenuate the signal considerably.

Electrical Grid Noise

For home networks relying on powerline communication technology, how to deal with electrical noise injected into the system from standard household appliances remains the largest challenge. Whenever any appliance is turned on or turned off it creates noise that could possibly disrupt data transfer through the wiring. IEEE products that are certified to be HomePlug 1.0 compliant have been engineered to no longer interfere with, or receive interference from other devices plugged into the same home's electrical grid.

Future

The convenience, availability, and reliability of externally managed cloud computing resources continues to become an appealing choice for many home-dwellers without interest or experience in IT. For these individuals, the subscription fees and/or privacy risks associated with such services are often perceived as lower cost than having to configure and maintain similar facilities within a home network.

There are increased offerings of service providers' triple play solutions which are usually bundled with Modem/Router/WiFi combination devices that require nothing but the setting of a password to complete configuration. In such situations the home-dweller no longer requires the purchase of an additional routing device to distribute internet access throughout the home—It also obviates the need for the home-dweller having even the most basic understanding of networking technology.

Storage Area Network

A storage area network (SAN) is a network which provides access to consolidated, block level data storage. SANs are primarily used to enhance storage devices, such as disk arrays, tape libraries, and optical jukeboxes, accessible to servers so that the devices appear to the operating system as locally attached devices. A SAN typically has its own network of storage devices that are generally not accessible through the local area network (LAN) by other devices. The cost and complexity of SANs dropped in the early 2000s to levels allowing wider adoption across both enterprise and small to medium-sized business environments.

A SAN does not provide file abstraction, only block-level operations. However, file systems built on top of SANs do provide file-level access, and are known as shared-disk file systems.

Storage

Historically, data centers first created "islands" of SCSI disk arrays as direct-attached storage (DAS), each dedicated to an application, and visible as a number of "virtual hard drives" (i.e. LUNs). Essentially, a SAN consolidates such storage islands together using a high-speed network.

Operating systems maintain their own file systems on their own dedicated, non-shared LUNs, as though they were local to themselves. If multiple systems were simply to attempt to share a LUN, these would interfere with each other and quickly corrupt the data. Any planned sharing of data on different computers within a LUN requires advanced solutions, such as SAN file systems or clustered computing.

Despite such issues, SANs help to increase storage capacity utilization, since multiple servers consolidate their private storage space onto the disk arrays.

Common uses of a SAN include provision of transactionally accessed data that require high-speed block-level access to the hard drives such as email servers, databases, and high usage file servers.

SAN Compared to NAS

Network-attached storage (NAS) was designed before the emergence of SAN as a solution to the limitations of the traditionally used direct-attached storage (DAS), in which individual storage devices such as disk drives are connected directly to each individual computer and not shared. In both a NAS and SAN solution the various computers in a network, such as individual users' desktop computers and dedicated servers running applications ("application servers"), can share a more centralized collection of storage devices via a network connection through the LAN.

Concentrating the storage on one or more NAS servers or in a SAN instead of placing storage devices on each application server allows application server configurations to be optimized for running their applications instead of also storing all the related data and moves the storage management task to the NAS or SAN system. Both NAS and SAN have the potential to reduce the amount of excess storage that must be purchased and provisioned as spare space. In a DAS-only architecture, each computer must be provisioned with enough excess storage to ensure that the computer does not run out of space at an untimely moment. In a DAS architecture the spare storage on one computer cannot be utilized by another. With a NAS or SAN architecture, where storage is shared across the needs of multiple computers, one normally provisions a pool of shared spare storage that will serve the peak needs of the connected computers, which typically is less than the total amount of spare storage that would be needed if individual storage devices were dedicated to each computer.

In a NAS solution the storage devices are directly connected to a "NAS-Server" that makes the storage available at a file-level to the other computers across the LAN. In a SAN solution the storage is made available via a server or other dedicated piece of hardware at a lower "block-level", leaving file system concerns to the "client" side. SAN protocols include Fibre Channel, iSCSI, ATA over Ethernet (AoE) and HyperSCSI. One way to loosely conceptualize the difference between a NAS and a SAN is that NAS appears to the client OS (operating system) as a file server (the client can map network drives to shares on that server) whereas a disk available through a SAN still appears to the client OS as a disk, visible in disk and volume management utilities (along with client's local disks), and available to be formatted with a file system and mounted.

One drawback to both the NAS and SAN architecture is that the connection between the various CPUs and the storage units are no longer dedicated high-speed busses tailored to the needs of storage access. Instead the CPUs use the LAN to communicate, potentially creating bandwidth as well as performance bottlenecks. Additional data security considerations are also required for NAS and SAN setups, as information is being transmitted via a network that potentially includes design flaws, security exploits and other vulnerabilities that may not exist in a DAS setup.

While it is possible to use the NAS or SAN approach to eliminate all storage at user or application computers, typically those computers still have some local Direct Attached Storage for the operating system, various program files and related temporary files used for a variety of purposes, including caching content locally.

To understand their differences, a comparison of SAN, DAS and NAS architectures may be helpful.

SAN-NAS Hybrid

Despite their differences, SAN and NAS are not mutually exclusive, and may be combined as a SAN-NAS hybrid, offering both file-level protocols (NAS) and block-level protocols (SAN) from the same system. An example of this is Openfiler, a free software product running on Linux-based systems. A shared disk file system can also be run on top of a SAN to provide filesystem services.

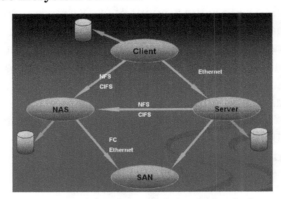

Hybrid using SAN, DAS and NAS technologies.

Benefits

Sharing storage usually simplifies storage administration and adds flexibility since cables and storage devices do not have to be physically moved to shift storage from one server to another.

Other benefits include the ability to allow servers to boot from the SAN itself. This allows for a quick and easy replacement of faulty servers since the SAN can be reconfigured so that a replacement server can use the LUN of the faulty server. While this area of technology is still new, many view it as being the future of the enterprise datacenter.

SANs also tend to enable more effective disaster recovery processes. A SAN could span a distant location containing a secondary storage array. This enables storage replication either implemented by disk array controllers, by server software, or by specialized SAN devices. Since IP WANs are often the least costly method of long-distance transport, the Fibre Channel over IP (FCIP) and iSCSI protocols have been developed to allow SAN extension over IP networks. The traditional physical SCSI layer could support only a few meters of distance - not nearly enough to ensure business continuance in a disaster.

The economic consolidation of disk arrays has accelerated the advancement of several features including I/O caching, snapshotting, and volume cloning (Business Continuance Volumes or BCVs).

Network Types

Most storage networks use the SCSI protocol for communication between servers and disk drive devices. A mapping layer to other protocols is used to form a network:

- ATA over Ethernet (AoE), mapping of ATA over Ethernet

- Fibre Channel Protocol (FCP), the most prominent one, is a mapping of SCSI over Fibre Channel

- Fibre Channel over Ethernet (FCoE)

- ESCON over Fibre Channel (FICON), used by mainframe computers

- HyperSCSI, mapping of SCSI over Ethernet

- iFCP or SANoIP mapping of FCP over IP

- iSCSI, mapping of SCSI over TCP/IP

- iSCSI Extensions for RDMA (iSER), mapping of iSCSI over InfiniBand

Storage networks may also be built using SAS and SATA technologies. SAS evolved from SCSI direct-attached storage. SATA evolved from IDE direct-attached storage. SAS and SATA devices can be networked using SAS Expanders.

Examples of stacked protocols using SCSI:

SAN Infrastructure

Qlogic SAN-switch with optical Fibre Channel connectors installed.

SANs often use a Fibre Channel fabric topology, an infrastructure specially designed to handle storage communications. It provides faster and more reliable access than higher-level protocols used in NAS. A fabric is similar in concept to a network segment in a local area network. A typical Fibre Channel SAN fabric is made up of a number of Fibre Channel switches.

Today, all major SAN equipment vendors also offer some form of Fibre Channel routing solution, and these bring substantial scalability benefits to the SAN architecture by allowing data to cross between different fabrics without merging them. These offerings use proprietary protocol elements, and the top-level architectures being promoted are radically different. They often enable mapping Fibre Channel traffic over IP or over SONET/SDH.

Compatibility

One of the early problems with Fibre Channel SANs was that the switches and other hardware from different manufacturers were not compatible. Although the basic storage protocols FCP were always quite standard, some of the higher-level functions did not interoperate well. Similarly, many host operating systems would react badly to other operating systems sharing the same fabric. Many solutions were pushed to the market before standards were finalized and vendors have since innovated around the standards.

In Media and Entertainment

Video editing workgroups require very high data transfer rates and very low latency. Outside of the enterprise market, this is one area that greatly benefits from SANs.

SANs in Media and Entertainment are often referred to as Serverless SANs due to the nature of the configuration which places the video workflow (ingest, editing, playout) clients directly on the SAN rather than attaching to servers. Control of data flow is managed by a distributed file system such as StorNext by Quantum.

Per-node bandwidth usage control, sometimes referred to as quality of service (QoS), is especially important in video workgroups as it ensures fair and prioritized bandwidth usage across the network, if there is insufficient open bandwidth available.

Storage Virtualization

Storage virtualization is the process of abstracting logical storage from physical storage. The physical storage resources are aggregated into storage pools, from which the logical storage is created. It presents to the user a logical space for data storage and transparently handles the process of mapping it to the physical location, a concept called location transparency. This is implemented in modern disk arrays, often using vendor proprietary solutions. However, the goal of storage virtualization is to group multiple disk arrays from different vendors, scattered over a network, into a single storage device. The single storage device can then be managed uniformly.

SAN Storage QoS (Quality of Service)

SAN Storage QoS (Quality of Service) is the coordination of capacity and performance in a dedicated storage area network. This enables the desired storage performance to be calculated and maintained for network customers accessing the device.

Key factors that affect Storage Area Network QoS(Quality of Service) are:

- Bandwidth – The rate of data throughput available on the system.

- Latency – The time delay for a read/write operation to execute.

- Queue depth – The number of outstanding operations waiting to execute to the underlying disks (Traditional or SSD).

QoS can be impacted in a SAN storage system by unexpected increase in data traffic (usage spike) from one network user that can cause performance to decrease for other users on the same network. This can be known as the "Noisy Neighbor Effect." When QoS services are enabled in a SAN storage system, the "Noisy Neighbor Effect" can be prevented and network storage performance can be accurately predicted.

Using SAN storage QoS is in contrast to using disk over-provisioning in a SAN environment. Over-provisioning can be used to provide additional capacity to compensate for peak network traffic loads. However, where network loads are not predictable, over-provisioning can eventually cause all bandwidth to be fully consumed and latency to increase significantly resulting in SAN performance degradation.

Campus Network

A campus network, campus area network, corporate area network or CAN is a computer network made up of an interconnection of local area networks (LANs) within a limited geographical area. The networking equipments (switches, routers) and transmission media (optical fiber, copper plant, Cat5 cabling etc.) are almost entirely owned by the campus tenant / owner: an enterprise, university, government etc.

University Campuses

College or university campus area networks often interconnect a variety of buildings, including administrative buildings, academic buildings, university libraries, campus or student centers, residence halls, gymnasiums, and other outlying structures, like conference centers, technology centers, and training institutes.

Early examples include the Stanford University Network at Stanford University, Project Athena at MIT, and the Andrew Project at Carnegie Mellon University.

Corporate Campuses

Much like a university campus network, a corporate campus network serves to connect buildings. Examples of such are the networks at Googleplex and Microsoft's campus. Campus networks are normally interconnected with high speed Ethernet links operating over optical fiber such as gigabit Ethernet and 10 Gigabit Ethernet.

Area Range

The range of CAN is 1 km to 5 km. If two buildings have the same domain and they are connected with a network, then it will be considered as CAN only. Though the CAN is mainly used for corporate campuses so the data link will be high speed.

Wide Area Network

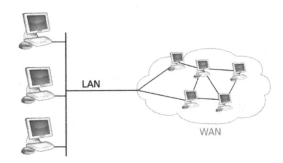

A wide area network (WAN) is a telecommunications network or computer network that extends over a large geographical distance. Wide area networks are often established with leased telecommunication circuits.

Business, education and government entities use wide area networks to relay data among staff, students, clients, buyers, and suppliers from various geographical locations. In essence, this mode of telecommunication allows a business to effectively carry out its daily function regardless of location. The Internet may be considered a WAN.

Related terms for other types of networks are personal area networks (PANs), local area networks (LANs), campus area networks (CANs), or metropolitan area networks (MANs) which are usually limited to a room, building, campus or specific metropolitan area respectively.

Design Options

The textbook definition of a WAN is a computer network spanning regions, countries, or even the world.However, in terms of the application of computer networking protocols and concepts, it may be best to view WANs as computer networking technologies used to transmit data over long distances, and between different LANs, MANs and other localised computer networking architectures. This distinction stems from the fact that common LAN technologies operating at Layer 1/2 (such as the forms of Ethernet or Wifi) are often designed for physically proximal networks, and thus cannot transmit data over tens, hundreds or even thousands of miles or kilometres.

WANs do not just necessarily connect physically disparate LANs. A CAN, for example, may have a localised backbone of a WAN technology, which connects different LANs within a campus. This could be to facilitate higher bandwidth applications, or provide better functionality for users in the CAN.

WANs are used to connect LANs and other types of networks together, so that users and computers in one location can communicate with users and computers in other locations. Many WANs are built for one particular organization and are private. Others, built by Internet service providers, provide connections from an organization's LAN to the Internet. WANs are often built using leased lines. At each end of the leased line, a router connects the LAN on one side with a second router within the LAN on the other. Leased lines can be very expensive. Instead of using leased lines, WANs can also be built using less costly circuit switching or packet switching methods. Network protocols including TCP/IP deliver transport and addressing functions. Protocols including Packet over SONET/SDH, MPLS, ATM and Frame Relay are often used by service providers to deliver the links that are used in WANs. X.25 was an important early WAN protocol, and is often considered to be the "grandfather" of Frame Relay as many of the underlying protocols and functions of X.25 are still in use today (with upgrades) by Frame Relay.

Academic research into wide area networks can be broken down into three areas: mathematical models, network emulation and network simulation.

Performance improvements are sometimes delivered via wide area file services or WAN optimization.

Connection Technology

Many technologies are available for wide area network links. Examples include circuit switched telephone lines, radio wave transmission, and optic fiber. New developments in technologies have successively increased transmission rates. In ca. 1960, a 110 bit/s (bits per second) line was normal on the edge of the WAN, while core links of 56 kbit/s to 64 kbit/s were considered fast. As of 2014, households are connected to the Internet with ADSL, Cable, Wimax, 4G or fiber at speeds ranging from 1 Mbit/s to 1 Gbit/s and the connections in the core of a WAN can range from 1 Gbit/s to 100 Gbit/s.

List of WAN Types

- ATM
- Cable modem
- Dial-up
- DSL

- Frame relay

- ISDN

- Leased line

- SONET

- X.25

- SD-WAN

Virtual Private Network

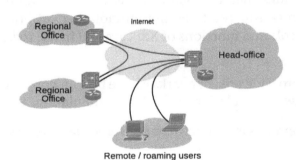

VPN connectivity overview

A virtual private network, also known as a VPN, is a private network that extends across a public network or internet. It enables users to send and receive data across shared or public networks as if their computing devices were directly connected to the private network.

VPNs can provide functionality, security and/or network management benefits to the user. But they can also lead to new issues, and some VPN services, especially "free" ones, can actually violate their users' privacy by logging their usage and making it available without their consent, or make money by selling the user's bandwidth to other users.

Some VPNs allow employees to securely access a corporate intranet while located outside the office. Some can securely connect geographically separated offices of an organization, creating one cohesive network. Individual Internet users can use some VPNs to secure their wireless transactions, to circumvent geo-restrictions and censorship, and/or to connect to proxy servers for the purpose of protecting personal identity and location. But some Internet sites block access via known VPNs to prevent the circumvention of their geo-restrictions.

A VPN is created by establishing a virtual point-to-point connection through the use of dedicated connections, virtual tunneling protocols, or traffic encryption. A VPN available from the public Internet can provide some of the benefits of a wide area network (WAN). From a user perspective, the resources available within the private network can be accessed remotely.

Traditional VPNs are characterized by a point-to-point topology, and they do not tend to support or connect broadcast domains, so services such as Microsoft Windows Net-BIOS may not be fully supported or work as they would on a local area network (LAN). Designers have developed VPN variants, such as Virtual Private LAN Service (VPLS), and layer-2 tunneling protocols, to overcome this limitation.

VPN Prehistory

The first incentive to VPN creation was a desire of different companies and corporations to remove a set of impediments of their successful business development.

Lots of business representatives were looking for the methods of boosting their data security. The question was how to keep information safe while transferring it to the other company departments located far away from the headquarter. In addition to these challenges, there arose the issue of Wi-Fi security. Business needed to make private Wi-Fi wireless network safe for their work. A necessity to economize on remote network access for employees was another reason to make use of a VPN. The X.25 Protocol and Frame Relay were the first steps to forthcoming of a VPN which later conquered not only business market but also became popular with common online users.

A range of events, including the Edward Snowden scandal, made Internet users consider their online privacy and security more seriously. Governments one by one have started adopting laws according to which all communication providers have to keep users' data up to 2 years. Users of countries with a highly censored Internet space like China also started looking for alternative ways of getting unrestricted access to the net. Another spur to VPN popularity was the blocking policy of renowned online streaming channels like Netflix, Hulu, Spotify, etc.

Types

Early data networks allowed VPN-style remote connectivity through dial-up modem or through leased line connections utilizing Frame Relay and Asynchronous Transfer Mode (ATM) virtual circuits, provisioned through a network owned and operated by telecommunication carriers. These networks are not considered true VPNs because they passively secure the data being transmitted by the creation of logical data streams. They have been replaced by VPNs based on IP and IP/Multi-protocol Label Switching (MPLS) Networks, due to significant cost-reductions and increased bandwidth provided by new technologies such as Digital Subscriber Line (DSL) and fiber-optic networks.

VPNs can be either remote-access (connecting a computer to a network) or site-to-site (connecting two networks). In a corporate setting, remote-access VPNs allow employees to access their company's intranet from home or while travelling outside the office, and site-to-site VPNs allow employees in geographically disparate offices to share one cohesive virtual network. A VPN can also be used to interconnect two similar networks over a dissimilar middle network; for example, two IPv6 networks over an IPv4 network.

VPN systems may be classified by:

- The protocols used to tunnel the traffic

- The tunnel's termination point location, e.g., on the customer edge or network-provider edge

- Whether they offer site-to-site or network-to-network connectivity

- The levels of security provided

- The OSI layer they present to the connecting network, such as Layer 2 circuits or Layer 3 network connectivity

- The number of simultaneous connections

Security Mechanisms

VPNs cannot make online connections completely anonymous, but they can usually increase privacy and security. To prevent disclosure of private information, VPNs typically allow only authenticated remote access using tunneling protocols and encryption techniques.

The VPN security model provides:

- Confidentiality such that even if the network traffic is sniffed at the packet level, an attacker would only see encrypted data

- Sender authentication to prevent unauthorized users from accessing the VPN

- Message integrity to detect any instances of tampering with transmitted messages

Secure VPN protocols include the following:

- Internet Protocol Security (IPsec) as initially developed by the Internet Engineering Task Force (IETF) for IPv6, which was required in all standards-compliant implementations of IPv6 before RFC 6434 made it only a recommendation. This standards-based security protocol is also widely used with IPv4 and the Layer 2 Tunneling Protocol. Its design meets most security goals: authentication, integrity, and confidentiality. IPsec uses encryption, encapsulating an IP packet inside an IPsec packet. De-encapsulation happens at the end of the tunnel, where the original IP packet is decrypted and forwarded to its intended destination.

- Transport Layer Security (SSL/TLS) can tunnel an entire network's traffic (as it does in the OpenVPN project and SoftEther VPN project) or secure an individual connection. A number of vendors provide remote-access VPN capabilities through SSL. An SSL VPN can connect from locations where IPsec runs into trouble with Network Address Translation and firewall rules.

- Datagram Transport Layer Security (DTLS) – used in Cisco AnyConnect VPN and in OpenConnect VPN to solve the issues SSL/TLS has with tunneling over UDP.

- Microsoft Point-to-Point Encryption (MPPE) works with the Point-to-Point Tunneling Protocol and in several compatible implementations on other platforms.

- Microsoft Secure Socket Tunneling Protocol (SSTP) tunnels Point-to-Point Protocol (PPP) or Layer 2 Tunneling Protocol traffic through an SSL 3.0 channel. (SSTP was introduced in Windows Server 2008 and in Windows Vista Service Pack 1.)

- Multi Path Virtual Private Network (MPVPN). Ragula Systems Development Company owns the registered trademark "MPVPN".

- Secure Shell (SSH) VPN – OpenSSH offers VPN tunneling (distinct from port forwarding) to secure remote connections to a network or to inter-network links. OpenSSH server provides a limited number of concurrent tunnels. The VPN feature itself does not support personal authentication.

Authentication

Tunnel endpoints must be authenticated before secure VPN tunnels can be established. User-created remote-access VPNs may use passwords, biometrics, two-factor authentication or other cryptographic methods. Network-to-network tunnels often use passwords or digital certificates. They permanently store the key to allow the tunnel to establish automatically, without intervention from the administrator.

Routing

Tunneling protocols can operate in a point-to-point network topology that would theoretically not be considered as a VPN, because a VPN by definition is expected to support arbitrary and changing sets of network nodes. But since most router implementations support a software-defined tunnel interface, customer-provisioned VPNs often are simply defined tunnels running conventional routing protocols.

Provider-provisioned VPN Building-blocks

Depending on whether a provider-provisioned VPN (PPVPN) operates in layer 2 or layer 3, the building blocks described below may be L2 only, L3 only, or combine them both. Multi-protocol label switching (MPLS) functionality blurs the L2-L3 identity.

RFC 4026 generalized the following terms to cover L2 and L3 VPNs, but they were introduced in RFC 2547. More information on the devices below can also be found in Lewis, Cisco Press.

Customer (C) devices

A device that is within a customer's network and not directly connected to the service provider's network. C devices are not aware of the VPN.

Customer Edge device (CE)

A device at the edge of the customer's network which provides access to the PPVPN. Sometimes it's just a demarcation point between provider and customer responsibility. Other providers allow customers to configure it.

Provider edge device (PE)

A PE is a device, or set of devices, at the edge of the provider network which connects to customer networks through CE devices and presents the provider's view of the customer site. PEs are aware of the VPNs that connect through them, and maintain VPN state.

Provider device (P)

A P device operates inside the provider's core network and does not directly interface to any customer endpoint. It might, for example, provide routing for many provider-operated tunnels that belong to different customers' PPVPNs. While the P device is a key part of implementing PPVPNs, it is not itself VPN-aware and does not maintain VPN state. Its principal role is allowing the service provider to scale its PPVPN offerings, for example, by acting as an aggregation point for multiple PEs. P-to-P connections, in such a role, often are high-capacity optical links between major locations of providers.

User-visible PPVPN Services

OSI Layer 2 services

Virtual LAN

A Layer 2 technique that allow for the coexistence of multiple LAN broadcast domains, interconnected via trunks using the IEEE 802.1Q trunking protocol. Other trunking protocols have been used but have become obsolete, including Inter-Switch Link (ISL), IEEE 802.10 (originally a security protocol but a subset was introduced for trunking), and ATM LAN Emulation (LANE).

Virtual private LAN service (VPLS)

Developed by Institute of Electrical and Electronics Engineers, VLANs allow multiple tagged LANs to share common trunking. VLANs frequently comprise only customer-owned facilities. Whereas VPLS as described in the above section (OSI Layer 1 services) supports emulation of both point-to-point and point-to-multipoint topologies, the method discussed here extends Layer 2 technologies such as 802.1d and 802.1q LAN trunking to run over transports such as Metro Ethernet.

As used in this context, a VPLS is a Layer 2 PPVPN, rather than a private line, emulating the full functionality of a traditional local area network (LAN). From a user standpoint, a VPLS makes it possible to interconnect several LAN segments over a packet-switched, or optical, provider core; a core transparent to the user, making the remote LAN segments behave as one single LAN.

In a VPLS, the provider network emulates a learning bridge, which optionally may include VLAN service.

Pseudo wire (PW)

PW is similar to VPLS, but it can provide different L2 protocols at both ends. Typically, its interface is a WAN protocol such as Asynchronous Transfer Mode or Frame Relay. In contrast, when aiming to provide the appearance of a LAN contiguous between two or more locations, the Virtual Private LAN service or IPLS would be appropriate.

Ethernet over IP tunneling

EtherIP (RFC 3378) is an Ethernet over IP tunneling protocol specification. EtherIP has only packet encapsulation mechanism. It has no confidentiality nor message integrity protection. EtherIP was introduced in the FreeBSD network stack and the SoftEther VPN server program.

IP-only LAN-like service (IPLS)

A subset of VPLS, the CE devices must have Layer 3 capabilities; the IPLS presents packets rather than frames. It may support IPv4 or IPv6.

OSI Layer 3 PPVPN Architectures

This section discusses the main architectures for PPVPNs, one where the PE disambiguates duplicate addresses in a single routing instance, and the other, virtual router, in which the PE contains a virtual router instance per VPN. The former approach, and its variants, have gained the most attention.

One of the challenges of PPVPNs involves different customers using the same address space, especially the IPv4 private address space. The provider must be able to disambiguate overlapping addresses in the multiple customers' PPVPNs.

BGP/MPLS PPVPN

In the method defined by RFC 2547, BGP extensions advertise routes in the IPv4 VPN address family, which are of the form of 12-byte strings, beginning with an 8-byte Route Distinguisher (RD) and ending with a 4-byte IPv4 address. RDs disambiguate otherwise duplicate addresses in the same PE.

PEs understand the topology of each VPN, which are interconnected with MPLS tunnels, either directly or via P routers. In MPLS terminology, the P routers are Label Switch Routers without awareness of VPNs.

Virtual router PPVPN

The virtual router architecture, as opposed to BGP/MPLS techniques, requires no modification to existing routing protocols such as BGP. By the provisioning of logically independent routing domains, the customer operating a VPN is completely responsible for the address space. In the various MPLS tunnels, the different PPVPNs are disambiguated by their label, but do not need routing distinguishers.

Unencrypted Tunnels

Some virtual networks may not use encryption to protect the privacy of data. While VPNs often provide security, an unencrypted overlay network does not neatly fit within the secure or trusted categorization. For example, a tunnel set up between two hosts that used Generic Routing Encapsulation (GRE) would in fact be a virtual private network, but neither secure nor trusted.

Native plaintext tunneling protocols include Layer 2 Tunneling Protocol (L2TP) when it is set up without IPsec and Point-to-Point Tunneling Protocol (PPTP) or Microsoft Point-to-Point Encryption (MPPE).

Trusted Delivery Networks

Trusted VPNs do not use cryptographic tunneling, and instead rely on the security of a single provider's network to protect the traffic.

- Multi-Protocol Label Switching (MPLS) often overlays VPNs, often with quality-of-service control over a trusted delivery network.

- Layer 2 Tunneling Protocol (L2TP) which is a standards-based replacement, and a compromise taking the good features from each, for two proprietary VPN protocols: Cisco's Layer 2 Forwarding (L2F) (obsolete as of 2009) and Microsoft's Point-to-Point Tunneling Protocol (PPTP).

From the security standpoint, VPNs either trust the underlying delivery network, or must enforce security with mechanisms in the VPN itself. Unless the trusted delivery network runs among physically secure sites only, both trusted and secure models need an authentication mechanism for users to gain access to the VPN.

VPNs in Mobile Environments

Mobile virtual private networks are used in settings where an endpoint of the VPN is not fixed to a single IP address, but instead roams across various networks such as data networks from cellular carriers or between multiple Wi-Fi access points. Mobile VPNs have been widely used in public safety, where they give law enforcement officers access to mission-critical applications, such as computer-assisted dispatch and criminal databases, while they travel between different subnets of a mobile network. They are also used in field service management and by healthcare organizations, among other industries.

Increasingly, mobile VPNs are being adopted by mobile professionals who need reliable connections. They are used for roaming seamlessly across networks and in and out of wireless coverage areas without losing application sessions or dropping the secure VPN session. A conventional VPN can not withstand such events because the network tunnel is disrupted, causing applications to disconnect, time out, or fail, or even cause the computing device itself to crash.

Instead of logically tying the endpoint of the network tunnel to the physical IP address, each tunnel is bound to a permanently associated IP address at the device. The mobile VPN software handles the necessary network authentication and maintains the network sessions in a manner transparent to the application and the user. The Host Identity Protocol (HIP), under study by the Internet Engineering Task Force, is designed to support mobility of hosts by separating the role of IP addresses for host identification from their locator functionality in an IP network. With HIP a mobile host maintains its logical connections established via the host identity identifier while associating with different IP addresses when roaming between access networks.

VPN on Routers

With the increasing use of VPNs, many have started deploying VPN connectivity on routers for additional security and encryption of data transmission by using various cryptographic techniques. Setting up VPN support on a router and establishing a VPN allows any networked device to have access to the entire network—all devices look like local devices with local addresses. Supported devices are not restricted to those capable of running a VPN client.

Many router manufacturers, including Asus, Cisco, Draytek, Linksys, Netgear, and Yamaha, supply routers with built-in VPN clients. Some use open-source firmware such as DD-WRT, OpenWRT and Tomato, in order to support additional protocols such as OpenVPN.

Setting up VPN services on a router requires a deep knowledge of network security and careful installation. Minor misconfiguration of VPN connections can leave the network vulnerable.Performance will vary depending on the ISP.

Networking limitations

One major limitation of traditional VPNs is that they are point-to-point, and do not tend to support or connect broadcast domains. Therefore, communication, software, and networking, which are based on layer 2 and broadcast packets, such as NetBIOS used in Windows networking, may not be fully supported or work exactly as they would on a real LAN. Variants on VPN, such as Virtual Private LAN Service (VPLS), and layer 2 tunneling protocols, are designed to overcome this limitation.

IEEE 802.20

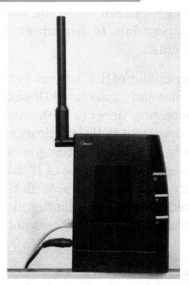

An iBurst desktop wireless modem by Kyocera in 2008 for IEEE 802.20 which provides an Ethernet interface

IEEE 802.20 or Mobile Broadband Wireless Access (MBWA) is a specification by the standard association of the Institute of Electrical and Electronics Engineers (IEEE) for mobile wireless Internet access networks. The main standard was published in 2008. MBWA is no longer being actively developed.

This wireless broadband technology is also known and promoted as iBurst (or HC-SD-MA, High Capacity Spatial Division Multiple Access). It was originally developed by ArrayComm and optimizes the use of its bandwidth with the help of smart antennas. Kyocera is the manufacturer of iBurst devices.

Description

iBurst is a mobile broadband wireless access system that was first developed by Array-Comm, and announced with partner Sony in April 2000. It was adopted as the High Capacity – Spatial Division Multiple Access (HC-SDMA) radio interface standard (ATIS-0700004-2005) by the Alliance for Telecommunications Industry Solutions (ATIS). The standard was prepared by ATIS' Wireless Technology and Systems Committee's Wireless Wideband Internet Access subcommittee and accepted as an American National Standard in 2005.

HC-SDMA was announced as considered by ISO TC204 WG16 for the continuous communications standards architecture, known as Communications, Air-interface, Long and Medium range (CALM), which ISO is developing for intelligent transport systems (ITS). ITS may include applications for public safety, network congestion management during traffic incidents, automatic toll booths, and more. An official liaison was established between WTSC and ISO TC204 WG16 for this in 2005.

The HC-SDMA interface provides wide-area broadband wireless data-connectivity for fixed, portable and mobile computing devices and appliances. The protocol is designed to be implemented with smart antenna array techniques (called MIMO for multiple-input multiple-output) to substantially improve the radio frequency (RF) coverage, capacity and performance for the system. In January 2006, the IEEE 802.20 Mobile Broadband Wireless Access Working Group adopted a technology proposal that included the use of the HC-SDMA standard for the 625kHz Multi-Carrier time division duplex (TDD) mode of the standard. One Canadian vendor operates at 1.8 GHz.

Technical Description

The HC-SDMA interface operates on a similar premise as cellular phones, with hand-offs between HC-SDMA cells repeatedly providing the user with a seamless wireless Internet access even when moving at the speed of a car or train.

The standard's proposed benefits:

- IP roaming & handoff (at more than 1 Mbit/s)

- New MAC and PHY with IP and adaptive antennas

- Optimized for full mobility up to vehicular speeds of 250 km/h

- Operates in Licensed Bands (below 3.5 GHz)

- Uses Packet Architecture

- Low Latency

Some technical details were:

- Bandwidths of 5, 10, and 20 MHz.

- Peak data rates of 80 Mbit/s.

- Spectral efficiency above 1 bit/sec/Hz using multiple input/multiple output technology (MIMO).

- Layered frequency hopping allocates OFDM carriers to near, middle, and far-away handsets, improving SNR (works best for SISO handsets.)

- Supports low-bit rates efficiently, carrying up to 100 phone calls per MHz.

- Hybrid ARQ with up to 6 transmissions and several choices for interleaving.

- Basic slot period of 913 microseconds carrying 8 OFDM symbols.

- One of the first standards to support both TDM (FL,RL) and separate-frequency (FL, RL) deployments.

The protocol:

- specifies base station and client device RF characteristics, including output power levels, transmit frequencies and timing error, pulse shaping, in-band and out-of band spurious emissions, receiver sensitivity and selectivity;

- defines associated frame structures for the various burst types including standard uplink and downlink traffic, paging and broadcast burst types;

- specifies the modulation, forward error correction, interleaving and scrambling for various burst types;

- describes the various logical channels (broadcast, paging, random access, configuration and traffic channels) and their roles in establishing communication over the radio link; and

- specifies procedures for error recovery and retry.

The protocol also supports Layer 3 (L3) mechanisms for creating and controlling logical connections (sessions) between client device and base including registration, stream start, power control, handover, link adaptation, and stream closure, as well as L3 mechanisms for client device authentication and secure transmission on the data links. Currently deployed iBurst systems allow connectivity up to 2 Mbit/s for each subscriber equipment. Apparently there will be future firmware upgrade possibilities to increase these speeds up to 5 Mbit/s, consistent with HC-SDMA protocol.

History

The 802.20 working group was proposed in response to products using technology originally developed by ArrayComm marketed under the iBurst brand name. The Alliance for Telecommunications Industry Solutions adopted iBurst as ATIS-0700004-2005. The Mobile Broadband Wireless Access (MBWA) Working Group was approved by IEEE Standards Board on December 11, 2002 to prepare a formal specification for a packet-based air interface designed for Internet Protocol-based services. At its height, the group had 175 participants.

On June 8, 2006, the IEEE-SA Standards Board directed that all activities of the 802.20 Working Group be temporarily suspended until October 1, 2006. The decision came from complaints of a lack of transparency, and that the group's chair, Jerry Upton, was favoring Qualcomm. The unprecedented step came after other working groups had also been subject to related allegations of large companies undermining the standard process. Intel and Motorola had filed appeals, claiming they were not given time to prepare proposals. These claims were cited in a 2007 lawsuit filed by Broadcom against Qualcomm.

On September 15, 2006, the IEEE-SA Standards Board approved a plan to enable the working group to move towards completion and approval by reorganizing. The chair at the November 2006 meeting was Arnold Greenspan. On July 17, 2007, the IEEE 802 Executive Committee along with its 802.20 Oversight Committee approved a change to voting in the 802.20 working group. Instead of a vote per attending individual, each entity would have a single vote.

On June 12, 2008, the IEEE approved the base standard to be published. Additional supporting standards included IEEE 802.20.2-2010, a protocol conformance statement, 802.20.3-2010, minimum performance characteristics, an amendment 802.20a-2010 for a Management Information Base and some corrections, and amendment 802.20b-2010 to support bridging.

802.20 standard was put to hibernation on March 2011 due to lack of activity.

In 2004 another wireless standard group had been formed as IEEE 802.22, for wireless regional networks using unused television station frequencies. Trials such as those in the Netherlands by T-Mobile International in 2004 were announced as "Pre-standard 802.20". These were based on an orthogonal frequency-division multiplexing technology known as FLASH-OFDM developed by Flarion (since 2006 owned by Qualcomm). However, other service providers soon adopted 802.16e (the mobile version of WiMAX).

In September 2008, the Association of Radio Industries and Businesses in Japan adopted the 802.20-2008 standard as ARIB STD-T97. Kyocera markets products supporting the standard under the iBurst name. As of March 2011, Kyocera claimed 15 operators offered service in 12 countries.

Commercial use

Various options are already commercially available using:

- Desktop modem with USB and Ethernet ports (with external power supply)
- Portable USB modem (using USB power supply)
- Laptop modem (PC card)
- Wireless Residential Gateway
- Mobile Broadband Router

iBurst was commercially available in twelve countries in 2011 including Azerbaijan, Lebanon, and United States.

iBurst (Pty) Ltd started operation in South Africa in 2005.

iBurst Africa International provided the service in Ghana in 2007, and then later in Mozambique, Democratic Republic of the Congo and Kenya.

MoBif Wireless Broadband Sdn Bhd, started service in Malaysia in 2007, changing its name to iZZinet. The provider ceased operations in March 2011.

In Australia, Veritel and Personal Broadband Australia (a subsidiary of Commander Australia Limited), offered iBurst services however both have since been shut down after the increase of 3.5G and 4G mobile data services. BigAir acquired Veritel's iBurst customers in 2006, and shut down the service in 2009. Personal Broadband Australia's iBurst service was shut down in December 2008.

Backbone Network

A backbone is a part of computer network that interconnects various pieces of network, providing a path for the exchange of information between different LANs or subnetworks. A backbone can tie together diverse networks in the same building, in different buildings in a campus environment, or over wide areas. Normally, the backbone's capacity is greater than the networks connected to it.

NSFNET T3 Network 1992

A diagram of a typical nationwide network backbone.

A large corporation that has many locations may have a backbone network that ties all of the locations together, for example, if a server cluster needs to be accessed by different departments of a company that are located at different geographical locations. The pieces of the network connections (for example: ethernet, wireless) that bring these departments together is often mentioned as network backbone. Network congestion is often taken into consideration while designing backbones.

One example of a backbone network is the Internet backbone.

Distributed Backbone

A distributed backbone is a backbone network that consists of a number of connectivity devices connected to a series of central connectivity devices, such as hubs, switches, or routers, in a hierarchy. This kind of topology allows for simple expansion and limited capital outlay for growth, because more layers of devices can be added to existing layers. In a distributed backbone network, all of the devices that access the backbone share the transmission media, as every device connected to this network is sent all transmissions placed on that network.

Distributed backbones, in all practicality, are in use by all large-scale networks. Applications in enterprise-wide scenarios confined to a single building are also practical, as certain connectivity devices can be assigned to certain floors or departments. Each floor or department possesses a LAN and a wiring closet with that workgroup's main hub or router connected to a bus-style network using backbone cabling . Another advantage of using a distributed backbone is the ability for network administrator to segregate workgroups for ease of management.

There is the possibility of single points of failure, referring to connectivity devices high in the series hierarchy. The distributed backbone must be designed to separate network traffic circulating on each individual LAN from the backbone network traffic by using access devices such as routers and bridges.

Collapsed Backbone

A collapsed backbone (inverted backbone, backbone-in-a-box) is a type of backbone network architecture. The traditional backbone network goes over the globe to provide interconnectivity to the remote hubs. In most cases, the backbones are the links while the switching or routing functions are done by the equipment at each hub. It is a distributed architecture.

In the case of a collapsed or inverted backbone, each hub provides a link back to a central location to be connected to a backbone-in-a-box. That box can be a switch or a router. The topology and architecture of a collapsed backbone is a star or a rooted tree.

The main advantages of the collapsed backbone approach are

1. ease of management since the backbone is in a single location and in a single box, and

2. since the backbone is essentially the back plane or internal switching matrix of the box, proprietary, high performance technology can be used.

However, the draw back of the collapsed backbone is that if the box housing the backbone is down or there are reachability problem to the central location, the entire network will crash. These problems can be minimized by having redundant backbone boxes as well as having secondary/backup backbone locations.

Parallel Backbone

There are a few different types of backbones that are used for an enterprise-wide network. When organizations are looking for a very strong and trustworthy backbone they should choose a parallel backbone. This backbone is a variation of a collapsed backbone in that it uses a central node (connection point). Although, with a parallel backbone, it allows for duplicate connections when there is more than one router or switch. Each switch and router are connected by two cables. By having more than one cable connecting each device, it ensures network connectivity to any area of the enterprise-wide network.

Parallel backbones are more expensive than other backbone networks because they require more cabling than the other network topologies. Although this can be a major factor when deciding which enterprise-wide topology to use, the expense of it makes up for the efficiency it creates by adding increased performance and fault tolerance. Most organizations use parallel backbones when there are critical devices on the network. For example, if there is important data, such as payroll, that should be accessed at all times by multiple departments, then your organization should choose to implement a Parallel Backbone to make sure that the connectivity is never lost.

Serial Backbone

A serial backbone is the simplest kind of backbone network. Serial backbones consist of two or more internet working devices connected to each other by a single cable in a daisy-chain fashion. A daisy chain is a group of connectivity devices linked together in a serial fashion. Hubs are often connected in this way to extend a network. However, hubs are not the only device that can be connected in a serial backbone. Gateways, routers, switches and bridges more commonly form part of the backbone. The serial backbone topology could be used for enterprise-wide networks, though it is rarely implemented for that purpose.

References

- Groth, David and Skandler, Toby (2005). Network+ Study Guide, Fourth Edition. Sybex, Inc. ISBN 0-7821-4406-3.

- Lewis, Mark (2006). Comparing, designing, and deploying VPNs (1st print. ed.). Indianapolis, Ind.: Cisco Press. pp. 5–6. ISBN 1587051796.

- Dean, Tamara (2010). Network+ Guide to Networks 5th Edition. Boston, MA: Cengage Course Technology. pp. 203–204. ISBN 1-4239-0245-9.

- Lamont Wood (2008-01-31). "The LAN turns 30, but will it reach 40?". Computerworld.com. Retrieved 2016-06-02.

- Henry, Alan. "Hola Better Internet Sells Your Bandwidth, Turning Its VPN into a Botnet". Lifehacker. Retrieved 2016-05-27.

- "Overview of Provider Provisioned Virtual Private Networks (PPVPN)". Secure Thoughts. Retrieved 29 August 2016.

- "StorNext Storage Manager - High-speed file sharing, Data Management and Digital Archiving Software". Quantum.com. Retrieved 2013-07-08.

- Turner, Brough (12 September 2007). "Congestion in the Backbone: Telecom and Internet Solutions". CircleID. Retrieved 2 October 2013.

- "Network (SUNet — The Stanford University Network)". Stanford University Information Technology Services. July 16, 2010. Retrieved May 4, 2011.

- "ATIS Standard Enables Seamless Wireless Wideband Connectivity at High Speeds". News release. ATIS. September 26, 2005. Retrieved August 21, 2011.

- Radhakrishna Canchi (March 11, 2011). "Mobile Broadband Wireless Access Systems Supporting Vehicular Mobility" (PDF). Retrieved August 21, 2011.

- "ATIS Standard Enables Seamless Wireless Wideband Connectivity at High Speeds". News release. ATIS. September 26, 2005. Retrieved August 21, 2011.

- Kathy Kowalenko (December 5, 2006). "Standards Uproar Leads to Working Group Overhaul". The Institute. IEEE. Retrieved August 21, 2011.

- Loring Wirbel (June 15, 2006). "IEEE 802.20 working group declares 'cooling off' period". EE Times. Retrieved August 19, 2011.

- Loring Wirbel (April 13, 2007). "Broadcom cites Qualcomm's standards moves in new lawsuit". EE Times. Retrieved August 19, 2011.

- "IEEE-SA Adopts Plan to Move 802.20 Broadband Wireless Standard Forward". News release. IEEE Standards Association. Archived from the original on December 10, 2008. Retrieved August 19, 2011.

- Loring Wirbel (July 18, 2007). "IEEE adopts 'one entity, one vote' for 802.20 mobile broadband". EE Times. Retrieved August 21, 2011.

- Stephen Lawson (July 22, 2007). "Wireless Standards Group Changes Rules for Parity". PC World. Retrieved August 21, 2011.

- "IEEE 802.20™: Mobile Broadband Wireless Access (MBWA)". Official standards free download web page. IEEE 802 committee. Retrieved August 20, 2011.

- Mobile Pipeline News (September 8, 2004). "Pre-standard 802.20 broadband trial starts in Holland". EE Times. Retrieved August 19, 2011.

- Patrick Mannion (April 15, 2004). "Navini dumps 802.20 mobile broadband for WiMax". EE Times. Retrieved August 19, 2011.

- Tim Lohman (March 16, 2010). "BigAir touts wireless market opportunities". Computerworld. Retrieved August 21, 2011.

Understanding Network Topology

There are various elements involved in computer networking, such as network links and network nodes. The arrangement of these elements is termed as network topology. Some of the classifications of network topology are ring network, bus network, star network and mesh networking. This section is an overview of the subject matter incorporating all the major aspects of network topology.

Network Topology

Network topology is the arrangement of the various elements (links, nodes, etc.) of a computer network. Essentially, it is the topological structure of a network and may be depicted physically or logically. *Physical topology* is the placement of the various components of a network, including device location and cable installation, while *logical topology* illustrates how data flows within a network, regardless of its physical design. Distances between nodes, physical interconnections, transmission rates, or signal types may differ between two networks, yet their topologies may be identical.

An example is a local area network (LAN). Any given node in the LAN has one or more physical links to other devices in the network; graphically mapping these links results in a geometric shape that can be used to describe the physical topology of the network. Conversely, mapping the data flow between the components determines the logical topology of the network.

Topology

Two basic categories of network topologies exist, physical topologies and logical topologies.

The cabling layout used to link devices is the physical topology of the network. This refers to the layout of cabling, the locations of nodes, and the interconnections between the nodes and the cabling. The physical topology of a network is determined by the capabilities of the network access devices and media, the level of control or fault tolerance desired, and the cost associated with cabling or telecommunications circuits.

In contrast, logical topology is the way that the signals act on the network media, or the way that the data passes through the network from one device to the next without regard to the physical interconnection of the devices. A network's logical topology is not necessarily the same as its physical topology. For example, the original twisted pair Ethernet using repeater hubs was a logical bus topology carried on a physical star topology. Token ring is a logical ring topology, but is wired as a physical star from the media access unit. Logical topologies are often closely associated with media access control methods and protocols. Some networks are able to dynamically change their logical topology through configuration changes to their routers and switches.

Classification

The study of network topology recognizes eight basic topologies: point-to-point, bus, star, ring or circular, mesh, tree, hybrid, or daisy chain.

Point-to-point

The simplest topology with a dedicated link between two endpoints. Easiest to understand, of the variations of point-to-point topology, is a point-to-point communications channel that appears, to the user, to be permanently associated with the two endpoints. A child's tin can telephone is one example of a *physical dedicated* channel.

Using circuit-switching or packet-switching technologies, a point-to-point circuit can be set up dynamically and dropped when no longer needed. Switched point-to-point topologies are the basic model of conventional telephony.

The value of a permanent point-to-point network is unimpeded communications between the two endpoints. The value of an on-demand point-to-point connection is proportional to the number of potential pairs of subscribers and has been expressed as Metcalfe's Law.

Bus

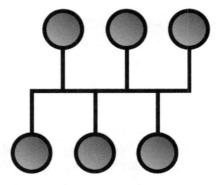

Bus network topology

In local area networks where bus topology is used, each node is connected to a single cable, by the help of interface connectors. This central cable is the backbone of the network and is known as the bus (thus the name). A signal from the source travels in both directions to all machines connected on the bus cable until it finds the intended recipient. If the machine address does not match the intended address for the data, the machine ignores the data. Alternatively, if the data matches the machine address, the data is accepted. Because the bus topology consists of only one wire, it is rather inexpensive to implement when compared to other topologies. However, the low cost of implementing the technology is offset by the high cost of managing the network. Additionally, because only one cable is utilized, it can be the single point of failure.

Linear Bus

The type of network topology in which all of the nodes of the network are connected to a common transmission medium which has exactly two endpoints (this is the 'bus', which is also commonly referred to as the backbone, or trunk) – all data that is transmitted between nodes in the network is transmitted over this common transmission medium and is able to be received by all nodes in the network simultaneously.

Note: When the electrical signal reaches the end of the bus, the signal is reflected back down the line, causing unwanted interference. As a solution, the two endpoints of the bus are normally terminated with a device called a terminator that prevents this reflection.

Distributed Bus

The type of network topology in which all of the nodes of the network are connected to a common transmission medium which has more than two endpoints that are created by adding branches to the main section of the transmission medium – the physical distributed bus topology functions in exactly the same fashion as the physical linear bus topology (i.e., all nodes share a common transmission medium).

Star

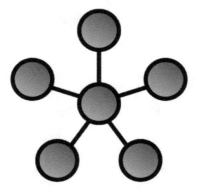

Star network topology

In local area networks with a star topology, each network host is connected to a central hub with a point-to-point connection. So it can be said that every computer is indirectly connected to every other node with the help of the hub. In Star topology, every node (computer workstation or any other peripheral) is connected to a central node called hub, router or switch. The switch is the server and the peripherals are the clients. The network does not necessarily have to resemble a star to be classified as a star network, but all of the nodes on the network must be connected to one central device. All traffic that traverses the network passes through the central hub. The hub acts as a signal repeater. The star topology is considered the easiest topology to design and implement. An advantage of the star topology is the simplicity of adding additional nodes. The primary disadvantage of the star topology is that the hub represents a single point of failure.

Extended Star

A type of network topology in which a network that is based upon the physical star topology has one or more repeaters between the central node and the peripheral or 'spoke' nodes, the repeaters being used to extend the maximum transmission distance of the point-to-point links between the central node and the peripheral nodes beyond that which is supported by the transmitter power of the central node or beyond that which is supported by the standard upon which the physical layer of the physical star network is based.

If the repeaters in a network that is based upon the physical extended star topology are replaced with hubs or switches, then a hybrid network topology is created that is referred to as a physical hierarchical star topology, although some texts make no distinction between the two topologies.

Distributed Star

A type of network topology that is composed of individual networks that are based upon the physical star topology connected in a linear fashion – i.e., 'daisy-chained' – with no central or top level connection point (e.g., two or more 'stacked' hubs, along with their associated star connected nodes or 'spokes').

Ring

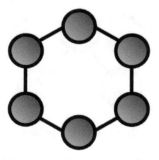

Ring network topology

A ring topology is a bus topology in a closed loop. Data travels around the ring in one direction. When one node sends data to another, the data passes through each intermediate node on the ring until it reaches its destination. The intermediate nodes repeat (retransmit) the data to keep the signal strong. Every node is a peer; there is no hierarchical relationship of clients and servers. If one node is unable to retransmit data, it severs communication between the nodes before and after it in the bus.

Mesh

The value of fully meshed networks is proportional to the exponent of the number of subscribers, assuming that communicating groups of any two endpoints, up to and including all the endpoints, is approximated by Reed's Law.

Fully Connected Network

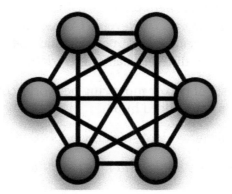

Fully connected mesh topology

In a *fully connected network*, all nodes are interconnected. (In graph theory this is called a complete graph.) The simplest fully connected network is a two-node network. A fully connected network doesn't need to use packet switching or broadcasting. However, since the number of connections grows quadratically with the number of nodes:

$$c = \frac{n(n-1)}{2}.$$

This makes it impractical for large networks.

Partially Connected Network

In a partially connected network, certain nodes are connected to exactly one other node; but some nodes are connected to two or more other nodes with a point-to-point link. This makes it possible to make use of some of the redundancy of mesh topology that is physically fully connected, without the expense and complexity required for a connection between every node in the network.

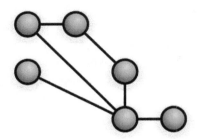

Partially connected mesh topology

Hybrid

Hybrid networks combine two or more topologies in such a way that the resulting network does not exhibit one of the standard topologies (e.g., bus, star, ring, etc.). For example, a tree network (or *star-bus network*) is a hybrid topology in which star networks are interconnected via bus networks. However, a tree network connected to another tree network is still topologically a tree network, not a distinct network type. A hybrid topology is always produced when two different basic network topologies are connected.

A *star-ring* network consists of two or more ring networks connected using a multistation access unit (MAU) as a centralized hub.

Snowflake topology is a star network of star networks.

Two other hybrid network types are *hybrid mesh* and *hierarchical star*.

Daisy Chain

Except for star-based networks, the easiest way to add more computers into a network is by daisy-chaining, or connecting each computer in series to the next. If a message is intended for a computer partway down the line, each system bounces it along in sequence until it reaches the destination. A daisy-chained network can take two basic forms: linear and ring.

- A linear topology puts a two-way link between one computer and the next. However, this was expensive in the early days of computing, since each computer (except for the ones at each end) required two receivers and two transmitters.

- By connecting the computers at each end, a ring topology can be formed. An advantage of the ring is that the number of transmitters and receivers can be cut in half, since a message will eventually loop all of the way around. When a node sends a message, the message is processed by each computer in the ring. If the ring breaks at a particular link then the transmission can be sent via the reverse path thereby ensuring that all nodes are always connected in the case of a single failure.

Centralization

The star topology reduces the probability of a network failure by connecting all of the peripheral nodes (computers, etc.) to a central node. When the physical star topology is applied to a logical bus network such as Ethernet, this central node (traditionally a hub) rebroadcasts all transmissions received from any peripheral node to all peripheral nodes on the network, sometimes including the originating node. All peripheral nodes may thus communicate with all others by transmitting to, and receiving from, the central node only. The failure of a transmission line linking any peripheral node to the central node will result in the isolation of that peripheral node from all others, but the remaining peripheral nodes will be unaffected. However, the disadvantage is that the failure of the central node will cause the failure of all of the peripheral nodes.

If the central node is *passive*, the originating node must be able to tolerate the reception of an echo of its own transmission, delayed by the two-way round trip transmission time (i.e. to and from the central node) plus any delay generated in the central node. An *active* star network has an active central node that usually has the means to prevent echo-related problems.

A tree topology (a.k.a. hierarchical topology) can be viewed as a collection of star networks arranged in a hierarchy. This tree has individual peripheral nodes (e.g. leaves) which are required to transmit to and receive from one other node only and are not required to act as repeaters or regenerators. Unlike the star network, the functionality of the central node may be distributed.

As in the conventional star network, individual nodes may thus still be isolated from the network by a single-point failure of a transmission path to the node. If a link connecting a leaf fails, that leaf is isolated; if a connection to a non-leaf node fails, an entire section of the network becomes isolated from the rest.

To alleviate the amount of network traffic that comes from broadcasting all signals to all nodes, more advanced central nodes were developed that are able to keep track of the identities of the nodes that are connected to the network. These network switches will "learn" the layout of the network by "listening" on each port during normal data transmission, examining the data packets and recording the address/identifier of each connected node and which port it is connected to in a lookup table held in memory. This lookup table then allows future transmissions to be forwarded to the intended destination only.

Decentralization

In a partially connected mesh topology, there are at least two nodes with two or more paths between them to provide redundant paths in case the link providing one of the paths fails. Decentralization is often used to compensate for the single-point-failure disadvantage that is present when using a single device as a central node (e.g., in star and tree networks). A special kind of mesh, limiting the number of hops between two nodes, is a hypercube. The number of arbitrary forks in mesh networks makes them more difficult to design and implement, but their decentralized nature makes them very useful. In 2012 the IEEE published the Shortest Path Bridging protocol to ease configuration tasks and allows all paths to be active which increases bandwidth and redundancy between all devices.

This is similar in some ways to a grid network, where a linear or ring topology is used to connect systems in multiple directions. A multidimensional ring has a toroidal topology, for instance.

A *fully connected network, complete topology,* or *full mesh topology* is a network topology in which there is a direct link between all pairs of nodes. In a fully connected network with n nodes, there are n(n-1)/2 direct links. Networks designed with this topology are usually very expensive to set up, but provide a high degree of reliability due to the multiple paths for data that are provided by the large number of redundant links between nodes. This topology is mostly seen in military applications.

Ring Network

A ring network is a network topology in which each node connects to exactly two other nodes, forming a single continuous pathway for signals through each node - a ring. Data travels from node to node, with each node along the way handling every packet.

Rings can be unidirectional, with all traffic travelling either clockwise or anticlockwise around the ring, or bidirectional (as in SONET/SDH). Because a unidirectional ring topology provides only one pathway between any two nodes, unidirectional ring networks may be disrupted by the failure of a single link. A node failure or cable break might isolate every node attached to the ring. In response, some ring networks add a "counter-rotating ring" (C-Ring) to form a redundant topology: in the event of a break, data are wrapped back onto the complementary ring before reaching the end of the cable, maintaining a path to every node along the resulting C-Ring. Such "dual ring" networks include Spatial Reuse Protocol, Fiber Distributed Data Interface (FDDI), and Resilient Packet Ring. 802.5 networks - also known as IBM token ring networks - avoid the weakness of a ring topology altogether: they actually use a *star* topology at the *physical* layer and a media access unit (MAU) to *imitate* a ring at the *datalink* layer.

Some SONET/SDH rings have two sets of bidirectional links between nodes. This allows maintenance or failures at multiple points of the ring usually without loss of the primary traffic on the outer ring by switching the traffic onto the inner ring past the failure points.

Advantages

- Very orderly network where every device has access to the token and the opportunity to transmit

- Performs better than a bus topology under heavy network load

- Does not require a central node to manage the connectivity between the computers

- Due to the point to point line configuration of devices with a device on either side (each device is connected to its immediate neighbor), it is quite easy to install and reconfigure since adding or removing a device requires moving just two connections.

- Point to point line configuration makes it easy to identify and isolate faults.

- Reconfiguration for line faults of bidirectional rings can be very fast, as switching happens at a high level, and thus the traffic does not require individual rerouting.

Disadvantages

- One malfunctioning workstation can create problems for the entire network. This can be solved by using a dual ring or a switch that closes off the break.

- Moving, adding and changing the devices can affect the network

- Communication delay is directly proportional to number of nodes in the network

- Bandwidth is shared on all links between devices

- More difficult to configure than a Star: node adjunction = Ring shutdown and reconfiguration

Misconceptions

- "Token Ring is an example of a ring topology." 802.5 (Token Ring) networks do not use a ring topology at layer 1. As explained above, IBM Token Ring (802.5) networks *imitate* a ring at layer 2 but use a physical star at layer 1.

- "Rings prevent collisions." The term "ring" only refers to the layout of the cables. It is true that there are no collisions on an IBM Token Ring, but this is because of the layer 2 Media Access Control method, not the physical topology (which again is a star, not a ring.) Token passing, not rings, prevent collisions.

- "Token passing happens on rings." Token passing is a way of managing access to the cable, implemented at the MAC sublayer of layer 2. Ring topology is the cable layout at layer one. It is possible to do token passing on a bus (802.4) a star (802.5) or a ring (FDDI). Token passing is not restricted to rings.

Bus Network

A bus network is a network topology in which nodes are directly connected to a common linear (or branched) half-duplex link called a bus.

Function

A host on a bus network is called a *Station* or *workstation*. In a bus network, every station receives all network traffic, and the traffic generated by each station has equal transmission priority. A bus network forms a single network segment and collision domain. In order for nodes to transmit on the same bus simultaneously, they use a media access control technology such as carrier sense multiple access (CSMA) or a bus master.

If any link or segment of the bus is severed, all network transmission ceases due to signal bounce caused by the lack of a terminating resistor.

Advantages and Disadvantages

Advantages

- Easy to connect a computer or peripheral to a linear bus
- Requires less cable length than a star topology resulting in lower costs
- It works well for small networks.

Disadvantages

- Entire network shuts down if there is a break in the main cable or one of the T connectors break.
- Large amount of packet collisions on the network, which results in high amounts of packet loss.

Star Network

Star networks are one of the most common computer network topologies. In its simplest form, a star network consists of one central node, typically a switch or hub, which acts as a conduit to transmit messages. In star topology, every node (computer workstation or any other peripheral) is connected to a central node. The switch is the server and the peripherals are the clients.

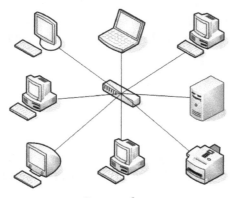

Star topology

A star network is an implementation of a Spoke–hub distribution paradigm in computer networks. Thus, the hub and leaf nodes, and the transmission lines between them, form a graph with the topology of a star. Data on a star network passes through the hub, switch, or concentrator before continuing to its destination. The hub, switch, or concentrator manages and controls all functions of the network. It also acts as a repeater for the data flow. This configuration is common with twisted pair cable and optical fibre cable. However, it can also be used with coaxial cable.

The star topology reduces the damage caused by line failure by connecting all of the systems to a central node. When applied to a bus-based network, this central hub rebroadcasts all transmissions received from any peripheral node to all peripheral nodes on the network, sometimes including the originating node. All peripheral nodes may thus communicate with all others by transmitting to, and receiving from, the central node only. The failure of a transmission line linking any peripheral node to the central node will result in the isolation of that peripheral node from all others, but the rest of the systems will be unaffected.

Advantages and Disadvantages

Advantages

- If one computer or its connection breaks it doesn't affect the other computers and their connections.

- Devices can be added or removed without disturbing the network

Disadvantages

- An expensive network layout to install because of the amount of cables needed

- The central hub is a single point of failure for the network

Passive Vs. Active

If the central node is *passive*, the originating node must be able to tolerate the reception of an echo of its own transmission, delayed by the two-way transmission time (i.e. to and from the central node) plus any delay generated in the central node. An *active* star network has an active central node that usually has the means to prevent echo-related problems.

Mesh Networking

A mesh network is a network topology in which each node relays data for the network. All mesh nodes cooperate in the distribution of data in the network.

Mesh networks can relay messages using either a *flooding* technique or a *routing* technique. With routing, the message is propagated along a path by *hopping* from node to node until it reaches its destination. To ensure all its paths' availability, the network must allow for continuous connections and must reconfigure itself around broken paths, using *self-healing* algorithms such as Shortest Path Bridging. Self-healing allows a routing-based network to operate when a node breaks down or when a connection becomes unreliable. As a result, the network is typically quite reliable, as there is often more than one path between a source and a destination in the network. Although mostly used in wireless situations, this concept can also apply to wired networks and to software interaction.

A mesh network whose nodes are all connected to each other is a fully connected network. Fully connected wired networks have the advantages of security and reliability: problems in a cable affect only the two nodes attached to it. However, in such networks, the number of cables, and therefore the cost, goes up rapidly as the number of nodes increases.

Mesh networks can be considered a type of an *ad-hoc* network. Thus, mesh networks are closely related to mobile ad hoc networks (MANETs), although MANETs also must deal with problems introduced by the mobility of the nodes.

Wired

Shortest path bridging allows Ethernet switches to be connected in a mesh topology and for all paths to be active.

Wireless

Wireless mesh networks were originally developed for military applications. Mesh networks are typically wireless. Over the past decade, the size, cost, and power requirements of radios has declined, enabling multiple radios to be contained within a single mesh node, thus allowing for greater modularity; each can handle multiple frequency bands and support a variety of functions as needed—such as client access, backhaul service, and scanning (required for high-speed handoff in mobile applications)—even customized sets of them.

Work in this field has been aided by the use of game theory methods to analyze strategies for the allocation of resources and routing of packets.

Early wireless mesh networks all use nodes that have a single half-duplex radio that, at any one instant, can either transmit or receive, but not both at the same time. This requires a shared mesh configuration.

Some later wireless mesh networks use nodes with more complex radio hardware that can receive packets from an upstream node and transmit packets to a downstream node simultaneously (on a different frequency or a different CDMA channel), which is a prerequisite for a switched mesh configuration.

Examples

- The first widely deployed mesh network was created for the military market. DoD JTRS radios are mesh networks (SRW). Harris ANW2 (2007), running on AN/PRC-117, AN/PRC-152A are mesh networks.

- In rural Catalonia, Guifi.net was developed in 2004 as a response to the lack of broadband internet, where commercial internet providers weren't providing a connection or a very poor one. Nowadays with more than 30,000 nodes it is only halfway a fully connected network, but following a peer to peer agreement it remained an open, free and neutral network with extensive redundancy.

- ZigBee digital radios are incorporated into some consumer appliances, including battery-powered appliances. ZigBee radios spontaneously organize a mesh network, using AODV routing; transmission and reception are synchronized. This means the radios can be off much of the time, and thus conserve power.

- Thread is a consumer wireless networking protocol built on open standards and IPv6/6LoWPAN protocols. Thread's features include a secure and reliable mesh network with no single point of failure, simple connectivity and low power. Thread networks are easy to set up and secure to use with banking-class encryption to close security holes that exist in other wireless protocols. In 2014 Google Inc's Nest Labs announced a working group with the companies Samsung, ARM Holdings, Freescale, Silicon Labs, Big Ass Fans and the lock company Yale to promote Thread.

Building a Rural Wireless Mesh Network

A do-it-yourself guide to planning and building
a Freifunk based mesh network

Version: 0.8

David Johnson, Karel Matthee, Dare Sokoya,
Lawrence Mboweni, Ajay Makan, and Henk Kotze

Wireless Africa, Meraka Institute, South Africa

30 October 2007

Building a Rural Wireless Mesh Network: A DIY Guide (PDF)

- In early 2007, the US-based firm Meraki launched a mini wireless mesh router. This is an example of a wireless mesh network (on a claimed speed of up to 50 megabits per second). The 802.11 radio within the Meraki Mini has been optimized for long-distance communication, providing coverage over 250 metres.

  This is an example of a single-radio mesh network being used within a community as opposed to multi-radio long range mesh networks like BelAir or MeshDynamics that provide multifunctional infrastructure, typically using tree based topologies and their advantages in O(n) routing.

- The Naval Postgraduate School, Monterey CA, demonstrated such wireless mesh networks for border security. In a pilot system, aerial cameras kept aloft by balloons relayed real time high resolution video to ground personnel via a mesh network.

- SPAWAR, a division of the US Navy, is prototyping and testing a scalable, secure Disruption Tolerant Mesh Network to protect strategic military assets, both stationary and mobile. Machine control applications, running on the mesh nodes, "take over", when internet connectivity is lost. Use cases include Internet of Things e.g. smart drone swarms.

- An MIT Media Lab project has developed the XO-1 laptop or "OLPC"(One Laptop per Child) which is intended for disadvantaged schools in developing nations and uses mesh networking (based on the IEEE 802.11s standard) to create a robust and inexpensive infrastructure. The instantaneous connections made by the laptops are claimed by the project to reduce the need for an external infrastructure such as the Internet to reach all areas, because a connected node could share the connection with nodes nearby. A similar concept has also been implemented by Greenpacket with its application called SONbuddy.

- In Cambridge, UK, on 3 June 2006, mesh networking was used at the "Strawberry Fair" to run mobile live television, radio and Internet services to an estimated 80,000 people.

- Broadband-Hamnet, a mesh networking project used in amateur radio, is a "a high-speed, self-discovering, self-configuring, fault-tolerant, wireless computer network" with very low power consumption and a focus on emergency communication.

- The Champaign-Urbana Community Wireless Network (CUWiN) project is developing mesh networking software based on open source implementations of the Hazy-Sighted Link State Routing Protocol and Expected Transmission Count metric. Additionally, the Wireless Networking Group in the University of Illinois at Urbana-Champaign are developing a multichannel, multi-radio wireless mesh testbed, called Net-X as a proof of concept implementation of some of the multichannel protocols being developed in that group. The implementations are based on an architecture that allows some of the radios to switch channels to maintain network connectivity, and includes protocols for channel allocation and routing.

- FabFi is an open-source, city-scale, wireless mesh networking system originally developed in 2009 in Jalalabad, Afghanistan to provide high-speed internet to parts of the city and designed for high performance across multiple hops. It is an inexpensive framework for sharing wireless internet from a central provider across a town or city. A second larger implementation followed a year later near Nairobi, Kenya with a freemium pay model to support network growth. Both projects were undertaken by the Fablab users of the respective cities.

- SMesh is an 802.11 multi-hop wireless mesh network developed by the Distributed System and Networks Lab at Johns Hopkins University. A fast handoff scheme allows mobile clients to roam in the network without interruption in connectivity, a feature suitable for real-time applications, such as VoIP.

- Many mesh networks operate across multiple radio bands. For example, Firetide and Wave Relay mesh networks have the option to communicate node to node on 5.2 GHz or 5.8 GHz, but communicate node to client on 2.4 GHz (802.11). This is accomplished using software-defined radio (SDR).

- The SolarMESH project examined the potential of powering 802.11-based mesh networks using solar power and rechargeable batteries. Legacy 802.11 access points were found to be inadequate due to the requirement that they be continuously powered. The IEEE 802.11s standardization efforts are considering power save options, but solar-powered applications might involve single radio nodes where relay-link power saving will be inapplicable.

- The WING project (sponsored by the Italian Ministry of University and Research and led by CREATE-NET and Technion) developed a set of novel algorithms and protocols for enabling wireless mesh networks as the standard access architecture for next generation Internet. Particular focus has been given to interference and traffic aware channel assignment, multi-radio/multi-interface support, and opportunistic scheduling and traffic aggregation in highly volatile environments.

- WiBACK Wireless Backhaul Technology has been developed by the Fraunhofer Institute for Open Communication Systems (FOKUS) in Berlin. Powered by solar cells and designed to support all existing wireless technologies, networks are due to be rolled out to several countries in sub-Saharan Africa in summer 2012.

- Recent standards for wired communications have also incorporated concepts from Mesh Networking. An example is ITU-T G.hn, a standard that specifies a high-speed (up to 1 Gbit/s) local area network using existing home wiring (power lines, phone lines and coaxial cables). In noisy environments such as power lines (where signals can be heavily attenuated and corrupted by noise) it's common that mutual visibility between devices in a network is not complete. In those situations, one of the nodes has to act as a relay and forward messages between those nodes that cannot communicate directly, effectively creating a mesh network. In G.hn, relaying is performed at the Data Link Layer.

References

- Bicsi, B. (2002). Network Design Basics for Cabling Professionals. McGraw-Hill Professional. ISBN 9780071782968.

- Sosinsky, Barrie A. (2009). "Network Basics". Networking Bible. Indianapolis: Wiley Publishing. p. 16. ISBN 978-0-470-43131-3. OCLC 359673774. Retrieved 2016-03-26.

- Bradley, Ray. Understanding Computer Science (for Advanced Level): The Study Guide. Cheltenham: Nelson Thornes. p. 244. ISBN 978-0-7487-6147-0. OCLC 47869750. Retrieved 2016-03-26.

- "Teach-ICT OCR GCSE Computing - computer network topologies, bus network, ring network, star network". teach-ict.com. Retrieved 2015-10-15.

- "Broadband-Hamnet wins International Association of Emergency Managers Awards". ARRL. Retrieved 2015-05-02.

- "What is star network? - Definition from WhatIs.com". Searchnetworking.techtarget.com. Retrieved 2014-06-24.

- "Avaya Extends the Automated Campus to End the Network Waiting Game". Avaya. 1 April 2014. Retrieved 18 April 2014.

- Peter Ashwood-Smith (24 February 2011). "Shortest Path Bridging IEEE 802.1aq Overview" (PDF). Huawei. Retrieved 11 May 2012.

- Jim Duffy (11 May 2012). "Largest Illinois healthcare system uproots Cisco to build $40M private cloud". PC Advisor. Retrieved 11 May 2012.

- "IEEE Approves New IEEE 802.1aq Shortest Path Bridging Standard". Tech Power Up. 7 May 2012. Retrieved 11 May 2012.

- D. Fedyk, Ed.,; P. Ashwood-Smith, Ed.,; D. Allan, A. Bragg,; P. Unbehagen (April 2012). "IS-IS Extensions Supporting IEEE 802.1aq". IETF. Retrieved 12 May 2012.

- Peter Ashwood-Smith (24 February 2011). "Shortest Path Bridging IEEE 802.1aq Overview" (PDF). Huawei. Retrieved 11 May 2012.

- Jim Duffy (11 May 2012). "Largest Illinois healthcare system uproots Cisco to build $40M private cloud". PC Advisor. Retrieved 11 May 2012.

- "IEEE Approves New IEEE 802.1aq Shortest Path Bridging Standard". Tech Power Up. 7 May 2012. Retrieved 11 May 2012.

- D. Fedyk, Ed.,; P. Ashwood-Smith, Ed.,; D. Allan, A. Bragg,; P. Unbehagen (April 2012). "IS-IS Extensions Supporting IEEE 802.1aq". IETF. Retrieved 12 May 2012.

Packet Switching: An Integrated Study

Packet switching is a technique by which all the data of networking communications are collected and grouped into blocks which are incidentally referred to as packets. The various packet switched networks are ARPANET, CYCLADES and IPSANET. This text provides the reader with an integrated understanding of packet switching.

Packet Switching

Packet switching is a digital networking communications method that groups all transmitted data into suitably sized blocks, called *packets*, which are transmitted via a medium that may be shared by multiple simultaneous communication sessions. Packet switching increases network efficiency, robustness and enables technological convergence of many applications operating on the same network.

Packets are composed of a header and payload. Information in the header is used by networking hardware to direct the packet to its destination where the payload is extracted and used by application software.

Starting in the late 1950s, American computer scientist Paul Baran developed the concept *Distributed Adaptive Message Block Switching* with the goal to provide a fault-tolerant, efficient routing method for telecommunication messages as part of a research program at the RAND Corporation, funded by the US Department of Defense. This concept contrasted and contradicted then-established principles of pre-allocation of network bandwidth, largely fortified by the development of telecommunications in the Bell System. The new concept found little resonance among network implementers until the independent work of British computer scientist Donald Davies at the National Physical Laboratory (United Kingdom) in the late 1960s. Davies is credited with coining the modern name *packet switching* and inspiring numerous packet switching networks in Europe in the decade following, including the incorporation of the concept in the early ARPANET in the United States.

Concept

A simple definition of packet switching is:

The routing and transferring of data by means of addressed packets so that a channel is occupied during the transmission of the packet only, and upon completion of the transmission the channel is made available for the transfer of other traffic

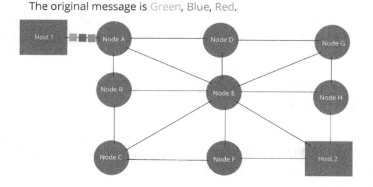

The original message is Green, Blue, Red.

An animation demonstrating data packet switching across a network

Packet switching features delivery of variable bit rate data streams, realized as sequences of packets, over a computer network which allocates transmission resources as needed using statistical multiplexing or dynamic bandwidth allocation techniques. As they traverse network nodes, such as switches and routers, packets are received, buffered, queued, and transmitted (stored and forwarded), resulting in variable latency and throughput depending on the link capacity and the traffic load on the network.

Packet switching contrasts with another principal networking paradigm, circuit switching, a method which pre-allocates dedicated network bandwidth specifically for each communication session, each having a constant bit rate and latency between nodes. In cases of billable services, such as cellular communication services, circuit switching is characterized by a fee per unit of connection time, even when no data is transferred, while packet switching may be characterized by a fee per unit of information transmitted, such as characters, packets, or messages.

Packet mode communication may be implemented with or without intermediate forwarding nodes (packet switches or routers). Packets are normally forwarded by intermediate network nodes asynchronously using first-in, first-out buffering, but may be forwarded according to some scheduling discipline for fair queuing, traffic shaping, or for differentiated or guaranteed quality of service, such as weighted fair queuing or leaky bucket. In case of a shared physical medium (such as radio or 10BASE5), the packets may be delivered according to a multiple access scheme.

History

In the late 1950s, the US Air Force established a wide area network for the Semi-Automatic Ground Environment (SAGE) radar defense system. They sought a system that might survive a nuclear attack to enable a response, thus diminishing the attractiveness of the first strike advantage by enemies.

Leonard Kleinrock conducted early research in queueing theory which proved important in packet switching, and published a book in the related field of digital message switching (without the packets) in 1961; he also later played a leading role in building and management of the world's first packet-switched network, the ARPANET.

The concept of switching small blocks of data was first explored independently by Paul Baran at the RAND Corporation in the US and Donald Davies at the National Physical Laboratory (NPL) in the UK in the early to mid-1960s.

Baran developed the concept of *distributed adaptive message block switching* during his research at the RAND Corporation for the US Air Force into communications networks, that could survive nuclear wars, first presented to the Air Force in the summer of 1961 as briefing B-265, later published as RAND report P-2626 in 1962, and finally in report RM 3420 in 1964. Report P-2626 described a general architecture for a large-scale, distributed, survivable communications network. The work focuses on three key ideas: use of a decentralized network with multiple paths between any two points, dividing user messages into *message blocks*, later called packets, and delivery of these messages by store and forward switching.

Baran's work was known to Robert Taylor and J.C.R. Licklider at the Information Processing Technology Office, who advocated wide area networks, and it influenced Lawrence Roberts to adopt the technology in the development of the ARPANET.

Starting in 1965, Donald Davies at the National Physical Laboratory, UK, independently developed the same message routing methodology as developed by Baran. He called it *packet switching*, a more accessible name than Baran's, and proposed to build a nationwide network in the UK. He gave a talk on the proposal in 1966, after which a person from the Ministry of Defence (MoD) told him about Baran's work. A member of Davies' team (Roger Scantlebury) met Lawrence Roberts at the 1967 ACM Symposium on Operating System Principles and suggested it for use in the ARPANET.

Davies had chosen some of the same parameters for his original network design as did Baran, such as a packet size of 1024 bits. In 1966, Davies proposed that a network should be built at the laboratory to serve the needs of NPL and prove the feasibility of packet switching. The NPL Data Communications Network entered service in 1970.

The first computer network and packet switching network deployed for computer resource sharing was the Octopus Network at the Lawrence Livermore National Laboratory that began connecting four Control Data 6600 computers to several shared storage devices (including an IBM 2321 Data Cell in 1968 and an IBM Photostore in 1970) and to several hundred Teletype Model 33 ASR terminals for time sharing use starting in 1968.

In 1973, Vint Cerf and Bob Kahn wrote the specifications for Transmission Control Protocol (TCP), an internetworking protocol for sharing resources using packet-switching among the nodes.

Connectionless and Connection-oriented Modes

Packet switching may be classified into connectionless packet switching, also known as datagram switching, and connection-oriented packet switching, also known as virtual circuit switching.

Examples of connectionless protocols are Ethernet, Internet Protocol (IP), and the User Datagram Protocol (UDP). Connection-oriented protocols include X.25, Frame Relay, Multiprotocol Label Switching (MPLS), and the Transmission Control Protocol (TCP).

In connectionless mode each packet includes complete addressing information. The packets are routed individually, sometimes resulting in different paths and out-of-order delivery. Each packet is labeled with a destination address, source address, and port numbers. It may also be labeled with the sequence number of the packet. This precludes the need for a dedicated path to help the packet find its way to its destination, but means that much more information is needed in the packet header, which is therefore larger, and this information needs to be looked up in power-hungry content-addressable memory. Each packet is dispatched and may go via different routes; potentially, the system has to do as much work for every packet as the connection-oriented system has to do in connection set-up, but with less information as to the application's requirements. At the destination, the original message/data is reassembled in the correct order, based on the packet sequence number. Thus a virtual connection, also known as a virtual circuit or byte stream is provided to the end-user by a transport layer protocol, although intermediate network nodes only provides a connectionless network layer service.

Connection-oriented transmission requires a setup phase in each involved node before any packet is transferred to establish the parameters of communication. The packets include a connection identifier rather than address information and are negotiated between endpoints so that they are delivered in order and with error checking. Address information is only transferred to each node during the connection set-up phase, when the route to the destination is discovered and an entry is added to the switching table in each network node through which the connection passes. The signaling protocols used allow the application to specify its requirements and discover link parameters. Acceptable values for service parameters may be negotiated. Routing a packet requires the node to look up the connection id in a table. The packet header can be small, as it only needs to contain this code and any information, such as length, timestamp, or sequence number, which is different for different packets.

Packet Switching in Networks

Packet switching is used to optimize the use of the channel capacity available in digital telecommunication networks such as computer networks, to minimize the transmission latency (the time it takes for data to pass across the network), and to increase robustness of communication.

The best-known use of packet switching is the Internet and most local area networks. The Internet is implemented by the Internet Protocol Suite using a variety of Link Layer technologies. For example, Ethernet and Frame Relay are common. Newer mobile phone technologies (e.g., GPRS, i-mode) also use packet switching.

X.25 is a notable use of packet switching in that, despite being based on packet switching methods, it provided virtual circuits to the user. These virtual circuits carry variable-length packets. In 1978, X.25 provided the first international and commercial packet switching network, the International Packet Switched Service (IPSS). Asynchronous Transfer Mode (ATM) also is a virtual circuit technology, which uses fixed-length cell relay connection oriented packet switching.

Datagram packet switching is also called connectionless networking because no connections are established. Technologies such as Multiprotocol Label Switching (MPLS) and the Resource Reservation Protocol (RSVP) create virtual circuits on top of datagram networks. Virtual circuits are especially useful in building robust failover mechanisms and allocating bandwidth for delay-sensitive applications.

MPLS and its predecessors, as well as ATM, have been called "fast packet" technologies. MPLS, indeed, has been called "ATM without cells". Modern routers, however, do not require these technologies to be able to forward variable-length packets at multigigabit speeds across the network.

X.25 vs. Frame Relay

Both X.25 and Frame Relay provide connection-oriented operations. X.25 provides it via the network layer of the OSI Model, whereas Frame Relay provides it via level two, the data link layer. Another major difference between X.25 and Frame Relay is that X.25 requires a handshake between the communicating parties before any user packets are transmitted. Frame Relay does not define any such handshakes. X.25 does not define any operations inside the packet network. It only operates at the user-network-interface (UNI). Thus, the network provider is free to use any procedure it wishes inside the network. X.25 does specify some limited re-transmission procedures at the UNI, and its link layer protocol (LAPB) provides conventional HDLC-type link management procedures. Frame Relay is a modified version of ISDN's layer two protocol, LAPD and LAPB. As such, its integrity operations pertain only between nodes on a link, not end-to-end. Any retransmissions must be carried out by higher layer protocols. The X.25 UNI protocol is part of the X.25 protocol suite, which consists of the lower three layers of the OSI Model. It was widely used at the UNI for packet switching networks during the 1980s and early 1990s, to provide a standardized interface into and out of packet networks. Some implementations used X.25 within the network as well, but its connection-oriented features made this setup cumbersome and inefficient. Frame relay operates principally at layer two of the OSI Model. However, its address field (the Data Link Connection ID, or DLCI) can be used at the OSI network layer, with a minimum set of procedures. Thus, it rids itself of many X.25 layer 3 encumbrances, but still has the DLCI as an ID beyond a node-to-node layer two link protocol. The simplicity of Frame Relay makes it faster and more efficient than X.25. Because Frame relay is a data link layer protocol, like X.25 it does not define internal network routing operations. For X.25 its packet IDs---the virtual circuit and virtual channel numbers have to be correlated to network addresses. The same is true for Frame Relays DLCI. How this is done is up to the network provider. Frame Relay, by virtue of having no network layer procedures is connection-oriented at layer two, by using the HDLC/LAPD/LAPB Set Asynchronous Balanced Mode (SABM). X.25 connections are typically established for each communication session, but it does have a feature allowing a limited amount of traffic to be passed across the UNI without the connection-oriented handshake. For a while, Frame Relay was used to interconnect LANs across wide area networks. However, X.25 and well as Frame Relay have been supplanted by the Internet Protocol (IP) at the network layer, and the Asynchronous Transfer Mode (ATM) and or versions of Multi-Protocol Label Switching (MPLS) at layer two. A typical configuration is to run IP over ATM or a version of MPLS. <Uyless Black, X.25 and Related Protocols, IEEE Computer Society, 1991> <Uyless Black, Frame Relay Networks, McGraw-Hill, 1998> <Uyless Black, MPLS and Label Switching Networks, Prentice Hall, 2001> < Uyless Black, ATM, Volume I, Prentice Hall, 1995>

Packet-switched Networks

The history of packet-switched networks can be divided into three overlapping eras: early networks before the introduction of X.25 and the OSI model, the X.25 era when many postal, telephone, and telegraph companies introduced networks with X.25 interfaces, and the Internet era.

Early Networks

ARPANET and SITA HLN became operational in 1969. Before the introduction of X.25 in 1973, about twenty different network technologies had been developed. Two fundamental differences involved the division of functions and tasks between the hosts at the edge of the network and the network core. In the datagram system, the hosts have the responsibility to ensure orderly delivery of packets. The User Datagram Protocol (UDP) is an example of a datagram protocol. In the virtual call system, the network guarantees sequenced delivery of data to the host. This results in a simpler host interface with less functionality than in the datagram model. The X.25 protocol suite uses this network type.

Appletalk

AppleTalk was a proprietary suite of networking protocols developed by Apple Inc. in 1985 for Apple Macintosh computers. It was the primary protocol used by Apple devices through the 1980s and 90s. AppleTalk included features that allowed local area networks to be established *ad hoc* without the requirement for a centralized router or server. The AppleTalk system automatically assigned addresses, updated the distributed namespace, and configured any required inter-network routing. It was a plug-n-play system.

AppleTalk versions were also released for the IBM PC and compatibles, and the Apple IIGS. AppleTalk support was available in most networked printers, especially laser printers, some file servers and routers. AppleTalk support was terminated in 2009, replaced by TCP/IP protocols.

ARPANET

The ARPANET was a progenitor network of the Internet and the first network to run the TCP/IP suite using packet switching technologies.

BNRNET

BNRNET was a network which Bell Northern Research developed for internal use. It initially had only one host but was designed to support many hosts. BNR later made major contributions to the CCITT X.25 project.

CYCLADES

The CYCLADES packet switching network was a French research network designed and directed by Louis Pouzin. First demonstrated in 1973, it was developed to explore alternatives to the early ARPANET design and to support network research generally. It was the first network to make the hosts responsible for reliable delivery of data, rather than the network itself, using unreliable datagrams and associated end-to-end protocol mechanisms. Concepts of this network influenced later ARPANET architecture.

DECnet

DECnet is a suite of network protocols created by Digital Equipment Corporation, originally released in 1975 in order to connect two PDP-11 minicomputers. It evolved into one of the first peer-to-peer network architectures, thus transforming DEC into a networking powerhouse in the 1980s. Initially built with three layers, it later (1982) evolved into a seven-layer OSI-compliant networking protocol. The DECnet protocols were designed entirely by Digital Equipment Corporation. However, DECnet Phase II (and later) were open standards with published specifications, and several implementations were developed outside DEC, including one for Linux.

DDX-1

This was an experimental network from Nippon PTT. It mixed circuit switching and packet switching. It was succeeded by DDX-2.

EIN née COST II

European Informatics Network was a project to link several national networks. It became operational in 1976.

EPSS

The Experimental Packet Switching System (EPSS) was an experiment of the UK Post Office. Ferranti supplied the hardware and software. The handling of link control messages (acknowledgements and flow control) was different from that of most other networks.

GEIS

As General Electric Information Services (GEIS), General Electric was a major international provider of information services. The company originally designed a telephone network to serve as its internal (albeit continent-wide) voice telephone network.

In 1965, at the instigation of Warner Sinback, a data network based on this voice-phone network was designed to connect GE's four computer sales and service centers (Schenectady, New York, Chicago, and Phoenix) to facilitate a computer time-sharing service, apparently the world's first commercial online service. (In addition to selling GE computers, the centers were computer service bureaus, offering batch processing services. They lost money from the beginning, and Sinback, a high-level marketing manager, was given the job of turning the business around. He decided that a time-sharing system, based on Kemney's work at Dartmouth—which used a computer on loan from GE—could be profitable. Warner was right.)

After going international some years later, GEIS created a network data center near Cleveland, Ohio. Very little has been published about the internal details of their network. (Though it has been stated by some that Tymshare copied the GEIS system to create their network, Tymnet.) The design was hierarchical with redundant communication links.

IPSANET

IPSANET was a semi-private network constructed by I. P. Sharp Associates to serve their time-sharing customers. It became operational in May 1976.

IPX/SPX

The Internetwork Packet Exchange (IPX) and Sequenced Packet Exchange (SPX) are Novell networking protocols derived from Xerox Network Systems' IDP and SPP protocols, respectively. They were used primarily on networks using the Novell NetWare operating systems.

Merit Network

Merit Network, Inc., an independent non-profit 501(c)(3) corporation governed by Michigan's public universities, was formed in 1966 as the Michigan Educational Research Information Triad to explore computer networking between three of Michigan's public universities as a means to help the state's educational and economic development. With initial support from the State of Michigan and the National Science Foundation (NSF), the packet-switched network was first demonstrated in December 1971 when an interactive host to host connection was made between the IBM mainframe computer systems at the University of Michigan in Ann Arbor and Wayne State University in Detroit. In October 1972 connections to the CDC mainframe at Michigan State University in East Lansing completed the triad. Over the next several years in addition to host to host interactive connections the network was enhanced to support terminal to host connections, host to host batch connections (remote job submission, remote printing, batch file transfer), interactive file transfer, gateways to the Tymnet and Telenet public data networks, X.25 host attachments, gateways to X.25 data networks, Ethernet attached hosts, and eventually TCP/IP and additional public universities in Michigan join the network. All of this set the stage for Merit's role in the NSFNET project starting in the mid-1980s.

NPL

Donald Davies of the National Physical Laboratory, UK made many important contributions to the theory of packet switching. NPL built a single node network to connect sundry hosts at NPL.

OCTOPUS

Octopus was a local network at Lawrence Livermore National Laboratory. It connected sundry hosts at the lab to interactive terminals and various computer peripherals including a bulk storage system.

Philips Research

Philips Research Laboratories in Redhill, Surrey developed a packet switching network for internal use. It was a datagram network with a single switching node.

PUP

PARC Universal Packet (PUP or Pup) was one of the two earliest internetwork protocol suites; it was created by researchers at Xerox PARC in the mid-1970s. The entire suite provided routing and packet delivery, as well as higher level functions such as a reliable byte stream, along with numerous applications. Further developments led to Xerox Network Systems (XNS).

RCP

RCP was an experimental network created by the French PTT. It was used to gain experience with packet switching technology before the specification of Transpac was frozen. RCP was a virtual-circuit network in contrast to CYCLADES which was based on datagrams. RCP emphasised terminal to host and terminal to terminal connection; CYCLADES was concerned with host-to-host communication. TRANSPAC was introduced as an X.25 network. RCP influenced the specification of X.25

RETD

Red Especial de Transmisión de Datos was a network developed by Compañía Telefónica Nacional de España. It became operational in 1972 and thus was the first public network.

SCANNET

"The experimental packet-switched Nordic telecommunication network SCANNET was implemented in Nordic technical libraries in 70's, and it included first Nordic electronic journal Extemplo. Libraries were also among first ones in universities to accommodate microcomputers for public use in early 80's."

SITA HLN

SITA is a consortium of airlines. Their High Level Network became operational in 1969 at about the same time as ARPANET. It carried interactive traffic and message-switching traffic. As with many non-academic networks very little has been published about it.

IBM Systems Network Architecture

IBM Systems Network Architecture (SNA) is IBM's proprietary networking architecture created in 1974. An IBM customer could acquire hardware and software from IBM and lease private lines from a common carrier to construct a private network.

Telenet

Telenet was the first FCC-licensed public data network in the United States. It was founded by former ARPA IPTO director Larry Roberts as a means of making ARPANET technology public. He had tried to interest AT&T in buying the technology, but the monopoly's reaction was that this was incompatible with their future. Bolt, Beranack and Newman (BBN) provided the financing. It initially used ARPANET technology but changed the host interface to X.25 and the terminal interface to X.29. Telenet designed these protocols and helped standardize them in the CCITT. Telenet was incorporated in 1973 and started operations in 1975. It went public in 1979 and was then sold to GTE.

Tymnet

Tymnet was an international data communications network headquartered in San Jose, CA that utilized virtual call packet switched technology and used X.25, SNA/SDLC, BSC and ASCII interfaces to connect host computers (servers)at thousands of large companies, educational institutions, and government agencies. Users typically connected via dial-up connections or dedicated async connections. The business consisted of a large public network that supported dial-up users and a private network business that allowed government agencies and large companies (mostly banks and airlines) to build their own dedicated networks. The private networks were often connected via gateways to the public network to reach locations not on the private network. Tymnet was also connected to dozens of other public networks in the U.S. and internationally via X.25/X.75 gateways. (Interesting note: Tymnet was not named after Mr. Tyme. Another employee suggested the name.)

XNS

Xerox Network Systems (XNS) was a protocol suite promulgated by Xerox, which provided routing and packet delivery, as well as higher level functions such as a reliable stream, and remote procedure calls. It was developed from PARC Universal Packet (PUP).

X.25 Era

There were two kinds of X.25 networks. Some such as DATAPAC and TRANSPAC were initially implemented with an X.25 external interface. Some older networks such as TELENET and TYMNET were modified to provide a X.25 host interface in addition to older host connection schemes. DATAPAC was developed by Bell Northern Research which was a joint venture of Bell Canada (a common carrier) and Northern Telecom (a telecommunications equipment supplier). Northern Telecom sold several DATAPAC clones to foreign PTTs including the Deutsche Bundespost. X.75 and X.121 allowed the interconnection of national X.25 networks. A user or host could call a host on a foreign network by including the DNIC of the remote network as part of the destination address.

AUSTPAC

AUSTPAC was an Australian public X.25 network operated by Telstra. Started by Telecom Australia in the early 1980s, AUSTPAC was Australia's first public packet-switched data network, supporting applications such as on-line betting, financial applications — the Australian Tax Office made use of AUSTPAC — and remote terminal access to academic institutions, who maintained their connections to AUSTPAC up until the mid-late 1990s in some cases. Access can be via a dial-up terminal to a PAD, or, by linking a permanent X.25 node to the network.

ConnNet

ConnNet was a packet-switched data network operated by the Southern New England Telephone Company serving the state of Connecticut.

Datanet 1

Datanet 1 was the public switched data network operated by the Dutch PTT Telecom (now known as KPN). Strictly speaking Datanet 1 only referred to the network and the connected users via leased lines (using the X.121 DNIC 2041), the name also referred to the public PAD service *Telepad* (using the DNIC 2049). And because the main Videotex service used the network and modified PAD devices as infrastructure the name Datanet 1 was used for these services as well. Although this use of the name was incorrect all these services were managed by the same people within one department of KPN contributed to the confusion.

Datapac

DATAPAC was the first operational X.25 network (1976). It covered major Canadian cities and was eventually extended to smaller centres.

Datex-P

Deutsche Bundespost operated this national network in Germany. The technology was acquired from Northern Telecom.

Eirpac

Eirpac is the Irish public switched data network supporting X.25 and X.28. It was launched in 1984, replacing Euronet. Eirpac is run by Eircom.

HIPA-NET

Hitachi designed a private network system for sale as a turnkey package to multi-national organizations. In addition to providing X.25 packet switching, message switching software was also included. Messages were buffered at the nodes adjacent to the sending and receiving terminals. Switched virtual calls were not supported, but through the use of "logical ports" an originating terminal could have a menu of pre-defined destination terminals.

Iberpac

Iberpac is the Spanish public packet-switched network, providing X.25 services. Iberpac is run by Telefonica.

JANET

JANET was the UK academic and research network, linking all universities, higher education establishments, publicly funded research laboratories. The X.25 network was based mainly on GEC 4000 series switches, and run X.25 links at up to 8 Mbit/s in its final phase before being converted to an IP based network. The JANET network grew out of the 1970s SRCnet (later called SERCnet) network.

PSS

Packet Switch Stream (PSS) was the UK Post Office (later to become British Telecom) national X.25 network with a DNIC of 2342. British Telecom renamed PSS under its GNS (Global Network Service) name, but the PSS name has remained better known. PSS also included public dial-up PAD access, and various InterStream gateways to other services such as Telex.

Transpac

Transpac was the national X.25 network in France. It was developed locally at about the same time as DataPac in Canada. The development was done by the French PTT and influenced by the experimental RCP network. It began operation in 1978.

VENUS-P

VENUS-P was an international X.25 network that operated from April 1982 through March 2006. At its subscription peak in 1999, VENUS-P connected 207 networks in 87 countries.

Venepaq

Venepaq is the national X.25 public network in Venezuela. It is run by Cantv and allow direct connection and dial up connections. Provides nationalwide access at very low cost. It provides national and international access. Venepaq allow connection from 19.2 kbit/s to 64 kbit/s in direct connections, and 1200, 2400 and 9600 bit/s in dial up connections.

Internet Era

When Internet connectivity was made available to anyone who could pay for an ISP subscription, the distinctions between national networks blurred. The user no longer saw network identifiers such as the DNIC. Some older technologies such as circuit switching have resurfaced with new names such as fast packet switching. Researchers have created some experimental networks to complement the existing Internet.

CSNET

The Computer Science Network (CSNET) was a computer network funded by the U.S. National Science Foundation (NSF) that began operation in 1981. Its purpose was to extend networking benefits, for computer science departments at academic and research institutions that could not be directly connected to ARPANET, due to funding or authorization limitations. It played a significant role in spreading awareness of, and access to, national networking and was a major milestone on the path to development of the global Internet.

Internet2

Internet2 is a not-for-profit United States computer networking consortium led by members from the research and education communities, industry, and government. The Internet2 community, in partnership with Qwest, built the first Internet2 Network, called Abilene, in 1998 and was a prime investor in the National LambdaRail (NLR) project. In 2006, Internet2 announced a partnership with Level 3 Communications to launch a brand new nationwide network, boosting its capacity from 10 Gbit/s to 100 Gbit/s. In October, 2007, Internet2 officially retired Abilene and now refers to its new, higher capacity network as the Internet2 Network.

NSFNET

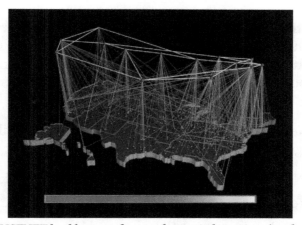

NSFNET Traffic 1991, NSFNET backbone nodes are shown at the top, regional networks below, traffic volume is depicted from purple (zero bytes) to white (100 billion bytes), visualization by NCSA using traffic data provided by the Merit Network.

The National Science Foundation Network (NSFNET) was a program of coordinated, evolving projects sponsored by the National Science Foundation (NSF) beginning in 1985 to promote advanced research and education networking in the United States. NSFNET was also the name given to several nationwide backbone networks operating at speeds of 56 kbit/s, 1.5 Mbit/s (T1), and 45 Mbit/s (T3) that were constructed to support NSF's networking initiatives from 1985-1995. Initially created to link researchers to the nation's

NSF-funded supercomputing centers, through further public funding and private industry partnerships it developed into a major part of the Internet backbone.

NSFNET Regional Networks

In addition to the five NSF supercomputer centers, NSFNET provided connectivity to eleven regional networks and through these networks to many smaller regional and campus networks in the United States. The NSFNET regional networks were:

- BARRNet, the Bay Area Regional Research Network in Palo Alto, California;

- CERFNET, California Education and Research Federation Network in San Diego, California, serving California and Nevada;

- CICNet, the Committee on Institutional Cooperation Network via the Merit Network in Ann Arbor, Michigan and later as part of the T3 upgrade via Argonne National Laboratory outside of Chicago, serving the Big Ten Universities and the University of Chicago in Illinois, Indiana, Michigan, Minnesota, Ohio, and Wisconsin;

- Merit/MichNet in Ann Arbor, Michigan serving Michigan, formed in 1966, still in operation as of 2016;

- MIDnet in Lincoln, Nebraska serving Arkansas, Iowa, Kansas, Missouri, Nebraska, Oklahoma, and South Dakota;

- NEARNET, the New England Academic and Research Network in Cambridge, Massachusetts, added as part of the upgrade to T3, serving Connecticut, Maine, Massachusetts, New Hampshire, Rhode Island, and Vermont, established in late 1988, operated by BBN under contract to MIT, BBN assumed responsibility for NEARNET on 1 July 1993;

- NorthWestNet in Seattle, Washington, serving Alaska, Idaho, Montana, North Dakota, Oregon, and Washington, founded in 1987;

- NYSERNet, New York State Education and Research Network in Ithaca, New York;

- JVNCNet, the John von Neumann National Supercomputer Center Network in Princeton, New Jersey, serving Delaware and New Jersey;

- SESQUINET, the Sesquicentennial Network in Houston, Texas, founded during the 150th anniversary of the State of Texas;

- SURAnet, the Southeastern Universities Research Association network in College Park, Maryland and later as part of the T3 upgrade in Atlanta, Georgia serving Alabama, Florida, Georgia, Kentucky, Louisiana, Maryland, Mississippi, North Carolina, South Carolina, Tennessee, Virginia, and West Virginia, sold to BBN in 1994; and

- Westnet in Salt Lake City, Utah and Boulder, Colorado, serving Arizona, Colorado, New Mexico, Utah, and Wyoming.

National LambdaRail

The National LambdaRail was launched in September 2003. It is a 12,000-mile high-speed national computer network owned and operated by the U.S. research and education community that runs over fiber-optic lines. It was the first transcontinental 10 Gigabit Ethernet network. It operates with high aggregate capacity of up to 1.6 Tbit/s and a high 40 Gbit/s bitrate, with plans for 100 Gbit/s.

TransPAC, TransPAC2, and TransPAC3

TransPAC2 and TransPAC3, continuations of the TransPAC project, a high-speed international Internet service connecting research and education networks in the Asia-Pacific region to those in the US. TransPAC is part of the NSF's International Research Network Connections (IRNC) program.

Very High-speed Backbone Network Service (vBNS)

The Very high-speed Backbone Network Service (vBNS) came on line in April 1995 as part of a National Science Foundation (NSF) sponsored project to provide high-speed interconnection between NSF-sponsored supercomputing centers and select access points in the United States. The network was engineered and operated by MCI Telecommunications under a cooperative agreement with the NSF. By 1998, the vBNS had grown to connect more than 100 universities and research and engineering institutions via 12 national points of presence with DS-3 (45 Mbit/s), OC-3c (155 Mbit/s), and OC-12c (622 Mbit/s) links on an all OC-12c backbone, a substantial engineering feat for that time. The vBNS installed one of the first ever production OC-48c (2.5 Gbit/s) IP links in February 1999 and went on to upgrade the entire backbone to OC-48c.

In June 1999 MCI WorldCom introduced vBNS+ which allowed attachments to the vBNS network by organizations that were not approved by or receiving support from NSF. After the expiration of the NSF agreement, the vBNS largely transitioned to providing service to the government. Most universities and research centers migrated to the Internet2 educational backbone. In January 2006, when MCI and Verizon merged, vBNS+ became a service of Verizon Business.

Various Packet Switched Networks

ARPANET

The Advanced Research Projects Agency Network (ARPANET) was an early packet switching network and the first network to implement the protocol suite TCP/IP. Both technologies became the technical foundation of the Internet. ARPANET was initially funded by the Advanced Research Projects Agency (ARPA) of the United States Department of Defense.

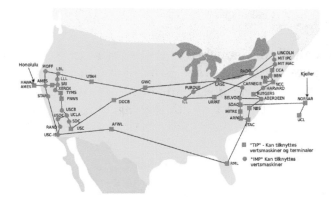

Arpanet 1974

The packet switching methodology employed in the ARPANET was based on concepts and designs by Americans Leonard Kleinrock and Paul Baran, British scientist Donald Davies, and Lawrence Roberts of the Lincoln Laboratory. The TCP/IP communications protocols were developed for ARPANET by computer scientists Robert Kahn and Vint Cerf, and incorporated concepts by Louis Pouzin for the French CYCLADES project.

As the project progressed, protocols for internetworking were developed by which multiple separate networks could be joined into a network of networks. Access to the ARPANET was expanded in 1981 when the National Science Foundation (NSF) funded the Computer Science Network (CSNET). In 1982, the Internet protocol suite (TCP/IP) was introduced as the standard networking protocol on the ARPANET. In the early 1980s the NSF funded the establishment for national supercomputing centers at several universities, and provided interconnectivity in 1986 with the NSFNET project, which also created network access to the supercomputer sites in the United States from research and education organizations. ARPANET was decommissioned in 1990.

History

Packet switching—today the dominant basis for data communications worldwide—was a new concept at the time of the conception of the ARPANET. Prior to the advent of packet switching, both voice and data communications had been based on the idea of circuit switching, as in the traditional telephone circuit, wherein each telephone call is allocated a dedicated, end to end, electronic connection between the two communicating stations. Such stations might be telephones or computers. The (temporarily) dedicated line is typically composed of many intermediary lines which are assembled into a chain that stretches all the way from the originating station to the destination station. With packet switching, a data system could use a single communication link to communicate with more than one machine by collecting data into datagrams and transmitting these as packets onto the attached network link, as soon as the link becomes idle. Thus, not only can the link be shared, much as a single post box can be used to post letters to different destinations, but each packet can be routed independently of other packets.

The earliest ideas for a computer network intended to allow general communications among computer users were formulated by computer scientist J. C. R. Licklider of Bolt, Beranek and Newman (BBN), in April 1963, in memoranda discussing the concept of the "Intergalactic Computer Network". Those ideas encompassed many of the features of the contemporary Internet. In October 1963, Licklider was appointed head of the Behavioral Sciences and Command and Control programs at the Defense Department's Advanced Research Projects Agency (ARPA). He convinced Ivan Sutherland and Bob Taylor that this network concept was very important and merited development, although Licklider left ARPA before any contracts were assigned for development.

Sutherland and Taylor continued their interest in creating the network, in part, to allow ARPA-sponsored researchers at various corporate and academic locales to utilize computers provided by ARPA, and, in part, to quickly distribute new software and other computer science results. Taylor had three computer terminals in his office, each connected to separate computers, which ARPA was funding: one for the System Development Corporation (SDC) Q-32 in Santa Monica, one for Project Genie at the University of California, Berkeley, and another for Multics at the Massachusetts Institute of Technology. Taylor recalls the circumstance: "For each of these three terminals, I had three different sets of user commands. So, if I was talking online with someone at S.D.C., and I wanted to talk to someone I knew at Berkeley, or M.I.T., about this, I had to get up from the S.D.C. terminal, go over and log into the other terminal and get in touch with them. I said, "Oh Man!", it's obvious what to do: If you have these three terminals, there ought to be one terminal that goes anywhere you want to go. That idea is the ARPANET".

Meanwhile, since the early 1960s, Paul Baran at the RAND Corporation had been researching systems that could survive nuclear war and developed the idea of *distributed adaptive message block switching*. Donald Davies at the United Kingdom's National Physical Laboratory (NPL) independently invented the same concept in 1965. His work, presented by a colleague, initially caught the attention of ARPANET developers at a conference in Gatlinburg, Tennessee, in October 1967. He gave the first public demonstration, having coined the term *packet switching*, on 5 August 1968 and incorporated it into the NPL network in England. Larry Roberts at ARPA applied Davies' concepts of packet switching for the ARPANET. The NPL network followed by ARPANET were the first two networks in the world to use packet switching, and were themselves connected together in 1973. The NPL network was using line speeds of 768 kbit/s, and the proposed line speed for ARPANET was upgraded from 2.4 kbit/s to 50 kbit/s.

Creation

By mid-1968, Taylor had prepared a complete plan for a computer network, and, after

ARPA's approval, a Request for Quotation (RFQ) was issued for 140 potential bidders. Most computer science companies regarded the ARPA–Taylor proposal as outlandish, and only twelve submitted bids to build a network; of the twelve, ARPA regarded only four as top-rank contractors. At year's end, ARPA considered only two contractors, and awarded the contract to build the network to BBN Technologies on 7 April 1969. The initial, seven-person BBN team were much aided by the technical specificity of their response to the ARPA RFQ, and thus quickly produced the first working system. This team was led by Frank Heart. The BBN-proposed network closely followed Taylor's ARPA plan: a network composed of small computers called Interface Message Processors (or IMPs), similar to the later concept of routers, that functioned as gateways interconnecting local resources. At each site, the IMPs performed store-and-forward packet switching functions, and were interconnected with leased lines via telecommunication data sets (modems), with initial data rates of 56kbit/s. The host computers were connected to the IMPs via custom serial communication interfaces. The system, including the hardware and the packet switching software, was designed and installed in nine months.

The first-generation IMPs were built by BBN Technologies using a rugged computer version of the Honeywell DDP-516 computer configured with 24KB of expandable magnetic-core memory, and a 16-channel Direct Multiplex Control (DMC) direct memory access unit. The DMC established custom interfaces with each of the host computers and modems. In addition to the front-panel lamps, the DDP-516 computer also features a special set of 24 indicator lamps showing the status of the IMP communication channels. Each IMP could support up to four local hosts, and could communicate with up to six remote IMPs via leased lines. The network connected one computer in Utah with three in California. Later, the Department of Defense allowed the universities to join the network for sharing hardware and software resources.

Debate on Design Goals

In *A Brief History of the Internet*, the Internet Society denies that ARPANET was designed to survive a nuclear attack:

> It was from the RAND study that the false rumor started, claiming that the ARPANET was somehow related to building a network resistant to nuclear war. This was never true of the ARPANET; only the unrelated RAND study on secure voice considered nuclear war. However, the later work on Internetting did emphasize robustness and survivability, including the capability to withstand losses of large portions of the underlying networks.

The RAND study was conducted by Paul Baran and pioneered packet switching. In an interview he confirmed that while ARPANET did not exactly share his project's goal, his work had greatly contributed to the development of ARPANET. Minutes taken by Elmer Shapiro of Stanford Research Institute at the ARPANET design meeting of 9–10

Oct. 1967 indicate that a version of Baran's routing method and suggestion of using a fixed packet size was expected to be employed.

According to Stephen J. Lukasik, who as Deputy Director and Director of DARPA (1967–1974) was "the person who signed most of the checks for Arpanet's development":

> The goal was to exploit new computer technologies to meet the needs of military command and control against nuclear threats, achieve survivable control of US nuclear forces, and improve military tactical and management decision making.

The ARPANET incorporated distributed computation (and frequent re-computation) of routing tables. This was a major contribution to the survivability of the ARPANET in the face of significant destruction - even by a nuclear attack. Such auto-routing was technically quite challenging to construct at the time. The fact that it was incorporated into the early ARPANET made many believe that this had been a design goal.

The ARPANET was designed to survive subordinate-network losses, since the principal reason was that the switching nodes and network links were unreliable, even without any nuclear attacks. Resource scarcity supported the creation of the ARPANET, according to Charles Herzfeld, ARPA Director (1965–1967):

> The ARPANET was not started to create a Command and Control System that would survive a nuclear attack, as many now claim. To build such a system was, clearly, a major military need, but it was not ARPA's mission to do this; in fact, we would have been severely criticized had we tried. Rather, the ARPANET came out of our frustration that there were only a limited number of large, powerful research computers in the country, and that many research investigators, who should have access to them, were geographically separated from them.

The ARPANET was operated by the military during the two decades of its existence, until 1990.

ARPANET Deployed

Historical document: First ARPANET IMP log: the first message ever sent via the AR-PANET, 10:30 pm, 29 October 1969. This IMP Log excerpt, kept at UCLA, describes setting up a message transmission from the UCLA SDS Sigma 7 Host computer to the SRI SDS 940 Host computer.

The initial ARPANET consisted of four IMPs:

- University of California, Los Angeles (UCLA), where Leonard Kleinrock had established a Network Measurement Center, with an SDS Sigma 7 being the first computer attached to it;

- The Augmentation Research Center at Stanford Research Institute (now SRI International), where Douglas Engelbart had created the ground-breaking NLS system, a very important early hypertext system, and would run the Network Information Center (NIC), with the SDS 940 that ran NLS, named "Genie", being the first host attached;

- University of California, Santa Barbara (UCSB), with the Culler-Fried Interactive Mathematics Center's IBM 360/75, running OS/MVT being the machine attached;

- The University of Utah's Computer Science Department, where Ivan Sutherland had moved, running a DEC PDP-10 operating on TENEX.

The first successful message on the ARPANET was sent by UCLA student programmer Charley Kline, at 10:30 pm on 29 October 1969, from Boelter Hall 3420. Kline transmitted from the university's SDS Sigma 7 Host computer to the Stanford Research Institute's SDS 940 Host computer. The message text was the word *login*; on an earlier attempt the *l* and the *o* letters were transmitted, but the system then crashed. Hence, the literal first message over the ARPANET was *lo*. About an hour later, after the programmers repaired the code that caused the crash, the SDS Sigma 7 computer effected a full *login*. The first permanent ARPANET link was established on 21 November 1969, between the IMP at UCLA and the IMP at the Stanford Research Institute. By 5 December 1969, the entire four-node network was established.

Growth and Evolution

In March 1970, the ARPANET reached the East Coast of the United States, when an IMP at BBN in Cambridge, Massachusetts was connected to the network. Thereafter, the ARPANET grew: 9 IMPs by June 1970 and 13 IMPs by December 1970, then 18 by September 1971 (when the network included 23 university and government hosts); 29 IMPs by August 1972, and 40 by September 1973. By June 1974, there were 46 IMPs, and in July 1975, the network numbered 57 IMPs. By 1981, the number was 213 host computers, with another host connecting approximately every twenty days.

In 1973 a transatlantic satellite link connected the Norwegian Seismic Array (NORSAR) to the ARPANET, making Norway the first country outside the US to be connected to the network. At about the same time a terrestrial circuit added a London IMP.

In 1975, the ARPANET was declared "operational". The Defense Communications Agency took control since ARPA was intended to fund advanced research.

In September 1984 work was completed on restructuring the ARPANET giving U.S. military sites their own Military Network (MILNET) for unclassified defense department communications. Controlled gateways connected the two networks. The combination was called the Defense Data Network (DDN). Separating the civil and military networks reduced the 113-node ARPANET by 68 nodes. The MILNET later became the NIPRNet.

Rules and Etiquette

Because of its government funding, certain forms of traffic were discouraged or prohibited. A 1982 handbook on computing at MIT's AI Lab stated regarding network etiquette:

It is considered illegal to use the ARPANet for anything which is not in direct support of Government business ... personal messages to other ARPANet subscribers (for example, to arrange a get-together or check and say a friendly hello) are generally not considered harmful ... Sending electronic mail over the ARPANet for commercial profit or political purposes is both anti-social and illegal. By sending such messages, you can offend many people, and it is possible to get MIT in serious trouble with the Government agencies which manage the ARPANet.

Technology

Support for inter-IMP circuits of up to 230.4 kbit/s was added in 1970, although considerations of cost and IMP processing power meant this capability was not actively used.

1971 saw the start of the use of the non-ruggedized (and therefore significantly lighter) Honeywell 316 as an IMP. It could also be configured as a Terminal Interface Processor (TIP), which provided terminal server support for up to 63 ASCII serial terminals through a multi-line controller in place of one of the hosts. The 316 featured a greater degree of integration than the 516, which made it less expensive and easier to maintain. The 316 was configured with 40 kB of core memory for a TIP. The size of core memory was later increased, to 32 kB for the IMPs, and 56 kB for TIPs, in 1973.

In 1975, BBN introduced IMP software running on the Pluribus multi-processor. These appeared in a few sites. In 1981, BBN introduced IMP software running on its own C/30 processor product.

In 1983, TCP/IP protocols replaced NCP as the ARPANET's principal protocol, and the ARPANET then became one subnet of the early Internet.

The original IMPs and TIPs were phased out as the ARPANET was shut down after the introduction of the NSFNet, but some IMPs remained in service as late as July 1990.

The *ARPANET Completion Report*, jointly published by BBN and ARPA, concludes that:

> ... it is somewhat fitting to end on the note that the ARPANET program has had a strong and direct feedback into the support and strength of computer science, from which the network, itself, sprang.

In the wake of ARPANET being formally decommissioned on 28 February 1990, Vinton Cerf wrote the following lamentation, entitled "Requiem of the ARPANET":

It was the first, and being first, was best, but now we lay it down to ever rest. Now pause with me a moment, shed some tears. For auld lang syne, for love, for years and years of faithful service, duty done, I weep. Lay down thy packet, now, O friend, and sleep.

-Vinton Cerf

Senator Albert Gore, Jr. began to craft the High Performance Computing and Communication Act of 1991 (commonly referred to as "The Gore Bill") after hearing the 1988 report toward a National Research Network submitted to Congress by a group chaired by Leonard Kleinrock, professor of computer science at UCLA. The bill was passed on 9 December 1991 and led to the National Information Infrastructure (NII) which Al Gore called the "information superhighway".

ARPANET was the subject of two IEEE Milestones, both dedicated in 2009.

Software and Protocols

The starting point for host-to-host communication on the ARPANET in 1969 was the 1822 protocol, which defined the transmission of messages to an IMP. The message format was designed to work unambiguously with a broad range of computer architectures. An 1822 message essentially consisted of a message type, a numeric host address, and a data field. To send a data message to another host, the transmitting host formatted a data message containing the destination host's address and the data message being sent, and then transmitted the message through the 1822 hardware interface. The IMP then delivered the message to its destination address, either by delivering it to a locally connected host, or by delivering it to another IMP. When the message was ultimately delivered to the destination host, the receiving IMP would transmit a *Ready for Next Message* (RFNM) acknowledgement to the sending, host IMP.

Unlike modern Internet datagrams, the ARPANET was designed to reliably transmit 1822 messages, and to inform the host computer when it loses a message; the contemporary IP is unreliable, whereas the TCP is reliable. Nonetheless, the 1822 protocol proved inadequate for handling multiple connections among different applications residing in a host computer. This problem was addressed with the Network Control Program (NCP), which provided a standard method to establish reliable, flow-controlled, bidirectional communications links among different processes in different host computers. The NCP interface allowed application software to connect across the ARPANET by implementing higher-level communication protocols, an early example of the *protocol layering* concept incorporated to the OSI model.

In 1983, TCP/IP protocols replaced NCP as the ARPANET's principal protocol, and the ARPANET then became one component of the early Internet.

Network Applications

NCP provided a standard set of network services that could be shared by several applications running on a single host computer. This led to the evolution of *application protocols* that operated, more or less, independently of the underlying network service, and permitted independent advances in the underlying protocols.

In 1971, Ray Tomlinson, of BBN sent the first network e-mail (RFC 524, RFC 561). By 1973, e-mail constituted 75 percent of ARPANET traffic.

By 1973, the File Transfer Protocol (FTP) specification had been defined (RFC 354) and implemented, enabling file transfers over the ARPANET.

The Network Voice Protocol (NVP) specifications were defined in 1977 (RFC 741), then implemented, but, because of technical shortcomings, conference calls over the ARPANET never worked well; the contemporary Voice over Internet Protocol (packet voice) was decades away.

Password Protection

The Purdy Polynomial hash algorithm was developed for ARPANET to protect passwords in 1971 at the request of Larry Roberts, head of ARPA at that time. It computed a polynomial of degree $2^{24} + 17$ modulo the 64-bit prime $p = 2^{64} - 59$. The algorithm was later used by Digital Equipment Corporation (DEC) to hash passwords in the VMS Operating System, and is still being used for this purpose.

ARPANET in Popular Culture

- *Computer Networks: The Heralds of Resource Sharing*, a 30-minute documentary film featuring Fernando J. Corbato, J.C.R. Licklider, Lawrence G. Roberts, Robert Kahn, Frank Heart, William R. Sutherland, Richard W. Watson, John R. Pasta, Donald W. Davies, and economist, George W. Mitchell.

- "Scenario", a February 1985 episode of the U.S. television sitcom *Benson* (season 6, episode 20), was the first incidence of a popular TV show directly referencing the Internet or its progenitors. The show includes a scene in which the ARPANET is accessed.

- There is an electronic music artist known as "Arpanet", Gerald Donald, one of the members of Drexciya. The artist's 2002 album *Wireless Internet* features commentary on the expansion of the internet via wireless communication, with songs such as *NTT DoCoMo*, dedicated to the mobile communications giant based in Japan.

- Thomas Pynchon mentions ARPANET in his 2009 novel *Inherent Vice*, which is set in Los Angeles in 1970, and in his 2013 novel *Bleeding Edge*.

- The 1993 television series *The X-Files* featured the ARPANET in a season 5 episode, titled "Unusual Suspects". John Fitzgerald Byers offers to help Susan Modeski (known as Holly . . . "just like the sugar") by hacking into the AR-PANET to obtain sensitive information.

- In the spy-drama television series *The Americans*, a Russian scientist defector offers access to ARPANET to the Russians in a plea to not be repatriated (Season 2 Episode 5 "The Deal"). Episode 7 of Season 2 is named 'ARPANET' and features Russian infiltration to bug the network.

- In the television series *Person of Interest*, main character Harold Finch hacked ARPANET in 1980 using a homemade computer during his first efforts to built a prototype of the Machine. This corresponds with the real life virus that occurred in October of that year that temporarily halted ARPANET functions. The ARPANET hack was first discussed in the episode *2PiR* where a computer science teacher called it the most famous hack in history and one that was never solved. Finch later mentioned it to Person of Interest Caleb Phipps and his role was first indicated when he showed knowledge that it was done by "a kid with a homemade computer" which Phipps, who had researched the hack, had never heard before.

- In the third season of the television series *Halt and Catch Fire*, the character Joe MacMillan explores the potential commercialization of ARPANET.

CYCLADES

The CYCLADES computer network was a French research network created in the early 1970s. It was one of the pioneering networks experimenting with the concept of packet switching, and was developed to explore alternatives to the ARPANET design. It supported general local network research.

The CYCLADES network was the first to make the hosts responsible for the reliable delivery of data, rather than this being a centralized service of the network itself. Datagrams were exchanged on the network using transport protocols that do not guarantee reliable delivery, but only attempt best-effort. To empower the network leaves, the hosts, to perform error-correction, the network ensured end-to-end protocol transparency, a concept later to be known as the end-to-end principle. This simplified network design, reduced network latency, and reduced the opportunities for single point failures. The experience with these concepts led to the design of key features of the Internet protocol in the ARPANET project.

The network was sponsored by the French government, through the *Institut de Recherche en Informatique et en Automatique* (IRIA), the national research laboratory for computer science in France, now known as INRIA, which served as the co-ordinating agency. Several French computer manufacturers, research institutes and universities contributed to the effort. CYCLADES was designed and directed by Louis Pouzin.

Conception and Deployment

Design and staffing started in 1972, and November 1973 saw the first demonstration, using three hosts and one packet switch. Deployment continued in 1974, with three packet switches installed by February, although at that point the network was only operational for three hours each day. By June the network was up to seven switches, and was available throughout the day for experimental use.

A terminal concentrator was also developed that year, since time-sharing was still a prevalent mode of computer use. In 1975, the network shrank slightly due to budgetary constraints, but the setback was only temporary. At that point, the network provided remote login, remote batch and file transfer user application services.

By 1976 the network was in full deployment, eventually numbering 20 nodes with connections to NPL in London, ESA in Rome, and to the European Informatics Network (EIN).

Technical Details

CYCLADES used a layered architecture, as did the Internet. The basic packet transmission like function, named CIGALE, was novel; however, it provided an unreliable *datagram* service (the word was coined by Louis Pouzin by combining *data* and *telegram*). Since the packet switches no longer had to ensure correct delivery of data, this greatly simplified their design.

"The inspiration for datagrams had two sources. One was Donald Davies' studies. He had done some simulation of datagram networks, although he had not built any, and it looked technically viable. The second inspiration was I like things simple. I didn't see any real technical motivation to overlay two levels of end-to-end protocols. I thought one was enough."

— Louis Pouzin

The CIGALE network featured a distance vector routing protocol, and allowed experimentation with various metrics. it also included a time synchronization protocol in all the packet switches. CIGALE included early attempts at performing congestion control by dropping excess packets.

The name CIGALE— which is French for *cicada*—originates from the fact that the developers installed a speaker at each computer, so that "it went 'chirp chirp chirp' like cicadas" when a packet passed a computer.

An end-to-end protocol built on top of that provided a reliable transport service, on top of which applications were built. It provided a reliable sequence of user-visible data units called *letters*, rather than the reliable byte stream of TCP. The transport protocol was able to deal with out-of-order and unreliable delivery of datagrams, using the now-standard mechanisms of end-end acknowledgments and timeouts; it also featured sliding windows and end-to-end flow control.

Demise

By 1976, the French PTT was developing Transpac, a packet network based on the emerging X.25 standard. The academic debates between datagram and virtual circuit networks continued for some time, but were eventually cut short by bureaucratic decisions.

Data transmission was a state monopoly in France at the time, and IRIA needed a special dispensation to run the CYCLADES network. The PTT did not agree to funding by the government of a competitor to their Transpac network, and insisted that the permission and funding be rescinded. By 1981, Cyclades was forced to shut down.

Legacy

The most important legacy of CYCLADES was in showing that moving the responsibility for reliability into the hosts was workable, and produced a well-functioning service network. It also showed that it greatly reduced the complexity of the packet switches. The concept became a cornerstone in the design of the Internet.

The network was also a fertile ground for experimentation, and allowed a generation of French computer scientists to experiment with networking concepts. Louis Pouzin and the CYCLADES alumni initiated a number of follow-on projects at IRIA to experiment with local area networks, satellite networks, the Unix operating system, and the message passing operating system Chorus.

Hubert Zimmermann used his experience in CYCLADES to influence the design of the OSI model, which is still a common pedagogical tool.

CYCLADES alumni and researchers at IRIA/INRIA were also influential in spreading adoption of the Internet in France, eventually witnessing the success of the data-gram-based Internet, and the demise of the X.25 and ATM virtual circuit networks.

IPSANET

IPSANET was a packet switching network written by I. P. Sharp Associates (IPSA). Operation began in May 1976. It initially used the IBM 3705 Communications Controller and Computer Automation LSI-2 computers as nodes. An Intel 80286 based-node was added in 1987. It was called the Beta node.

The original purpose was to connect low-speed dumb terminals to a central time sharing host in Toronto. It was soon modified to allow a terminal to connect to an alternate host running the SHARP APL software under license. Terminals were initially either 2741-type machines based on the 14.8 characters/s IBM Selectric typewriter or 30 character/s ASCII machines. Link speed was limited to 9600 bit/s until about 1984.

Other services including 2780/3780 Bisync support, remote printing, X.25 gateway and SDLC pipe lines were added in the 1978 to 1984 era. There was no general purpose data transport facility until the introduction of *Network Shared Variable Processor* (NSVP) in 1984. This allowed APL programs running on different hosts to communicate via Shared Variables.

The Beta node improved performance and provided new services not tied to APL. An X.25 interface was the most important of these. It allowed connection to a host which was not running SHARP APL.

IPSANET allowed for the development of an early yet advanced e-mail service, *666 BOX*, which also became a major product for some time, originally hosted on IPSA's system, and later sold to end users to run on their own machines. NSVP allowed these remote e-mail systems to exchange traffic.

The network reached its maximum size of about 300 nodes before it was shut down in 1993.

Network Packet

A network packet is a formatted unit of data carried by a packet-switched network. Computer communications links that do not support packets, such as traditional point-to-point telecommunications links, simply transmit data as a bit stream. When data is formatted into packets, packet switching is possible and the bandwidth of the communication medium can be better shared among users than with circuit switching.

A packet consists of control information and user data, which is also known as the payload. Control information provides data for delivering the payload, for example: source and destination network addresses, error detection codes, and sequencing information. Typically, control information is found in packet headers and trailers.

Terminology

In the seven-layer OSI model of computer networking, *packet* strictly refers to a data unit at layer 3, the Network Layer. The correct term for a data unit at Layer 2, the Data Link Layer, is a *frame*, and at Layer 4, the Transport Layer, the correct term is a *segment* or *datagram*. For the case of TCP/IP communication over Ethernet, a TCP segment is carried in one or more IP packets, which are each carried in one or more Ethernet frames.

Packet Framing

Different communications protocols use different conventions for distinguishing between the elements and for formatting the data. For example, in Point-to-Point Protocol, the packet is formatted in 8-bit bytes, and special characters are used to delimit the different elements. Other protocols like Ethernet, establish the start of the header and data elements by their location relative to the start of the packet. Some protocols format the information at a bit level instead of a byte level.

A good analogy is to consider a packet to be like a letter: the header is like the envelope, and the data area is whatever the person puts inside the envelope.

A network design can achieve two major results by using packets: *error detection* and *multiple host addressing*. A packet has the following components.

Addresses

The routing of network packets requires two network addresses, the source address of the sending host, and the destination address of the receiving host.

Error Detection and Correction

Error detection and correction is performed at various layers in the protocol stack. Network packets may contain a checksum, parity bits or cyclic redundancy checks to detect errors that occur during transmission.

At the transmitter, the calculation is performed before the packet is sent. When received at the destination, the checksum is recalculated, and compared with the one in the packet. If discrepancies are found, the packet may be corrected or discarded. Any packet loss is dealt with by the network protocol.

In some cases modifications of the network packet may be necessary while routing, in which cases checksums are recalculated.

Hop Counts

Under fault conditions packets can end up traversing a closed circuit. If nothing was done, eventually the number of packets circulating would build up until the network was congested to the point of failure. A time to live is a field that is decreased by one each time a packet goes through a network node. If the field reaches zero, routing has failed, and the packet is discarded.

Ethernet packets have no time-to-live field and so are subject to broadcast radiation in the presence of a switch loop.

Length

There may be a field to identify the overall packet length. However, in some types of networks, the length is implied by the duration of transmission.

Priority

Some networks implement quality of service which can prioritize some types of packets above others. This field indicates which packet queue should be used; a high priority queue is emptied more quickly than lower priority queues at points in the network where congestion is occurring.

Payload

In general, payload is the data that is carried on behalf of an application. It is usually of variable length, up to a maximum that is set by the network protocol and sometimes the equipment on the route. Some networks can break a larger packet into smaller packets when necessary.

Example: IP Packets

IP packets are composed of a header and payload. The IPv4 packet header consists of:

00	01	02	03	04	05	06	07	08	09	10	11	12	13	14	15	16	17	18	19	20	21	22	23	24	25	26	27	28	29	30	31
Version				IHL				QoS								Length															
ID																0	DF	MF	Fragment Offset												
TTL								Protocol								Checksum															
Source IP																															
Destination IP																															

4 bits that contain the *version*, that specifies if it's an IPv4 or IPv6 packet,

1. 4 bits that contain the *Internet Header Length*, which is the length of the header in multiples of 4 bytes (e.g., 5 means 20 bytes).

2. 8 bits that contain the *Type of Service*, also referred to as Quality of Service (QoS), which describes what priority the packet should have,

3. 16 bits that contain the *length* of the packet in bytes,

4. 16 bits that contain an *identification tag* to help reconstruct the packet from several fragments,

5. 3 bits. The first contains a zero, followed by a flag that says whether the packet is allowed to be *fragmented* or not (DF: Don't fragment), and a flag to state whether more fragments of a packet follow (MF: More Fragments)

6. 13 bits that contain the *fragment offset*, a field to identify position of fragment within original packet

7. 8 bits that contain the *Time to live* (TTL), which is the number of hops (router, computer or device along a network) the packet is allowed to pass before it dies (for example, a packet with a TTL of 16 will be allowed to go across 16 routers to get to its destination before it is discarded),

8. 8 bits that contain the *protocol* (TCP, UDP, ICMP, etc.)

9. 16 bits that contain the *Header Checksum,* a number used in error detection,

10. 32 bits that contain the *source IP address,*

11. 32 bits that contain the *destination address.*

After those 160 bits, optional flags can be added of varied length, which can change based on the protocol used, then the data that packet carries is added. An IP packet has no trailer. However, an IP packet is often carried as the payload inside an Ethernet frame, which has its own header and trailer.

Many networks do not provide guarantees of delivery, nonduplication of packets, or in-order delivery of packets, e.g., the UDP protocol of the Internet. However, it is possible to layer a transport protocol on top of the packet service that can provide such protection; TCP and UDP are the best examples of layer 4, the Transport Layer, of the seven layered OSI model.

Example: the NASA Deep Space Network

The Consultative Committee for Space Data Systems (CCSDS) packet telemetry standard defines the protocol used for the transmission of spacecraft instrument data over the deep-space channel. Under this standard, an image or other data sent from a spacecraft instrument is transmitted using one or more packets.

CCSDS Packet Definition

A packet is a block of data with length that can vary between successive packets, ranging from 7 to 65,542 bytes, including the packet header.

- Packetized data is transmitted via frames, which are fixed-length data blocks. The size of a frame, including frame header and control information, can range up to 2048 bytes.

- Packet sizes are fixed during the development phase.

Because packet lengths are variable but frame lengths are fixed, packet boundaries usually do not coincide with frame boundaries.

Telecom Processing Notes

Data in a frame is typically protected from channel errors by error-correcting codes.

- Even when the channel errors exceed the correction capability of the error-correcting code, the presence of errors is nearly always detected by the error-correcting code or by a separate error-detecting code.

- Frames for which uncorrectable errors are detected are marked as undecodable and typically are deleted.

Handling Data Loss

Deleted undecodable whole frames are the principal type of data loss that affects compressed data sets. In general, there would be little to gain from attempting to use compressed data from a frame marked as undecodable.

- When errors are present in a frame, the bits of the subband pixels are already decoded before the first bit error will remain intact, but all subsequent decoded bits in the segment usually will be completely corrupted; a single bit error is often just as disruptive as many bit errors.

- Furthermore, compressed data usually are protected by powerful, long-block-length error-correcting codes, which are the types of codes most likely to yield substantial fractions of bit errors throughout those frames that are undecodable.

Thus, frames with detected errors would be essentially unusable even if they were not deleted by the frame processor.

This data loss can be compensated for with the following mechanisms.

- If an erroneous frame escapes detection, the decompressor will blindly use the frame data as if they were reliable, whereas in the case of detected erroneous frames, the decompressor can base its reconstruction on incomplete, but not misleading, data.

- However, it is extremely rare for an erroneous frame to go undetected.

- For frames coded by the CCSDS Reed–Solomon code, fewer than 1 in 40,000 erroneous frames can escape detection.

- All frames not employing the Reed–Solomon code use a cyclic redundancy check (CRC) error-detecting code, which has an undetected frame-error rate of less than 1 in 32,000.

Example: Radio and TV broadcasting

MPEG Packetized Stream

Packetized Elementary Stream (PES) is a specification defined by the MPEG communication protocol that allows an elementary stream to be divided into packets. The elementary stream is packetized by encapsulating sequential data bytes from the elementary stream inside PES packet headers.

A typical method of transmitting elementary stream data from a video or audio encoder is to first create PES packets from the elementary stream data and then to encapsulate these PES packets inside an MPEG transport stream (TS) packets or an MPEG program stream (PS). The TS packets can then be multiplexed and transmitted using broadcasting techniques, such as those used in an ATSC and DVB.

PES Packet Header

Name	Size	Description
Packet start code prefix	3 bytes	0x000001
Stream id	1 byte	Examples: Audio streams (0xC0-0xDF), Video streams (0xE0-0xEF)
		Note: The above 4 bytes is called the 32-bit start code.
PES Packet length	2 bytes	Can be zero as in not specified for video streams in MPEG transport streams
Optional PES header	variable length	
Stuffing bytes	variable length	
Data		See elementary stream. In the case of private streams the first byte of the payload is the sub-stream number.

Optional PES Header

Name	Number of Bits	Description
Marker bits	2	**10** binary or 0x2 hex
Scrambling control	2	00 implies not scrambled
Priority	1	
Data alignment indicator	1	1 indicates that the PES packet header is immediately followed by the video start code or audio syncword
Copyright	1	1 implies copyrighted
Original or Copy	1	1 implies original
PTS DTS indicator	2	11 = both present, 10 = only PTS
ESCR flag	1	
ES rate flag	1	
DSM trick mode flag	1	
Additional copy info flag	1	
CRC flag	1	
extension flag	1	
PES header length	8	gives the length of the remainder of the PES header
Optional fields	variable length	presence is determined by flag bits above
Stuffing Bytes	variable length	0xff

NICAM

In order to provide mono "compatibility", the NICAM signal is transmitted on a sub-carrier alongside the sound carrier. This means that the FM or AM regular mono sound carrier is left alone for reception by monaural receivers.

A NICAM-based stereo-TV infrastructure can transmit a stereo TV programme as well as the mono "compatibility" sound at the same time, or can transmit two or three entirely different sound streams. This latter mode could be used to transmit audio in different languages, in a similar manner to that used for in-flight movies on international flights. In this mode, the user can select which soundtrack to listen to when watching the content by operating a "sound-select" control on the receiver.

NICAM offers the following possibilities. The mode is auto-selected by the inclusion of a 3-bit type field in the data-stream

- One digital stereo sound channel.

- Two completely different digital mono sound channels.

- One digital mono sound channel and a 352 kbit/s data channel.

- One 704 kbit/s data channel.

The four other options could be implemented at a later date. Only the first two of the ones listed are known to be in general use however.

NICAM Packet Transmission

The NICAM packet (except for the header) is scrambled with a nine-bit pseudo-random bit-generator before transmission.

- The topology of this pseudo-random generator yields a bitstream with a repetition period of 511 bits.

- The pseudo-random generator's polynomial is: $x^9 + x^4 + 1$.

- The pseudo-random generator is initialized with: 111111111.

Making the NICAM bitstream look more like white noise is important because this reduces signal patterning on adjacent TV channels.

- The NICAM header is not subject to scrambling. This is necessary so as to aid in locking on to the NICAM data stream and resynchronisation of the data stream at the receiver.

- At the start of each NICAM packet the pseudo-random bit generator's shift-register is reset to all-ones.

References

- Martin Weik - Fiber Optics Standard Dictionary Springer Science & Business Media 6 Dec 2012, 1219 pages, ISBN 1461560233 [Retrieved 2015-08-04]

- Inside AppleTalk, Second Edition, Gursharan Sidhu, Richard Andrews and Alan Oppenheiner, Addison-Wesley, 1989, ISBN 0-201-55021-0

- L.A Lievrouw - Handbook of New Media: Student Edition (p.253) (edited by L.A Lievrouw, S.M. Livingstone), published by SAGE 2006 (abridged, reprint, revised), 475 pages, ISBN 1412918731 [Retrieved 2015-08-15]

- R. Oppliger. Internet and Intranet Security (p.12). Artech House, 1 Jan 2001, 403 pages, Artech House computer security series, ISBN 1580531660. Retrieved 2015-08-15.

- (ed. by H. Bidgoli). The Internet Encyclopedia, G Â– O. published by John Wiley & Sons 11 May 2004, 840 pages, ISBN 0471689963, Volume 2 of The Internet Encyclopedia. Retrieved 2015-08-15.

- Isaacson, Walter (2014). The Innovators: How a Group of Hackers, Geniuses, and Geeks Created the Digital Revolution. Simon & Schuster. p. 237. ISBN 9781476708690.

- M. Ziewitz & I. Brown (2013). Research Handbook on Governance of the Internet. Edward Elgar Publishing. p. 7. ISBN 1849805040. Retrieved 2015-08-16.

- Fritz E. Froehlich; Allen Kent (1990). "ARPANET, the Defense Data Network, and Internet". The Froehlich/Kent Encyclopedia of Telecommunications. 1. CRC Press. pp. 341–375. ISBN 978-0-8247-2900-4.

- Abbate, Janet (11 June 1999). Inventing the Internet. Cambridge, MA: MIT Press. ASIN B003VP-WY6E. ISBN 0-262-01172-7.

- Baran, Paul (May 27, 1960). "Reliable Digital Communications Using Unreliable Network Repeater Nodes" (PDF). The RAND Corporation: 1. Retrieved July 7, 2016.

- G. Schneider; J. Evans; K. Pinard. The Internet - Illustrated. published by Cengage Learning 26 Oct 2009, 296 pages, ISBN 0538750987, Available Titles Skills Assessment Manager (SAM) - Office 2010 Series Illustrated (Course Technology). Retrieved 2015-08-15.

- Scantlebury, Roger (25 June 2013). "Internet pioneers airbrushed from history". The Guardian. Retrieved 1 August 2015.

- Davies, D. W. (17 March 1986), Oral History 189: D. W. Davies interviewed by Martin Campbell-Kelly at the National Physical Laboratory, Charles Babbage Institute University of Minnesota, Minneapolis, retrieved 21 July 2014

- "Digital Equipment Corporation, Nineteen Fifty-Seven to the Present", Digital Equipment Corporation, 1978, page 53. Retrieved 3 September 2013.

- "Maintaining IPX Compatibility During a Migration to TCP/IP on a NetWare Network", Rich Lee, Novell, 1 March 1998. Retrieved 3 September 2013.

- "KDDI to Close VENUS-P International Public Data Communications Service", KDDI, 9 November 2005. Retrieved 3 September 2013.

- "TransPAC3 - Asia-US High Performance International Networking", International Research Network Connections Program (IRNC), U.S. National Science Foundation, October 2011. Retrieved 3 September 2013.

Internet Protocol Suite: An Overview

The Internet protocol suite or TCP/IP is the abstract model on which the Internet functions. It is mainly used in protocols, and specifies how data should be grouped, directed and then received. Some of the key principles of Internet protocol suite are also elucidated in this chapter, such as End- to- end principle and robustness principle.

Internet Protocol Suite

The Internet protocol suite is the computer networking model and set of communications protocols used on the Internet and similar computer networks. It is commonly known as TCP/IP, because its most commonly used protocols, the Transmission Control Protocol (TCP) and the Internet Protocol (IP) were the first networking protocols defined during its development. It is occasionally known as the Department of Defense (DoD) model, because the development of the networking model was funded by DARPA, an agency of the United States Department of Defense.

The Internet protocol suite provides end-to-end data communication specifying how data should be packetized, addressed, transmitted, routed and received. This functionality is organized into four abstraction layers which are used to sort all related protocols according to the scope of networking involved. From lowest to highest, the layers are the link layer, containing communication methods for data that remains within a single network segment (link); the internet layer, connecting independent networks, thus providing internetworking; the transport layer handling host-to-host communication; and the application layer, which provides process-to-process data exchange for applications.

Technical standards specifying the Internet protocol suite and many of its constituent protocols are maintained by the Internet Engineering Task Force (IETF).

History

Early Research

The Internet protocol suite resulted from research and development conducted by the Defense Advanced Research Projects Agency (DARPA) in the late 1960s. After initiating the pioneering ARPANET in 1969, DARPA started work on a number of other data transmission technologies. In 1972, Robert E. Kahn joined the DARPA Information Processing Technology Office, where he worked on both satellite packet networks and ground-based radio packet networks, and recognized the value of being able to communicate across both. In the spring of 1973, Vinton Cerf, the developer of the existing ARPANET Network Control Program (NCP) protocol, joined Kahn to work on open-architecture interconnection models with the goal of designing the next protocol generation for the ARPANET.

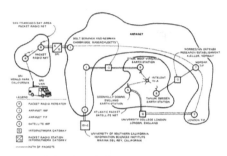

Diagram of the first internetworked connection

A Stanford Research Institute Packet Radio Van, used for the first three-way internetworked transmission.

By the summer of 1973, Kahn and Cerf had worked out a fundamental reformulation, in which the differences between network protocols were hidden by using a common internetwork protocol, and, instead of the network being responsible for reliability, as in the ARPANET, this function was delegated to the hosts. Cerf credits Hubert Zimmermann and Louis Pouzin, designer of the CYCLADES network, with important influences on this design. The protocol was implemented as the *Transmission Control Program* (TCP), first published in 1974.

Initially, the TCP managed both datagram transmissions and routing, but as the protocol grew, other researchers recommended a division of functionality into protocol layers. Advocates included Jonathan Postel of the University of Southern California's Information Sciences Institute, who edited the Request for Comments (RFCs), the technical and strategic series that both documented and catalyzed Internet development. Postel stated, *"we are screwing up in our design of Internet protocols by violating the principle of layering"*. Encapsulation of different mechanisms was intended to create an environment where the upper layers could access only what was needed from the lower layers. A monolithic design would be inflexible and lead to scalability issues. The Transmission Control Program was split into two distinct protocols, the Transmission Control Protocol and the Internet Protocol. The new suite replaced all protocols used previously., PRnet, and SATnet

The design of the network included the recognition that it should provide only the functions of efficiently transmitting and routing traffic between end nodes and that all other intelligence should be located at the edge of the network, in the end nodes. This design is known as the end-to-end principle. Using this design, it became possible to connect almost any network to the ARPANET, irrespective of the local characteristics, thereby solving Kahn's initial problem. One popular expression is that TCP/IP, the eventual product of Cerf and Kahn's work, will run over *two tin cans and a string.* (Years later, as a joke, the IP over Avian Carriers formal protocol specification was created and successfully tested.)

A computer called a router is provided with an interface to each network. It forwards packets back and forth between them. Originally a router was called *gateway*, but the term was changed to avoid confusion with other types of gateways.

Specification

From 1973 to 1974, Cerf's networking research group at Stanford worked out details of the idea, resulting in the first TCP specification. A significant technical influence was the early networking work at Xerox PARC, which produced the PARC Universal Packet protocol suite, much of which existed around that time.

DARPA then contracted with BBN Technologies, Stanford University, and the University College London to develop operational versions of the protocol on different hardware platforms. Four versions were developed: TCP v1, TCP v2, TCP v3 and IP v3, and TCP/IP v4. The last protocol is still in use today.

In 1975, a two-network TCP/IP communications test was performed between Stanford and University College London (UCL). In November, 1977, a three-network TCP/IP test was conducted between sites in the US, the UK, and Norway. Several other TCP/IP prototypes were developed at multiple research centers between 1978 and 1983. The migration of the ARPANET to TCP/IP was officially completed on flag day January 1, 1983, when the new protocols were permanently activated.

Adoption

In March 1982, the US Department of Defense declared TCP/IP as the standard for all military computer networking. In 1985, the Internet Advisory Board (later renamed the Internet Architecture Board) held a three-day workshop on TCP/IP for the computer industry, attended by 250 vendor representatives, promoting the protocol and leading to its increasing commercial use.

In 1985, the first Interop conference focused on network interoperability by broader adoption of TCP/IP. The conference was founded by Dan Lynch, an early Internet activist. From the beginning, large corporations, such as IBM and DEC, attended the meeting. Interoperability conferences have been held every year since then. Every year from 1985 through 1993, the number of attendees tripled.

IBM, AT&T and DEC were the first major corporations to adopt TCP/IP, despite having competing internal protocols (SNA, XNS, DECNET). In IBM, from 1984, Barry Appelman's group did TCP/IP development. (Appelman later moved to AOL to be the head of all its development efforts.) They navigated the corporate politics to get a stream of TCP/IP products for various IBM systems, including MVS, VM, and OS/2. At the same time, several smaller companies began offering TCP/IP stacks for DOS and MS Windows, such as the company FTP Software, and the Wollongong Group. The first VM/CMS TCP/IP stack came from the University of Wisconsin.

Some of these TCP/IP stacks were written single-handedly by a few programmers. Jay Elinsky and Oleg Vishnepolsky of IBM Research wrote TCP/IP stacks for VM/CMS and OS/2, respectively. In 1984 Donald Gillies at MIT wrote a 'ntcp' multi-connection TCP which ran atop the IP/PacketDriver layer maintained by John Romkey at MIT in 1983-4. Romkey leveraged this TCP in 1986 when FTP Software was founded. Phil Karn created KA9Q TCP (a multi-connection TCP for ham radio applications) starting in 1985.

The spread of TCP/IP was fueled further in June 1989, when AT&T agreed to place the TCP/IP code developed for UNIX into the public domain. Various vendors, including IBM, included this code in their own TCP/IP stacks. Many companies sold TCP/IP stacks for Windows until Microsoft released a native TCP/IP stack in Windows 95. This event was a little late in the evolution of the Internet, but it cemented TCP/IP's dominance over other protocols, which began to lose ground. These protocols included IBM Systems Network Architecture (SNA), Open Systems Interconnection (OSI), Microsoft's native NetBIOS, and Xerox Network Systems (XNS).

Key Architectural Principles

An early architectural document, RFC 1122, emphasizes architectural principles over layering.

- End-to-end principle: This principle has evolved over time. Its original expression put the maintenance of state and overall intelligence at the edges, and assumed the Internet that connected the edges retained no state and concentrated on speed and simplicity. Real-world needs for firewalls, network address translators, web content caches and the like have forced changes in this principle.

- Robustness Principle: "In general, an implementation must be conservative in its sending behavior, and liberal in its receiving behavior. That is, it must be careful to send well-formed datagrams, but must accept any datagram that it can interpret (e.g., not object to technical errors where the meaning is still clear)." "The second part of the principle is almost as important: software on other hosts may contain deficiencies that make it unwise to exploit legal but obscure protocol features." (Postel famously summarized the principle as, "Be conservative in what you do, be liberal in what you accept from others" -- a saying that came to known as "Postel's Law.")

Abstraction Layers

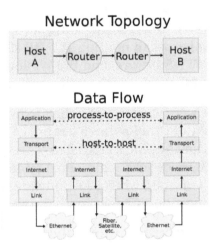

Two Internet hosts connected via two routers and the corresponding layers used at each hop. The application on each host executes read and write operations as if the processes were directly connected to each other by some kind of data pipe. Every other detail of the communication is hidden from each process. The underlying mechanisms that transmit data between the host computers are located in the lower protocol layers.

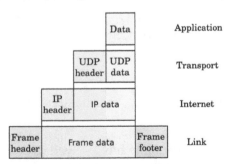

Encapsulation of application data descending through the layers described in RFC 1122

Encapsulation is used to provide abstraction of protocols and services. Encapsulation is usually aligned with the division of the protocol suite into layers of general functionality. In general, an application (the highest level of the model) uses a set of protocols to send its data down the layers, being further encapsulated at each level.

The layers of the protocol suite near the top are logically closer to the user application, while those near the bottom are logically closer to the physical transmission of the data. Viewing layers as providing or consuming a service is a method of abstraction to isolate upper layer protocols from the details of transmitting bits over, for example, Ethernet and collision detection, while the lower layers avoid having to know the details of each and every application and its protocol.

Even when the layers are examined, the assorted architectural documents—there is no single architectural model such as ISO 7498, the Open Systems Interconnection (OSI) model—have fewer and less rigidly defined layers than the OSI model, and thus provide an easier fit for real-world protocols. One frequently referenced document, RFC 1958, does not contain a stack of layers. The lack of emphasis on layering is a major difference between the IETF and OSI approaches. It only refers to the existence of the internetworking layer and generally to *upper layers*; this document was intended as a 1996 snapshot of the architecture: "The Internet and its architecture have grown in evolutionary fashion from modest beginnings, rather than from a Grand Plan. While this process of evolution is one of the main reasons for the technology's success, it nevertheless seems useful to record a snapshot of the current principles of the Internet architecture."

RFC 1122, entitled *Host Requirements*, is structured in paragraphs referring to layers, but the document refers to many other architectural principles not emphasizing layering. It loosely defines a four-layer model, with the layers having names, not numbers, as follows:

- The application layer is the scope within which applications create user data and communicate this data to other applications on another or the same host. The applications, or processes, make use of the services provided by the underlying, lower layers, especially the Transport Layer which provides reliable or unreliable *pipes* to other processes. The communications partners are characterized by the application architecture, such as the client-server model and peer-to-peer networking. This is the layer in which all *higher level* protocols, such as SMTP, FTP, SSH, HTTP, operate. Processes are addressed via ports which essentially represent services.

- The transport layer performs host-to-host communications on either the same or different hosts and on either the local network or remote networks separated by routers. It provides a channel for the communication needs of applications. UDP is the basic transport layer protocol, providing an unreliable datagram service. The Transmission Control Protocol provides flow-control, connection establishment, and reliable transmission of data.

- The internet layer has the task of exchanging datagrams across network boundaries. It provides a uniform networking interface that hides the actual topology (layout) of the underlying network connections. It is therefore also referred to as the layer that establishes internetworking, indeed, it defines and establishes the Internet. This layer defines the addressing and routing structures used for the TCP/IP protocol suite. The primary protocol in this scope is the Internet Protocol, which defines IP addresses. Its function in routing is to transport datagrams to the next IP router that has the connectivity to a network closer to the final data destination.

- The link layer defines the networking methods within the scope of the local network link on which hosts communicate without intervening routers. This layer includes the protocols used to describe the local network topology and the interfaces needed to effect transmission of Internet layer datagrams to next-neighbor hosts.

The Internet protocol suite and the layered protocol stack design were in use before the OSI model was established. Since then, the TCP/IP model has been compared with the OSI model in books and classrooms, which often results in confusion because the two models use different assumptions and goals, including the relative importance of strict layering.

This abstraction also allows upper layers to provide services that the lower layers do not provide. While the original OSI model was extended to include connectionless services (OSIRM CL), IP is not designed to be reliable and is a best effort delivery protocol. This means that all transport layer implementations must choose whether or how to provide reliability. UDP provides data integrity via a checksum but does not guarantee delivery; TCP provides both data integrity and delivery guarantee by retransmitting until the receiver acknowledges the reception of the packet.

This model lacks the formalism of the OSI model and associated documents, but the IETF does not use a formal model and does not consider this a limitation, as illustrated in the comment by David D. Clark, "We reject: kings, presidents and voting. We believe in: rough consensus and running code." Criticisms of this model, which have been made with respect to the OSI model, often do not consider ISO's later extensions to that model.

For multi-access links with their own addressing systems (e.g. Ethernet) an address mapping protocol is needed. Such protocols can be considered to be below IP but above the existing link system. While the IETF does not use the terminology, this is a subnetwork dependent convergence facility according to an extension to the OSI model, the internal organization of the network layer (IONL).

ICMP & IGMP operate on top of IP but do not transport data like UDP or TCP. Again, this functionality exists as layer management extensions to the OSI model, in its *Management Framework* (OSIRM MF)

The SSL/TLS library operates above the transport layer (uses TCP) but below application protocols. Again, there was no intention, on the part of the designers of these protocols, to comply with OSI architecture.

The link is treated as a black box. The IETF explicitly does not intend to discuss transmission systems, which is a less academic but practical alternative to the OSI model.

The following is a description of each layer in the TCP/IP networking model starting from the lowest level.

Link Layer

The link layer has the networking scope of the local network connection to which a host is attached. This regime is called the *link* in TCP/IP literature. It is the lowest component layer of the Internet protocols, as TCP/IP is designed to be hardware independent. As a result, TCP/IP may be implemented on top of virtually any hardware networking technology.

The link layer is used to move packets between the Internet layer interfaces of two different hosts on the same link. The processes of transmitting and receiving packets on a given link can be controlled both in the software device driver for the network card, as well as on firmware or specialized chipsets. These perform data link functions such as adding a packet header to prepare it for transmission, then actually transmit the frame over a physical medium. The TCP/IP model includes specifications of translating the network addressing methods used in the Internet Protocol to data link addressing, such as Media Access Control (MAC). All other aspects below that level, however, are implicitly assumed to exist in the link layer, but are not explicitly defined.

This is also the layer where packets may be selected to be sent over a virtual private network or other networking tunnel. In this scenario, the link layer data may be considered application data which traverses another instantiation of the IP stack for transmission or reception over another IP connection. Such a connection, or virtual link, may be established with a transport protocol or even an application scope protocol that serves as a tunnel in the link layer of the protocol stack. Thus, the TCP/IP model does not dictate a strict hierarchical encapsulation sequence.

The TCP/IP model's link layer corresponds to the Open Systems Interconnection (OSI) model physical and data link layers, layers one and two of the OSI model.

Internet Layer

The internet layer has the responsibility of sending packets across potentially multiple networks. Internetworking requires sending data from the source network to the destination network. This process is called routing.

The Internet Protocol performs two basic functions:

- Host addressing and identification: This is accomplished with a hierarchical IP addressing system.

- Packet routing: This is the basic task of sending packets of data (datagrams) from source to destination by forwarding them to the next network router closer to the final destination.

The internet layer is not only agnostic of data structures at the transport layer, but it also does not distinguish between operation of the various transport layer protocols. IP carries data for a variety of different upper layer protocols. These protocols are each identified by a unique protocol number: for example, Internet Control Message Protocol (ICMP) and Internet Group Management Protocol (IGMP) are protocols 1 and 2, respectively.

Some of the protocols carried by IP, such as ICMP which is used to transmit diagnostic information, and IGMP which is used to manage IP Multicast data, are layered on top of IP but perform internetworking functions. This illustrates the differences in the architecture of the TCP/IP stack of the Internet and the OSI model. The TCP/IP model's internet layer corresponds to layer three of the Open Systems Interconnection (OSI) model, where it is referred to as the network layer.

The internet layer provides an unreliable datagram transmission facility between hosts located on potentially different IP networks by forwarding the transport layer datagrams to an appropriate next-hop router for further relaying to its destination. With this functionality, the internet layer makes possible internetworking, the interworking of different IP networks, and it essentially establishes the Internet. The Internet Protocol is the principal component of the internet layer, and it defines two addressing systems to identify network hosts' computers, and to locate them on the network. The original address system of the ARPANET and its successor, the Internet, is Internet Protocol version 4 (IPv4). It uses a 32-bit IP address and is therefore capable of identifying approximately four billion hosts. This limitation was eliminated in 1998 by the standardization of Internet Protocol version 6 (IPv6) which uses 128-bit addresses. IPv6 production implementations emerged in approximately 2006.

Transport Layer

The transport layer establishes basic data channels that applications use for task-specific data exchange. The layer establishes process-to-process connectivity, meaning it provides end-to-end services that are independent of the structure of user data and the logistics of exchanging information for any particular specific purpose. Its responsibility includes end-to-end message transfer independent of the underlying network, along with error control, segmentation, flow control, congestion control, and application addressing (port numbers). End-to-end message transmission or connecting applications at the transport layer can be categorized as either connection-oriented, implemented in TCP, or connectionless, implemented in UDP.

For the purpose of providing process-specific transmission channels for applications, the layer establishes the concept of the port. This is a numbered logical construct allocated specifically for each of the communication channels an application needs. For many types of services, these port numbers have been standardized so that client computers may address specific services of a server computer without the involvement of service announcements or directory services.

Because IP provides only a best effort delivery, some transport layer protocols offer reliability. However, IP can run over a reliable data link protocol such as the High-Level Data Link Control (HDLC).

For example, the TCP is a connection-oriented protocol that addresses numerous reliability issues in providing a reliable byte stream:

- data arrives in-order

- data has minimal error (i.e., correctness)

- duplicate data is discarded

- lost or discarded packets are resent

- includes traffic congestion control

The newer Stream Control Transmission Protocol (SCTP) is also a reliable, connection-oriented transport mechanism. It is message-stream-oriented—not byte-stream-oriented like TCP—and provides multiple streams multiplexed over a single connection. It also provides multi-homing support, in which a connection end can be represented by multiple IP addresses (representing multiple physical interfaces), such that if one fails, the connection is not interrupted. It was developed initially for telephony applications (to transport SS7 over IP), but can also be used for other applications.

The User Datagram Protocol is a connectionless datagram protocol. Like IP, it is a best effort, "unreliable" protocol. Reliability is addressed through error detection using a weak checksum algorithm. UDP is typically used for applications such as streaming media (audio, video, Voice over IP etc.) where on-time arrival is more important than reliability, or for simple query/response applications like DNS lookups, where the overhead of setting up a reliable connection is disproportionately large. Real-time Transport Protocol (RTP) is a datagram protocol that is designed for real-time data such as streaming audio and video.

The applications at any given network address are distinguished by their TCP or UDP port. By convention certain *well known ports* are associated with specific applications.

The TCP/IP model's transport or host-to-host layer corresponds to the fourth layer in the Open Systems Interconnection (OSI) model, also called the transport layer.

Application Layer

The application layer includes the protocols used by most applications for providing user services or exchanging application data over the network connections established by the lower level protocols, but this may include some basic network support services, such as many routing protocols, and host configuration protocols. Examples of application layer protocols include the Hypertext Transfer Protocol (HTTP), the File Transfer Protocol (FTP), the Simple Mail Transfer Protocol (SMTP), and the Dynamic Host Configuration Protocol (DHCP). Data coded according to application layer protocols are encapsulated into transport layer protocol units (such as TCP or UDP messages), which in turn use lower layer protocols to effect actual data transfer.

The TCP/IP model does not consider the specifics of formatting and presenting data, and does not define additional layers between the application and transport layers as in the OSI model (presentation and session layers). Such functions are the realm of libraries and application programming interfaces.

Application layer protocols generally treat the transport layer (and lower) protocols as black boxes which provide a stable network connection across which to communicate, although the applications are usually aware of key qualities of the transport layer connection such as the end point IP addresses and port numbers. Application layer protocols are often associated with particular client–server applications, and common services have *well-known* port numbers reserved by the Internet Assigned Numbers Authority (IANA). For example, the HyperText Transfer Protocol uses server port 80 and Telnet uses server port 23. Clients connecting to a service usually use ephemeral ports, i.e., port numbers assigned only for the duration of the transaction at random or from a specific range configured in the application.

The transport layer and lower-level layers are unconcerned with the specifics of application layer protocols. Routers and switches do not typically examine the encapsulated traffic, rather they just provide a conduit for it. However, some firewall and bandwidth throttling applications must interpret application data. An example is the Resource Reservation Protocol (RSVP). It is also sometimes necessary for network address translator (NAT) traversal to consider the application payload.

The application layer in the TCP/IP model is often compared as equivalent to a combination of the fifth (Session), sixth (Presentation), and the seventh (Application) layers of the Open Systems Interconnection (OSI) model.

Furthermore, the TCP/IP reference model distinguishes between *user protocols* and *support protocols*. Support protocols provide services to a system. User protocols are used for actual user applications. For example, FTP is a user protocol and DNS is a support protocol.

Layer Names and Number of Layers in the Literature

The following table shows various networking models. The number of layers varies between three and seven.

RFC 1122, Internet STD 3 (1989)	Cisco Academy	Kurose, Forouzan	Comer, Kozierok	Stallings	Tanenbaum	Mike Padlipsky's 1982 "Arpanet Reference Model" (RFC 871)	OSI model
Four layers	Four layers	Five layers	Four+one layers	Five layers	Five layers	Three layers	Seven layers
"Internet model"	"Internet model"	"Five-layer Internet model" or "TCP/IP protocol suite"	"TCP/IP 5-layer reference model"	"TCP/IP model"	"TCP/IP 5-layer reference model"	"Arpanet reference model"	OSI model
Application	Application	Application	Application	Application	Application	Application/ Process	Application
							Presentation
							Session
Transport	Transport	Transport	Transport	Host-to-host or transport	Transport	Host-to-host	Transport
Internet	Internetwork	Network	Internet	Internet	Internet		Network
Link	Network interface	Data link	Data link (Network interface)	Network access	Data link	Network interface	Data link
		Physical	(Hardware)	Physical	Physical		Physical

Some of the networking models are from textbooks, which are secondary sources that may conflict with the intent of RFC 1122 and other IETF primary sources.

Comparison of TCP/IP and OSI Layering

The three top layers in the OSI model, i.e. the application layer, the presentation layer and the session layer, are not distinguished separately in the TCP/IP model which only has an application layer above the transport layer. While some pure OSI protocol applications, such as X.400, also combined them, there is no requirement that a TCP/IP protocol stack must impose monolithic architecture above the transport layer. For example, the NFS application protocol runs over the eXternal Data Representation (XDR) presentation protocol, which, in turn, runs over a protocol called Remote Procedure Call (RPC). RPC provides reliable record transmission, so it can safely use the best-effort UDP transport.

Different authors have interpreted the TCP/IP model differently, and disagree whether the link layer, or the entire TCP/IP model, covers OSI layer 1 (physical layer) issues, or whether a hardware layer is assumed below the link layer.

Several authors have attempted to incorporate the OSI model's layers 1 and 2 into the TCP/IP model, since these are commonly referred to in modern standards (for example, by IEEE and ITU). This often results in a model with five layers, where the link layer or network access layer is split into the OSI model's layers 1 and 2.

The IETF protocol development effort is not concerned with strict layering. Some of its protocols may not fit cleanly into the OSI model, although RFCs sometimes refer to it and often use the old OSI layer numbers. The IETF has repeatedly stated that Internet protocol and architecture development is not intended to be OSI-compliant. RFC 3439, addressing Internet architecture, contains a section entitled: "Layering Considered Harmful".

For example, the session and presentation layers of the OSI suite are considered to be included to the application layer of the TCP/IP suite. The functionality of the session layer can be found in protocols like HTTP and SMTP and is more evident in protocols like Telnet and the Session Initiation Protocol (SIP). Session layer functionality is also realized with the port numbering of the TCP and UDP protocols, which cover the transport layer in the TCP/IP suite. Functions of the presentation layer are realized in the TCP/IP applications with the MIME standard in data exchange.

Conflicts are apparent also in the original OSI model, ISO 7498, when not considering the annexes to this model, e.g., the ISO 7498/4 Management Framework, or the ISO 8648 Internal Organization of the Network layer (IONL). When the IONL and Management Framework documents are considered, the ICMP and IGMP are defined as layer management protocols for the network layer. In like manner, the IONL provides a structure for "subnetwork dependent convergence facilities" such as ARP and RARP.

IETF protocols can be encapsulated recursively, as demonstrated by tunneling protocols such as Generic Routing Encapsulation (GRE). GRE uses the same mechanism that OSI uses for tunneling at the network layer.

Implementations

The Internet protocol suite does not presume any specific hardware or software environment. It only requires that hardware and a software layer exists that is capable of sending and receiving packets on a computer network. As a result, the suite has been implemented on essentially every computing platform. A minimal implementation of TCP/IP includes the following: Internet Protocol (IP), Address Resolution Protocol (ARP), Internet Control Message Protocol (ICMP), Transmission Control Protocol (TCP), User Datagram Protocol (UDP), and IGMP. In addition to IP, ICMP, TCP, UDP, Internet Protocol version 6 requires Neighbor Discovery Protocol (NDP), ICMPv6, and IGMPv6 and is often accompanied by an integrated IPSec security layer.

Application programmers are typically concerned only with interfaces in the application layer and often also in the transport layer, while the layers below are services provided by the TCP/IP stack in the operating system. Most IP implementations are accessible to programmers through sockets and APIs.

Unique implementations include Lightweight TCP/IP, an open source stack designed for embedded systems, and KA9Q NOS, a stack and associated protocols for amateur packet radio systems and personal computers connected via serial lines.

Microcontroller firmware in the network adapter typically handles link issues, supported by driver software in the operating system. Non-programmable analog and digital electronics are normally in charge of the physical components below the link layer, typically using an application-specific integrated circuit (ASIC) chipset for each network interface or other physical standard. High-performance routers are to a large extent based on fast non-programmable digital electronics, carrying out link level switching.

Key Architectural Principles

End-to-end Principle

The end-to-end principle is a classic design principle in computer networking. In networks designed according to the principle, application-specific features reside in the communicating end nodes of the network, rather than in intermediary nodes, such as gateways and routers, that exist to establish the network. The end-to-end principle originated in the work by Paul Baran in the 1960s, which addressed the requirement of network reliability when the building blocks are inherently unreliable. It was first articulated explicitly in 1981 by Saltzer, Reed, and Clark.

A basic premise of the principle is that the payoffs from adding features to a simple network quickly diminish, especially in cases in which the end hosts have to implement those functions only for reasons of conformance, i.e. completeness and correctness based on a specification. Furthermore, as implementing any specific function incurs some resource penalties regardless of whether the function is used or not, implementing a specific function *in the network* distributes these penalties among all clients, regardless of whether they use that function or not.

The canonical example for the end-to-end principle is that of an arbitrarily reliable file transfer between two end-points in a distributed network of some nontrivial size: The only way two end-points can obtain a completely reliable transfer is by transmitting and acknowledging a checksum for the entire data stream; in such a setting, lesser checksum and acknowledgement (ACK/NACK) protocols are justified only for the purpose of optimizing performance - they are useful to the vast majority of clients, but are not enough to fulfil the reliability requirement of this particular application. Thorough checksum is hence best done at the end-points, and the network maintains a relatively low level of complexity and reasonable performance for all clients.

The end-to-end principle is closely related, and sometimes seen as a direct precursor to the principle of net neutrality.

Concept

The fundamental notion behind the end-to-end principle is that for two processes communicating with each other via some communication means, the *reliability* obtained from that means cannot be expected to be perfectly aligned with the reliability requirements of the processes. In particular, meeting or exceeding very high reliability requirements of communicating processes separated by networks of nontrivial size is more costly than obtaining the required degree of reliability by positive end-to-end acknowledgements and retransmissions (referred to as PAR or ARQ). Put differently, it is far easier and more tractable to obtain reliability beyond a certain margin by mechanisms in the *end hosts* of a network rather than in the *intermediary nodes*, especially when the latter are beyond the control of and accountability to the former. An end-to-end PAR protocol with infinite retries can obtain arbitrarily high reliability from any network with a higher than zero probability of successfully transmitting data from one end to another.

The end-to-end principle does not trivially extend to functions beyond end-to-end error control and correction. E.g., no straightforward end-to-end arguments can be made for communication parameters such as latency and throughput. Based on a personal communication with Saltzer (lead author of the original end-to-end paper) Blumenthal and Clark in a 2001 paper note: *[F]rom the beginning, the end-to-end arguments revolved around requirements that could be implemented correctly at the end-points; if implementation inside the network is the only way to accomplish the requirement, then an end-to-end argument isn't appropriate in the first place. (p. 80).*

The meaning of the end-to-end principle has been continuously reinterpreted ever since its initial articulation. Also, noteworthy formulations of the end-to-end principle can be found prior to the seminal 1981 Saltzer, Reed, and Clark paper.

The Basic Notion: Reliability from Unreliable Parts

In the 1960s, Paul Baran and Donald Davies in their pre-ARPANET elaborations of networking made brief comments about reliability that capture the essence of the later end-to-end principle. To quote from a 1964 Baran paper: *Reliability and raw error rates are secondary. The network must be built with the expectation of heavy damage anyway.*

Powerful error removal methods exist. (p. 5). Similarly, Davies notes on end-to-end error control: *It is thought that all users of the network will provide themselves with some kind of error control and that without difficulty this could be made to show up a missing packet. Because of this, loss of packets, if it is sufficiently rare, can be tolerated. (p. 2.3).*

Early Trade-offs: Experiences in the ARPANET

The ARPANET was the first large-scale general-purpose packet switching network – implementing several of the basic notions previously touched on by Baran and Davies, and demonstrating several important aspects of the end-to-end principle:

Packet switching pushes some logical functions toward the communication end points

> If the basic premise of a distributed network is packet switching, then functions such as reordering and duplicate detection inevitably have to be implemented at the logical end points of such network. Consequently, the ARPANET featured two distinct levels of functionality – (1) a lower level concerned with transporting data packets between neighboring network nodes (called IMPs), and (2) a higher level concerned with various end-to-end aspects of the data transmission. Dave Clark, one of the authors of the end-to-end principle paper, concludes: "The discovery of packets is not a consequence of the end-to-end argument. It is the success of packets that make the end-to-end argument relevant" (slide 31).

No arbitrarily reliable data transfer without end-to-end acknowledgment and retransmission mechanisms

> The ARPANET was designed to provide reliable data transport between any two end points of the network – much like a simple I/O channel between a computer and a nearby peripheral device. In order to remedy any potential failures of packet transmission normal ARPANET messages were handed from one node to the next node with a positive acknowledgment and retransmission scheme; after a successful handover they were then discarded, no source to destination retransmission in case of packet loss was catered for. However, in spite of significant efforts, perfect reliability as envisaged in the initial ARPANET specification turned out to be impossible to provide – a reality that became increasingly obvious once the ARPANET grew well beyond its initial four node topology. The ARPANET thus provided a strong case for the inherent limits of network based hop-by-hop reliability mechanisms in pursuit of true end-to-end reliability.

Trade-off between reliability, latency, and throughput

> The pursuit of perfect reliability may hurt other relevant parameters of a data transmission – most importantly latency and throughput. This is particularly important for applications that require no perfect reliability, but rather value

predictable throughput and low latency – the classic example being interactive real-time voice applications. This use case was catered for in the ARPANET by providing a raw message service that dispensed with various reliability measures so as to provide faster and lower latency data transmission service to the end hosts.

The Canonical Case: TCP/IP

On the Internet the Internet Protocol – a connectionless datagram service with no delivery guarantees and effectively no QoS parameters – is used for nearly all communications. Arbitrary protocols may sit on top of IP. It turns out that some applications (such as voice, in many cases) do not need reliable retransmission, and so the only reliability in IP is in the checksum of the IP header (which is necessary to prevent bit errors from sending packets on wild routing paths.) End-to-end acknowledgment and retransmission is relegated to the connection-oriented TCP which sits on top of IP. The functional split between IP and TCP exemplifies proper application of the end-to-end principle to transport protocol design.

Limitations

The most important limitation of the end-to-end principle is that its basic conclusion, placing functions in the application end points rather than in the intermediary nodes, is not trivial to operationalize. Specifically:

- The principle assumes a notion of distinct application end points as opposed to intermediary nodes, which makes little sense when considering the structure of distributed applications;

- The principle assumes a dichotomy between non-application-specific and application-specific functions, the former to be part of the operations between application end points and the latter to be implemented by the application end points themselves, while arguably no function to be performed in a network is fully orthogonal to all possible application needs;

- The principle is silent on functions that may not be implemented completely and correctly in the application end points and places no upper bound on the amount of application specific functions that may be placed with intermediary nodes on grounds of performance considerations, or economic trade-offs.

An example of the limitations of the end-to-end principle exists in mobile devices. Pushing service-specific complexity to the endpoints can cause issues with mobile devices if the device has unreliable access to network channels. Further problems can be seen with a decrease in network transparency from the addition of network address translation.

The implementation of new protocols such as Internet Protocol version 6 also has potential consequences for the end-to-end principle.

Robustness Principle

In computing, the robustness principle is a general design guideline for software:

> *Be conservative in what you do, be liberal in what you accept from others* (often reworded as "Be conservative in what you send, be liberal in what you accept").

The principle is also known as Postel's law, after internet pioneer Jon Postel, who wrote in an early specification of the Transmission Control Protocol that:

> TCP implementations should follow a general principle of robustness: be conservative in what you do, be liberal in what you accept from others.

In other words, code that sends commands or data to other machines (or to other programs on the same machine) should conform completely to the specifications, but code that receives input should accept non-conformant input as long as the meaning is clear.

Among programmers, to produce compatible functions, the principle is popularized in the form be contravariant in the input type and covariant in the output type.

Interpretation

RFC 1122 (1989) expanded on Postel's principle by recommending that programmers "assume that the network is filled with malevolent entities that will send in packets designed to have the worst possible effect". Protocols should allow for the addition of new codes for existing fields in future versions of protocols by accepting messages with unknown codes (possibly logging them). Programmers should avoid sending messages with "legal but obscure protocol features" that might expose deficiencies in receivers, and design their code "not just to survive other misbehaving hosts, but also to cooperate to limit the amount of disruption such hosts can cause to the shared communication facility".

Criticism

In RFC 3117, Marshall Rose characterized several deployment problems when applying Postel's principle in the design of a new application protocol. For example, a defective implementation that sends non-conforming messages might be used only with implementations that tolerate those deviations from the specification until, possibly several years later, it is connected with a less tolerant application that rejects its messages. In such a situation, identifying the problem is often difficult, and deploying a solution can be costly. Rose therefore recommended "explicit consistency checks in a protocol ... even if they impose implementation overhead".

Transmission Control Protocol

The Transmission Control Protocol (TCP) is one of the main protocols of the Internet protocol suite. It originated in the initial network implementation in which it complemented the Internet Protocol (IP). Therefore, the entire suite is commonly referred to as *TCP/IP*. TCP provides reliable, ordered, and error-checked delivery of a stream of octets between applications running on hosts communicating by an IP network. Major Internet applications such as the World Wide Web, email, remote administration, and file transfer rely on TCP. Applications that do not require reliable data stream service may use the User Datagram Protocol (UDP), which provides a connectionless datagram service that emphasizes reduced latency over reliability.

Historical Origin

During May 1974, the Institute of Electrical and Electronic Engineers (IEEE) published a paper titled "*A Protocol for Packet Network Intercommunication.*" The paper's authors, Vint Cerf and Bob Kahn, described an internetworking protocol for sharing resources using packet-switching among the nodes. A central control component of this model was the *Transmission Control Program* that incorporated both connection-oriented links and datagram services between hosts. The monolithic Transmission Control Program was later divided into a modular architecture consisting of the *Transmission Control Protocol* at the connection-oriented layer and the *Internet Protocol* at the internetworking (datagram) layer. The model became known informally as *TCP/IP*, although formally it was henceforth termed the *Internet Protocol Suite*.

Network Function

The Transmission Control Protocol provides a communication service at an intermediate level between an application program and the Internet Protocol. It provides host-to-host connectivity at the Transport Layer of the Internet model. An application does not need to know the particular mechanisms for sending data via a link to another host, such as the required packet fragmentation on the transmission medium. At the transport layer, the protocol handles all handshaking and transmission details and just presents an abstraction of the network connection to the application.

At the lower levels of the protocol stack, due to network congestion, traffic load balancing, or other unpredictable network behaviour, IP packets may be lost, duplicated, or delivered out of order. TCP detects these problems, requests re-transmission of lost data, rearranges out-of-order data and even helps minimise network congestion to reduce the occurrence of the other problems. If the data still remains undelivered, its source is notified of this failure. Once the TCP receiver has reassembled the sequence of octets originally transmitted, it passes them to the receiving application. Thus, TCP abstracts the application's communication from the underlying networking details.

TCP is used extensively by many applications available by internet, including the World Wide Web (WWW), E-mail, File Transfer Protocol, Secure Shell, peer-to-peer file sharing, and streaming media applications.

TCP is optimised for accurate delivery rather than timely delivery. Therefore, TCP sometimes incurs relatively long delays (on the order of seconds) while waiting for out-of-order messages or re-transmissions of lost messages. It is not particularly suitable for real-time applications such as Voice over IP. For such applications, protocols like the Real-time Transport Protocol (RTP) operating over the User Datagram Protocol (UDP) are usually recommended instead.

TCP is a reliable stream delivery service which guarantees that all bytes received will be identical with bytes sent and in the correct order. Since packet transfer by many networks is not reliable, a technique known as 'positive acknowledgement with re-transmission' is used to guarantee reliability of packet transfers. This fundamental technique requires the receiver to respond with an acknowledgement message as it receives the data. The sender keeps a record of each packet it sends and maintains a timer from when the packet was sent. The sender re-transmits a packet if the timer expires before the message has been acknowledged. The timer is needed in case a packet gets lost or corrupted.

While IP handles actual delivery of the data, TCP keeps track of 'segments' - the individual units of data transmission that a message is divided into for efficient routing through the network. For example, when an HTML file is sent from a web server, the TCP software layer of that server divides the sequence of file octets into segments and forwards them individually to the IP software layer (Internet Layer). The Internet Layer encapsulates each TCP segment into an IP packet by adding a header that includes (among other data) the destination IP address. When the client program on the destination computer receives them, the TCP layer (Transport Layer) re-assembles the individual segments and ensures they are correctly ordered and error-free as it streams them to an application.

TCP Segment Structure

Transmission Control Protocol accepts data from a data stream, divides it into chunks, and adds a TCP header creating a TCP segment. The TCP segment is then encapsulated into an Internet Protocol (IP) datagram, and exchanged with peers.

The term *TCP packet* appears in both informal and formal usage, whereas in more precise terminology *segment* refers to the TCP protocol data unit (PDU), *datagram* to the IP PDU, and *frame* to the data link layer PDU:

Processes transmit data by calling on the TCP and passing buffers of data as arguments. The TCP packages the data from these buffers into segments and calls on the internet module [e.g. IP] to transmit each segment to the destination TCP.

A TCP segment consists of a segment *header* and a *data* section. The TCP header contains 10 mandatory fields, and an optional extension field (*Options*, pink background in table).

The data section follows the header. Its contents are the payload data carried for the application. The length of the data section is not specified in the TCP segment header. It can be calculated by subtracting the combined length of the TCP header and the encapsulating IP header from the total IP datagram length (specified in the IP header).

Source port (16 bits)

> identifies the sending port

Destination port (16 bits)

> identifies the receiving port

Sequence number (32 bits)

> has a dual role:
>
> - If the SYN flag is set (1), then this is the initial sequence number. The sequence number of the actual first data byte and the acknowledged number in the corresponding ACK are then this sequence number plus 1.
>
> - If the SYN flag is clear (0), then this is the accumulated sequence number of the first data byte of this segment for the current session.

Acknowledgment number (32 bits)

> if the ACK flag is set then the value of this field is the next sequence number that the sender is expecting. This acknowledges receipt of all prior bytes (if any). The first ACK sent by each end acknowledges the other end's initial sequence number itself, but no data.

Data offset (4 bits)

> specifies the size of the TCP header in 32-bit words. The minimum size header is 5 words and the maximum is 15 words thus giving the minimum size of 20 bytes and maximum of 60 bytes, allowing for up to 40 bytes of options in the header. This field gets its name from the fact that it is also the offset from the start of the TCP segment to the actual data.

Reserved (3 bits)

> for future use and should be set to zero

Flags (9 bits) (aka Control bits)

contains 9 1-bit flags

- NS (1 bit) – ECN-nonce concealment protection

- CWR (1 bit) – Congestion Window Reduced (CWR) flag is set by the sending host to indicate that it received a TCP segment with the ECE flag set and had responded in congestion control mechanism (added to header by RFC 3168).

- ECE (1 bit) – ECN-Echo has a dual role, depending on the value of the SYN flag. It indicates:

- If the SYN flag is set (1), that the TCP peer is ECN capable.

- If the SYN flag is clear (0), that a packet with Congestion Experienced flag set (ECN=11) in IP header received during normal transmission (added to header by RFC 3168). This serves as an indication of network congestion (or impending congestion) to the TCP sender.

- URG (1 bit) – indicates that the Urgent pointer field is significant

- ACK (1 bit) – indicates that the Acknowledgment field is significant. All packets after the initial SYN packet sent by the client should have this flag set.

- PSH (1 bit) – Push function. Asks to push the buffered data to the receiving application.

- RST (1 bit) – Reset the connection

- SYN (1 bit) – Synchronize sequence numbers. Only the first packet sent from each end should have this flag set. Some other flags and fields change meaning based on this flag, and some are only valid for when it is set, and others when it is clear.

- FIN (1 bit) – No more data from sender

Window size (16 bits)

the size of the *receive window*, which specifies the number of window size units (by default, bytes) (beyond the segment identified by the sequence number in the acknowledgment field) that the sender of this segment is currently willing to receive

Checksum (16 bits)

The 16-bit checksum field is used for error-checking of the header and data

Urgent pointer (16 bits)

> if the URG flag is set, then this 16-bit field is an offset from the sequence number indicating the last urgent data byte

Options (Variable 0–320 bits, divisible by 32)

> The length of this field is determined by the data offset field. Options have up to three fields: Option-Kind (1 byte), Option-Length (1 byte), Option-Data (variable). The Option-Kind field indicates the type of option, and is the only field that is not optional. Depending on what kind of option we are dealing with, the next two fields may be set: the Option-Length field indicates the total length of the option, and the Option-Data field contains the value of the option, if applicable. For example, an Option-Kind byte of 0x01 indicates that this is a No-Op option used only for padding, and does not have an Option-Length or Option-Data byte following it. An Option-Kind byte of 0 is the End Of Options option, and is also only one byte. An Option-Kind byte of 0x02 indicates that this is the Maximum Segment Size option, and will be followed by a byte specifying the length of the MSS field (should be 0x04). This length is the total length of the given options field, including Option-Kind and Option-Length bytes. So while the MSS value is typically expressed in two bytes, the length of the field will be 4 bytes (+2 bytes of kind and length). In short, an MSS option field with a value of 0x05B4 will show up as (0x02 0x04 0x05B4) in the TCP options section.

> Some options may only be sent when SYN is set; they are indicated below as . Option-Kind and standard lengths given as (Option-Kind,Option-Length).

> - 0 (8 bits) – End of options list
>
> - 1 (8 bits) – No operation (NOP, Padding) This may be used to align option fields on 32-bit boundaries for better performance.
>
> - 2,4,SS (32 bits) – Maximum segment size
>
> - 3,3,S (24 bits) – Window scale
>
> - 4,2 (16 bits) – Selective Acknowledgement permitted.
>
> - 5,N,$BBBB$,$EEEE$,... (variable bits, N is either 10, 18, 26, or 34)- Selective ACKnowledgement (SACK) These first two bytes are followed by a list of 1–4 blocks being selectively acknowledged, specified as 32-bit begin/end pointers.
>
> - 8,10,$TTTT$,$EEEE$ (80 bits)- Timestamp and echo of previous timestamp

(The remaining options are historical, obsolete, experimental, not yet standardized, or unassigned)

Padding

The TCP header padding is used to ensure that the TCP header ends and data begins on a 32 bit boundary. The padding is composed of zeros.

Protocol Operation

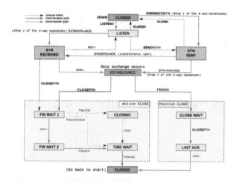

A Simplified TCP State Diagram. TCP EFSM diagram for a more detailed state diagram including the states inside the ESTABLISHED state.

TCP protocol operations may be divided into three phases. Connections must be properly established in a multi-step handshake process (*connection establishment*) before entering the *data transfer* phase. After data transmission is completed, the *connection termination* closes established virtual circuits and releases all allocated resources.

A TCP connection is managed by an operating system through a programming interface that represents the local end-point for communications, the *Internet socket*. During the lifetime of a TCP connection the local end-point undergoes a series of state changes:

LISTEN

(server) represents waiting for a connection request from any remote TCP and port.

SYN-SENT

(client) represents waiting for a matching connection request after having sent a connection request.

SYN-RECEIVED

(server) represents waiting for a confirming connection request acknowledgment after having both received and sent a connection request.

ESTABLISHED

(both server and client) represents an open connection, data received can be delivered to the user. The normal state for the data transfer phase of the connection.

FIN-WAIT-1

> (both server and client) represents waiting for a connection termination request from the remote TCP, or an acknowledgment of the connection termination request previously sent.

FIN-WAIT-2

> (both server and client) represents waiting for a connection termination request from the remote TCP.

CLOSE-WAIT

> (both server and client) represents waiting for a connection termination request from the local user.

CLOSING

> (both server and client) represents waiting for a connection termination request acknowledgment from the remote TCP.

LAST-ACK

> (both server and client) represents waiting for an acknowledgment of the connection termination request previously sent to the remote TCP (which includes an acknowledgment of its connection termination request).

TIME-WAIT

> (either server or client) represents waiting for enough time to pass to be sure the remote TCP received the acknowledgment of its connection termination request. [According to RFC 793 a connection can stay in TIME-WAIT for a maximum of four minutes known as two MSL (maximum segment lifetime).]

CLOSED

> (both server and client) represents no connection state at all.

Connection Establishment

To establish a connection, TCP uses a three-way handshake. Before a client attempts to connect with a server, the server must first bind to and listen at a port to open it up for connections: this is called a passive open. Once the passive open is established, a client may initiate an active open. To establish a connection, the three-way (or 3-step) handshake occurs:

1. SYN: The active open is performed by the client sending a SYN to the server. The client sets the segment's sequence number to a random value A.

2. SYN-ACK: In response, the server replies with a SYN-ACK. The acknowledgment number is set to one more than the received sequence number i.e. A+1, and the sequence number that the server chooses for the packet is another random number, B.

3. ACK: Finally, the client sends an ACK back to the server. The sequence number is set to the received acknowledgement value i.e. A+1, and the acknowledgement number is set to one more than the received sequence number i.e. B+1.

At this point, both the client and server have received an acknowledgment of the connection. The steps 1, 2 establish the connection parameter (sequence number) for one direction and it is acknowledged. The steps 2, 3 establish the connection parameter (sequence number) for the other direction and it is acknowledged. With these, a full-duplex communication is established.

Connection Termination

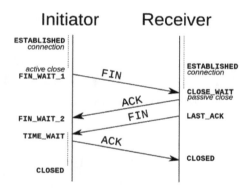

Connection termination

The connection termination phase uses a four-way handshake, with each side of the connection terminating independently. When an endpoint wishes to stop its half of the connection, it transmits a FIN packet, which the other end acknowledges with an ACK. Therefore, a typical tear-down requires a pair of FIN and ACK segments from each TCP endpoint. After the side that sent the first FIN has responded with the final ACK, it waits for a timeout before finally closing the connection, during which time the local port is unavailable for new connections; this prevents confusion due to delayed packets being delivered during subsequent connections.

A connection can be "half-open", in which case one side has terminated its end, but the other has not. The side that has terminated can no longer send any data into the connection, but the other side can. The terminating side should continue reading the data until the other side terminates as well.

It is also possible to terminate the connection by a 3-way handshake, when host A sends a FIN and host B replies with a FIN & ACK (merely combines 2 steps into one) and host A replies with an ACK.

Some host TCP stacks may implement a half-duplex close sequence, as Linux or HP-UX do. If such a host actively closes a connection but still has not read all the incoming data the stack already received from the link, this host sends a RST instead of a FIN (Section 4.2.2.13 in RFC 1122). This allows a TCP application to be sure the remote application has read all the data the former sent—waiting the FIN from the remote side, when it actively closes the connection. But the remote TCP stack cannot distinguish between a *Connection Aborting RST* and *Data Loss RST*. Both cause the remote stack to lose all the data received.

Some application protocols may violate the OSI model layers, using the TCP open/close handshaking for the application protocol open/close handshaking — these may find the RST problem on active close. As an example:

s = connect(remote);

send(s, data);

close(s);

For a usual program flow like above, a TCP/IP stack like that described above does not guarantee that all the data arrives to the other application.

Resource Usage

Most implementations allocate an entry in a table that maps a session to a running operating system process. Because TCP packets do not include a session identifier, both endpoints identify the session using the client's address and port. Whenever a packet is received, the TCP implementation must perform a lookup on this table to find the destination process. Each entry in the table is known as a Transmission Control Block or TCB. It contains information about the endpoints (IP and port), status of the connection, running data about the packets that are being exchanged and buffers for sending and receiving data.

The number of sessions in the server side is limited only by memory and can grow as new connections arrive, but the client must allocate a random port before sending the first SYN to the server. This port remains allocated during the whole conversation, and effectively limits the number of outgoing connections from each of the client's IP addresses. If an application fails to properly close unrequired connections, a client can run out of resources and become unable to establish new TCP connections, even from other applications.

Both endpoints must also allocate space for unacknowledged packets and received (but unread) data.

Data Transfer

There are a few key features that set TCP apart from User Datagram Protocol:

- Ordered data transfer — the destination host rearranges according to sequence number

- Retransmission of lost packets — any cumulative stream not acknowledged is retransmitted

- Error-free data transfer

- Flow control — limits the rate a sender transfers data to guarantee reliable delivery. The receiver continually hints the sender on how much data can be received (controlled by the sliding window). When the receiving host's buffer fills, the next acknowledgment contains a 0 in the window size, to stop transfer and allow the data in the buffer to be processed.

- Congestion control

Reliable Transmission

TCP uses a *sequence number* to identify each byte of data. The sequence number identifies the order of the bytes sent from each computer so that the data can be reconstructed in order, regardless of any packet reordering, or packet loss that may occur during transmission. The sequence number of the first byte is decided during the initial 3-way handshake. This number can be arbitrary, and should in fact be unpredictable to defend against TCP sequence prediction attacks.

Acknowledgements (Acks) are sent by the receiver of data to tell the sender that data has been received. Acks do not imply that the data has been delivered to the application. They merely signify that it is now the receiver's responsibility to deliver the data. In TCP Acks are cumulative. That is, if the ith byte is acknowledged, it means that all previous bytes have been received too.

Reliability is achieved by the sender detecting lost data and retransmitting it. TCP uses two primary techniques to identify loss. Retransmission timeout (abbreviated as RTO) and duplicate cumulative acknowledgements (DupAcks).

Dupack Based Retransmission

If a single packet (say packet 100) in a stream is lost, then the receiver cannot acknowledge packets above 100 because it uses cumulative acks. Hence the receiver acknowledges packet 100 again on the receipt of another data packet. This duplicate acknowledgement is used as a signal for packet loss. That is, if the sender receives three duplicate acknowledgements, it retransmits the last unacknowledged packet. A threshold of three is used because the network may reorder packets causing duplicate acknowledgements. This threshold has been demonstrated to avoid spurious retransmissions due to reordering. Sometimes selective acknowledgements (SACKs) are used to give more explicit feedback on which packets have been received. This greatly improves TCP's ability to retransmit the right packets.

Timeout Based Retransmission

Whenever a packet is sent, the sender sets a timer that is a conservative estimate of when that packet will be acked. If the sender does not receive an ack by then, it transmits that packet again. The timer is reset every time the sender receives an acknowledgement. This means that the retransmit timer fires only when the sender has received *no* acknowledgement for a long time. Typically the timer value is set to $smoothedRTT + max(G, 4 * RTTvariation)$ where G is the clock granularity. Further, in case a retransmit timer has fired and still no acknowledgement is received, the next timer is set to twice the previous value (up to a certain threshold). Among other things, this helps defend against a man-in-the-middle denial of service attack that tries to fool the sender into making so many retransmissions that the receiver is overwhelmed.

If the sender infers that data has been lost in the network using one of the two techniques described above, it retransmits the data.

Error Detection

Sequence numbers allow receivers to discard duplicate packets and properly sequence reordered packets. Acknowledgments allow senders to determine when to retransmit lost packets.

To assure correctness a checksum field is included; section for details on checksumming. The TCP checksum is a weak check by modern standards. Data Link Layers with high bit error rates may require additional link error correction/detection capabilities. The weak checksum is partially compensated for by the common use of a CRC or better integrity check at layer 2, below both TCP and IP, such as is used in PPP or the Ethernet frame. However, this does not mean that the 16-bit TCP checksum is redundant: remarkably, introduction of errors in packets between CRC-protected hops is common, but the end-to-end 16-bit TCP checksum catches most of these simple errors. This is the end-to-end principle at work.

Flow Control

TCP uses an end-to-end flow control protocol to avoid having the sender send data too fast for the TCP receiver to receive and process it reliably. Having a mechanism for flow control is essential in an environment where machines of diverse network speeds communicate. For example, if a PC sends data to a smartphone that is slowly processing received data, the smartphone must regulate the data flow so as not to be overwhelmed.

TCP uses a sliding window flow control protocol. In each TCP segment, the receiver specifies in the *receive window* field the amount of additionally received data (in bytes) that it is willing to buffer for the connection. The sending host can send only up to that amount of data before it must wait for an acknowledgment and window update from the receiving host.

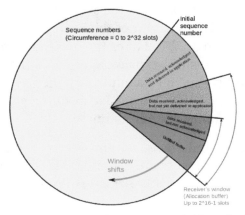

TCP sequence numbers and receive windows behave very much like a clock. The receive window shifts each time the receiver receives and acknowledges a new segment of data. Once it runs out of sequence numbers, the sequence number loops back to 0.

When a receiver advertises a window size of 0, the sender stops sending data and starts the *persist timer*. The persist timer is used to protect TCP from a deadlock situation that could arise if a subsequent window size update from the receiver is lost, and the sender cannot send more data until receiving a new window size update from the receiver. When the persist timer expires, the TCP sender attempts recovery by sending a small packet so that the receiver responds by sending another acknowledgement containing the new window size.

If a receiver is processing incoming data in small increments, it may repeatedly advertise a small receive window. This is referred to as the silly window syndrome, since it is inefficient to send only a few bytes of data in a TCP segment, given the relatively large overhead of the TCP header.

Congestion Control

The final main aspect of TCP is congestion control. TCP uses a number of mechanisms to achieve high performance and avoid congestion collapse, where network performance can fall by several orders of magnitude. These mechanisms control the rate of data entering the network, keeping the data flow below a rate that would trigger collapse. They also yield an approximately max-min fair allocation between flows.

Acknowledgments for data sent, or lack of acknowledgments, are used by senders to infer network conditions between the TCP sender and receiver. Coupled with timers, TCP senders and receivers can alter the behavior of the flow of data. This is more generally referred to as congestion control and/or network congestion avoidance.

Modern implementations of TCP contain four intertwined algorithms: slow-start, congestion avoidance, fast retransmit, and fast recovery (RFC 5681).

In addition, senders employ a *retransmission timeout* (RTO) that is based on the estimated round-trip time (or RTT) between the sender and receiver, as well as the variance in this round trip time. The behavior of this timer is specified in RFC 6298. There are subtleties in the estimation of RTT. For example, senders must be careful when calculating RTT samples for retransmitted packets; typically they use Karn's Algorithm or TCP timestamps. These individual RTT samples are then averaged over time to create a Smoothed Round Trip Time (SRTT) using Jacobson's algorithm. This SRTT value is what is finally used as the round-trip time estimate.

Enhancing TCP to reliably handle loss, minimize errors, manage congestion and go fast in very high-speed environments are ongoing areas of research and standards development. As a result, there are a number of TCP congestion avoidance algorithm variations.

Maximum Segment Size

The maximum segment size (MSS) is the largest amount of data, specified in bytes, that TCP is willing to receive in a single segment. For best performance, the MSS should be set small enough to avoid IP fragmentation, which can lead to packet loss and excessive retransmissions. To try to accomplish this, typically the MSS is announced by each side using the MSS option when the TCP connection is established, in which case it is derived from the maximum transmission unit (MTU) size of the data link layer of the networks to which the sender and receiver are directly attached. Furthermore, TCP senders can use path MTU discovery to infer the minimum MTU along the network path between the sender and receiver, and use this to dynamically adjust the MSS to avoid IP fragmentation within the network.

MSS announcement is also often called "MSS negotiation". Strictly speaking, the MSS is not "negotiated" between the originator and the receiver, because that would imply that both originator and receiver will negotiate and agree upon a single, unified MSS that applies to all communication in both directions of the connection. In fact, two completely independent values of MSS are permitted for the two directions of data flow in a TCP connection. This situation may arise, for example, if one of the devices participating in a connection has an extremely limited amount of memory reserved (perhaps even smaller than the overall discovered Path MTU) for processing incoming TCP segments.

Selective Acknowledgments

Relying purely on the cumulative acknowledgment scheme employed by the original TCP protocol can lead to inefficiencies when packets are lost. For example, suppose 10,000 bytes are sent in 10 different TCP packets, and the first packet is lost during transmission. In a pure cumulative acknowledgment protocol, the receiver cannot say that it received bytes 1,000 to 9,999 successfully, but failed to receive the first packet, containing bytes 0 to 999. Thus the sender may then have to resend all 10,000 bytes.

To alleviate this issue TCP employs the *selective acknowledgment (SACK)* option, defined in RFC 2018, which allows the receiver to acknowledge discontinuous blocks of packets which were received correctly, in addition to the sequence number of the last contiguous byte received successively, as in the basic TCP acknowledgment. The acknowledgement can specify a number of *SACK blocks*, where each SACK block is conveyed by the starting and ending sequence numbers of a contiguous range that the receiver correctly received. In the example above, the receiver would send SACK with sequence numbers 1000 and 9999. The sender would accordingly retransmit only the first packet (bytes 0 to 999).

A TCP sender can interpret an out-of-order packet delivery as a lost packet. If it does so, the TCP sender will retransmit the packet previous to the out-of-order packet and slow its data delivery rate for that connection. The duplicate-SACK option, an extension to the SACK option that was defined in RFC 2883, solves this problem. The TCP receiver sends a D-ACK to indicate that no packets were lost, and the TCP sender can then reinstate the higher transmission-rate.

The SACK option is not mandatory, and comes into operation only if both parties support it. This is negotiated when a connection is established. SACK uses the optional part of the TCP header. The use of SACK has become widespread — all popular TCP stacks support it. Selective acknowledgment is also used in Stream Control Transmission Protocol (SCTP).

Window Scaling

For more efficient use of high-bandwidth networks, a larger TCP window size may be used. The TCP window size field controls the flow of data and its value is limited to between 2 and 65,535 bytes.

Since the size field cannot be expanded, a scaling factor is used. The TCP window scale option, as defined in RFC 1323, is an option used to increase the maximum window size from 65,535 bytes to 1 gigabyte. Scaling up to larger window sizes is a part of what is necessary for TCP tuning.

The window scale option is used only during the TCP 3-way handshake. The window scale value represents the number of bits to left-shift the 16-bit window size field. The window scale value can be set from 0 (no shift) to 14 for each direction independently. Both sides must send the option in their SYN segments to enable window scaling in either direction.

Some routers and packet firewalls rewrite the window scaling factor during a transmission. This causes sending and receiving sides to assume different TCP window sizes. The result is non-stable traffic that may be very slow. The problem is visible on some sites behind a defective router.

TCP Timestamps

TCP timestamps, defined in RFC 1323, can help TCP determine in which order packets were sent. TCP timestamps are not normally aligned to the system clock and start at some random value. Many operating systems will increment the timestamp for every elapsed millisecond; however the RFC only states that the ticks should be proportional.

There are two timestamp fields:

> a 4-byte sender timestamp value (my timestamp)

> a 4-byte echo reply timestamp value (the most recent timestamp received from you).

TCP timestamps are used in an algorithm known as *Protection Against Wrapped Sequence* numbers, or *PAWS*. PAWS is used when the receive window crosses the sequence number wraparound boundary. In the case where a packet was potentially retransmitted it answers the question: "Is this sequence number in the first 4 GB or the second?" And the timestamp is used to break the tie.

Also, the Eifel detection algorithm (RFC 3522) uses TCP timestamps to determine if retransmissions are occurring because packets are lost or simply out of order.

Out-of-band Data

It is possible to interrupt or abort the queued stream instead of waiting for the stream to finish. This is done by specifying the data as *urgent*. This tells the receiving program to process it immediately, along with the rest of the urgent data. When finished, TCP informs the application and resumes back to the stream queue. An example is when TCP is used for a remote login session, the user can send a keyboard sequence that interrupts or aborts the program at the other end. These signals are most often needed when a program on the remote machine fails to operate correctly. The signals must be sent without waiting for the program to finish its current transfer.

TCP OOB data was not designed for the modern Internet. The *urgent* pointer only alters the processing on the remote host and doesn't expedite any processing on the network itself. When it gets to the remote host there are two slightly different interpretations of the protocol, which means only single bytes of OOB data are reliable. This is assuming it is reliable at all as it is one of the least commonly used protocol elements and tends to be poorly implemented.

Forcing Data Delivery

Normally, TCP waits for 200 ms for a full packet of data to send (Nagle's Algorithm tries to group small messages into a single packet). This wait creates small, but potentially serious delays if repeated constantly during a file transfer. For example, a typical send block would be 4 KB, a typical MSS is 1460, so 2 packets go out on a 10 Mbit/s ethernet taking ~1.2 ms each followed by a third carrying the remaining 1176 after a 197 ms pause because TCP is waiting for a full buffer.

In the case of telnet, each user keystroke is echoed back by the server before the user can see it on the screen. This delay would become very annoying.

Setting the socket option TCP_NODELAY overrides the default 200 ms send delay. Application programs use this socket option to force output to be sent after writing a character or line of characters.

The RFC defines the PSH push bit as "a message to the receiving TCP stack to send this data immediately up to the receiving application". There is no way to indicate or control it in user space using Berkeley sockets and it is controlled by protocol stack only.

Vulnerabilities

TCP may be attacked in a variety of ways. The results of a thorough security assessment of TCP, along with possible mitigations for the identified issues, were published in 2009, and is currently being pursued within the IETF.

Denial of Service

By using a spoofed IP address and repeatedly sending purposely assembled SYN packets, followed by many ACK packets, attackers can cause the server to consume large amounts of resources keeping track of the bogus connections. This is known as a SYN flood attack. Proposed solutions to this problem include SYN cookies and cryptographic puzzles, though SYN cookies come with their own set of vulnerabilities. Sockstress is a similar attack, that might be mitigated with system resource management. An advanced DoS attack involving the exploitation of the TCP Persist Timer was analyzed in Phrack #66.

Connection Hijacking

An attacker who is able to eavesdrop a TCP session and redirect packets can hijack a TCP connection. To do so, the attacker learns the sequence number from the ongoing communication and forges a false segment that looks like the next segment in the stream. Such a simple hijack can result in one packet being erroneously accepted at one end. When the receiving host acknowledges the extra segment to the other side of the connection, synchronization is lost. Hijacking might be combined with Address Resolution Protocol (ARP) or routing attacks that allow taking control of the packet flow, so as to get permanent control of the hijacked TCP connection.

Impersonating a different IP address was not difficult prior to RFC 1948, when the initial *sequence number* was easily guessable. That allowed an attacker to blindly send a sequence of packets that the receiver would believe to come from a different IP address, without the need to deploy ARP or routing attacks: it is enough to ensure that the legitimate host of the impersonated IP address is down, or bring it to that condition using denial-of-service attacks. This is why the initial sequence number is now chosen at random.

TCP Veto

An attacker who can eavesdrop and predict the size of the next packet to be sent can cause the receiver to accept a malicious payload without disrupting the existing connection. The attacker injects a malicious packet with the sequence number and a payload size of the next expected packet. When the legitimate packet is ultimately received, it is found to have the same sequence number and length as a packet already received and is silently dropped as a normal duplicate packet—the legitimate packet is "vetoed" by the malicious packet. Unlike in connection hijacking, the connection is never desynchronized and communication continues as normal after the malicious payload is accepted. TCP veto gives the attacker less control over the communication, but makes the attack particularly resistant to detection. The large increase in network traffic from the ACK storm is avoided. The only evidence to the receiver that something is amiss is a single duplicate packet, a normal occurrence in an IP network. The sender of the vetoed packet never sees any evidence of an attack.

Another vulnerability is TCP reset attack.

TCP Ports

TCP and UDP use port numbers to identify sending and receiving application endpoints on a host, often called Internet sockets. Each side of a TCP connection has an associated 16-bit unsigned port number (0-65535) reserved by the sending or receiving application. Arriving TCP packets are identified as belonging to a specific TCP connection by its sockets, that is, the combination of source host address, source port, destination host address, and destination port. This means that a server computer can provide several clients with several services simultaneously, as long as a client takes care of initiating any simultaneous connections to one destination port from different source ports.

Port numbers are categorized into three basic categories: well-known, registered, and dynamic/private. The well-known ports are assigned by the Internet Assigned Numbers Authority (IANA) and are typically used by system-level or root processes. Well-known applications running as servers and passively listening for connections typically use these ports. Some examples include: FTP (20 and 21), SSH (22), TELNET (23), SMTP (25), HTTP over SSL/TLS (443), and HTTP (80). Registered ports are typically used by end user applications as ephemeral source ports when contacting servers, but they can also identify named services that have been registered by a third party. Dynamic/private ports can also be used by end user applications, but are less commonly so. Dynamic/private ports do not contain any meaning outside of any particular TCP connection.

Network Address Translation (NAT), typically uses dynamic port numbers, on the ("Internet-facing") public side, to disambiguate the flow of traffic that is passing between a public network and a private subnetwork, thereby allowing many IP addresses (and their ports) on the subnet to be serviced by a single public-facing address.

Development

TCP is a complex protocol. However, while significant enhancements have been made and proposed over the years, its most basic operation has not changed significantly since its first specification RFC 675 in 1974, and the v4 specification RFC 793, published in September 1981. RFC 1122, Host Requirements for Internet Hosts, clarified a number of TCP protocol implementation requirements. A list of the 8 required specifications and over 20 strongly encouraged enhancements is available in RFC 7414. Among this list is RFC 2581, TCP Congestion Control, one of the most important TCP-related RFCs in recent years, describes updated algorithms that avoid undue congestion. In 2001, RFC 3168 was written to describe Explicit Congestion Notification (ECN), a congestion avoidance signaling mechanism.

The original TCP congestion avoidance algorithm was known as "TCP Tahoe", but many alternative algorithms have since been proposed (including TCP Reno, TCP Vegas, FAST TCP, TCP New Reno, and TCP Hybla).

TCP Interactive (iTCP) is a research effort into TCP extensions that allows applications to subscribe to TCP events and register handler components that can launch applications for various purposes, including application-assisted congestion control.

Multipath TCP (MPTCP) is an ongoing effort within the IETF that aims at allowing a TCP connection to use multiple paths to maximize resource usage and increase redundancy. The redundancy offered by Multipath TCP in the context of wireless networks enables statistical multiplexing of resources, and thus increases TCP throughput dramatically. Multipath TCP also brings performance benefits in datacenter environments. The reference implementation of Multipath TCP is being developed in the Linux kernel.

TCP Cookie Transactions (TCPCT) is an extension proposed in December 2009 to secure servers against denial-of-service attacks. Unlike SYN cookies, TCPCT does not conflict with other TCP extensions such as window scaling. TCPCT was designed due to necessities of DNSSEC, where servers have to handle large numbers of short-lived TCP connections.

tcpcrypt is an extension proposed in July 2010 to provide transport-level encryption directly in TCP itself. It is designed to work transparently and not require any configuration. Unlike TLS (SSL), tcpcrypt itself does not provide authentication, but provides simple primitives down to the application to do that. As of 2010, the first tcpcrypt IETF draft has been published and implementations exist for several major platforms.

TCP Fast Open is an extension to speed up the opening of successive TCP connections between two endpoints. It works by skipping the three-way handshake using a cryptographic "cookie". It is similar to an earlier proposal called T/TCP, which was not widely adopted due to security issues. As of July 2012, it is an IETF Internet draft.

Proposed in May 2013, Proportional Rate Reduction (PRR) is a TCP extension developed by Google engineers. PRR ensures that the TCP window size after recovery is as close to the Slow-start threshold as possible. The algorithm is designed to improve the speed of recovery and is the default congestion control algorithm in Linux 3.2+ kernels.

TCP Over Wireless Networks

TCP was originally designed for wired networks. Packet loss is considered to be the result of network congestion and the congestion window size is reduced dramatically as a precaution. However, wireless links are known to experience sporadic and usually temporary losses due to fading, shadowing, hand off, interference, and other radio effects, that are not strictly congestion. After the (erroneous) back-off of the congestion window size, due to wireless packet loss, there may be a congestion avoidance phase with a conservative decrease in window size. This causes the radio link to be underutilized. Extensive research on combating these harmful effects has been conducted. Suggested solutions can be categorized as end-to-end solutions, which require modifications at the client or server, link layer solutions, such as Radio Link Protocol (RLP) in cellular networks, or proxy-based solutions which require some changes in the network without modifying end nodes.

A number of alternative congestion control algorithms, such as Vegas, Westwood, Veno, and Santa Cruz, have been proposed to help solve the wireless problem.

Hardware Implementations

One way to overcome the processing power requirements of TCP is to build hardware implementations of it, widely known as TCP offload engines (TOE). The main problem of TOEs is that they are hard to integrate into computing systems, requiring extensive changes in the operating system of the computer or device. One company to develop such a device was Alacritech.

Debugging

A packet sniffer, which intercepts TCP traffic on a network link, can be useful in debugging networks, network stacks, and applications that use TCP by showing the user what packets are passing through a link. Some networking stacks support the SO_DEBUG socket option, which can be enabled on the socket using setsockopt. That option dumps all the packets, TCP states, and events on that socket, which is helpful in debugging. Netstat is another utility that can be used for debugging.

Alternatives

For many applications TCP is not appropriate. One problem (at least with normal implementations) is that the application cannot access the packets coming after a lost packet until the retransmitted copy of the lost packet is received. This causes problems for real-time applications such as streaming media, real-time multiplayer games and voice over IP (VoIP) where it is generally more useful to get most of the data in a timely fashion than it is to get all of the data in order.

For historical and performance reasons, most storage area networks (SANs) use Fibre Channel Protocol (FCP) over Fibre Channel connections.

Also, for embedded systems, network booting, and servers that serve simple requests from huge numbers of clients (e.g. DNS servers) the complexity of TCP can be a problem. Finally, some tricks such as transmitting data between two hosts that are both behind NAT (using STUN or similar systems) are far simpler without a relatively complex protocol like TCP in the way.

Generally, where TCP is unsuitable, the User Datagram Protocol (UDP) is used. This provides the application multiplexing and checksums that TCP does, but does not handle streams or retransmission, giving the application developer the ability to code them in a way suitable for the situation, or to replace them with other methods like forward error correction or interpolation.

Stream Control Transmission Protocol (SCTP) is another protocol that provides reliable stream oriented services similar to TCP. It is newer and considerably more complex than TCP, and has not yet seen widespread deployment. However, it is especially designed to be used in situations where reliability and near-real-time considerations are important.

Venturi Transport Protocol (VTP) is a patented proprietary protocol that is designed to replace TCP transparently to overcome perceived inefficiencies related to wireless data transport.

TCP also has issues in high-bandwidth environments. The TCP congestion avoidance algorithm works very well for ad-hoc environments where the data sender is not known in advance. If the environment is predictable, a timing based protocol such as Asynchronous Transfer Mode (ATM) can avoid TCP's retransmits overhead.

UDP-based Data Transfer Protocol (UDT) has better efficiency and fairness than TCP in networks that have high bandwidth-delay product.

Multipurpose Transaction Protocol (MTP/IP) is patented proprietary software that is designed to adaptively achieve high throughput and transaction performance in a wide variety of network conditions, particularly those where TCP is perceived to be inefficient.

Checksum Computation

TCP checksum for IPv4

When TCP runs over IPv4, the method used to compute the checksum is defined in RFC 793:

The checksum field is the 16 bit one's complement of the one's complement sum of all 16-bit words in the header and text. If a segment contains an odd number of header and text octets to be checksummed, the last octet is padded on the right with zeros to form a 16-bit word for checksum purposes. The pad is not transmitted as part of the segment. While computing the checksum, the checksum field itself is replaced with zeros.

In other words, after appropriate padding, all 16-bit words are added using one's complement arithmetic. The sum is then bitwise complemented and inserted as the checksum field. A pseudo-header that mimics the IPv4 packet header used in the checksum computation is shown in the table below.

TCP pseudo-header for checksum computation (IPv4)				
Bit offset	**0–3**	**4–7**	**8–15**	**16–31**
0	Source address			
32	Destination address			
64	Zeros		Protocol	TCP length
96	Source port			Destination port
128	Sequence number			

160	Acknowledgement number			
192	Data offset	Reserved	Flags	Window
224	Checksum			Urgent pointer
256	Options (optional)			
256/288+	Data			

The source and destination addresses are those of the IPv4 header. The protocol value is 6 for TCP (cf. List of IP protocol numbers). The TCP length field is the length of the TCP header and data (measured in octets).

TCP Checksum for IPv6

When TCP runs over IPv6, the method used to compute the checksum is changed, as per RFC 2460:

> Any transport or other upper-layer protocol that includes the addresses from the IP header in its checksum computation must be modified for use over IPv6, to include the 128-bit IPv6 addresses instead of 32-bit IPv4 addresses.

A pseudo-header that mimics the IPv6 header for computation of the checksum is shown below.

TCP pseudo-header for checksum computation (IPv6)				
Bit offset	0–7	8–15	16–23	24–31
0	Source address			
32				
64				
96				
128	Destination address			
160				
192				
224				
256	TCP length			
288	Zeros			Next header
320	Source port		Destination port	
352	Sequence number			

384	Acknowledgement number			
416	Data offset	Reserved	Flags	Window
448	Checksum			Urgent pointer
480	Options (optional)			
480/512+	Data			

Source address – the one in the IPv6 header

- Destination address – the final destination; if the IPv6 packet doesn't contain a Routing header, TCP uses the destination address in the IPv6 header, otherwise, at the originating node, it uses the address in the last element of the Routing header, and, at the receiving node, it uses the destination address in the IPv6 header.

- TCP length – the length of the TCP header and data

- Next Header – the protocol value for TCP

Checksum Offload

Many TCP/IP software stack implementations provide options to use hardware assistance to automatically compute the checksum in the network adapter prior to transmission onto the network or upon reception from the network for validation. This may relieve the OS from using precious CPU cycles calculating the checksum. Hence, overall network performance is increased.

This feature may cause packet analyzers detecting outbound network traffic upstream of the network adapter that are unaware or uncertain about the use of checksum offload to report invalid checksum in outbound packets.

Internet Protocol

The Internet Protocol (IP) is the principal communications protocol in the Internet protocol suite for relaying datagrams across network boundaries. Its routing function enables internetworking, and essentially establishes the Internet.

IP has the task of delivering packets from the source host to the destination host solely based on the IP addresses in the packet headers. For this purpose, IP defines packet structures that encapsulate the data to be delivered. It also defines addressing methods that are used to label the datagram with source and destination information.

Historically, IP was the connectionless datagram service in the original *Transmission Control Program* introduced by Vint Cerf and Bob Kahn in 1974; the other being the connection-oriented Transmission Control Protocol (TCP). The Internet protocol suite is therefore often referred to as TCP/IP.

The first major version of IP, Internet Protocol Version 4 (IPv4), is the dominant protocol of the Internet. Its successor is Internet Protocol Version 6 (IPv6).

Function

The Internet Protocol is responsible for addressing hosts and for routing datagrams (packets) from a source host to a destination host across one or more IP networks. For this purpose, the Internet Protocol defines the format of packets and provides an addressing system that has two functions: Identifying hosts and providing a logical location service.

Datagram Construction

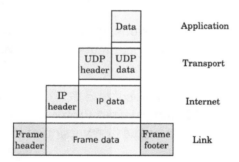

Sample encapsulation of application data from UDP to a Link protocol frame

Each datagram has two components: a header and a payload. The IP header is tagged with the source IP address, the destination IP address, and other meta-data needed to route and deliver the datagram. The payload is the data that is transported. This method of nesting the data payload in a packet with a header is called encapsulation.

IP addressing and Routing

IP addressing entails the assignment of IP addresses and associated parameters to host interfaces. The address space is divided into networks and subnetworks, involving the designation of network or routing prefixes. IP routing is performed by all hosts, as well as routers, whose main function is to transport packets across network boundaries. Routers communicate with one another via specially designed routing protocols, either interior gateway protocols or exterior gateway protocols, as needed for the topology of the network.

IP routing is also common in local networks. For example, many Ethernet switches support IP multicast operations. These switches use IP addresses and Internet Group Management Protocol to control multicast routing but use MAC addresses for the actual routing.

Version History

The versions currently relevant are IPv4 and IPv6.

In May 1974, the Institute of Electrical and Electronic Engineers (IEEE) published a paper entitled "A Protocol for Packet Network Intercommunication". The paper's authors, Vint Cerf and Bob Kahn, described an internetworking protocol for sharing resources using packet switching among network nodes. A central control component of this model was the "Transmission Control Program" that incorporated both connection-oriented links and datagram services between hosts. The monolithic Transmission Control Program was later divided into a modular architecture consisting of the Transmission Control Protocol and User Datagram Protocol at the transport layer and the Internet Protocol at the network layer. The model became known as the *Department of Defense (DoD) Internet Model* and *Internet protocol suite*, and informally as *TCP/IP*.

IP versions 0 to 3 were experimental versions, used between 1977 and 1979. The following Internet Experiment Note (IEN) documents describe versions of the Internet Protocol prior to the modern version of IPv4:

- IEN 2 (*Comments on Internet Protocol and TCP*), dated August 1977 describes the need to separate the TCP and Internet Protocol functionalities (which were previously combined.) It proposes the first version of the IP header, using 0 for the version field.

- IEN 26 (*A Proposed New Internet Header Format*), dated February 1978 describes a version of the IP header that uses a 1-bit version field.

- IEN 28 (*Draft Internetwork Protocol Description Version 2*), dated February 1978 describes IPv2.

- IEN 41 (*Internetwork Protocol Specification Version 4*), dated June 1978 describes the first protocol to be called IPv4. The IP header is different from the modern IPv4 header.

- IEN 44 (*Latest Header Formats*), dated June 1978 describes another version of IPv4, also with a header different from the modern IPv4 header.

- IEN 54 (*Internetwork Protocol Specification Version 4*), dated September 1978 is the first description of IPv4 using the header that would be standardized in RFC 760.

The dominant internetworking protocol in the Internet Layer in use today is IPv4; the number 4 is the protocol version number carried in every IP datagram. IPv4 is described in RFC 791 (1981).

Version 5 was used by the Internet Stream Protocol, an experimental streaming protocol.

The successor to IPv4 is IPv6. Its most prominent difference from version 4 is the size of the addresses. While IPv4 uses 32 bits for addressing, yielding c. 4.3 billion (4.3×10^9) addresses, IPv6 uses 128-bit addresses providing ca. 340 undecillion, or 3.4×10^{38} addresses. Although adoption of IPv6 has been slow, as of June 2008, all United States government systems have demonstrated basic infrastructure support for IPv6. IPv6 was a result of several years of experimentation and dialog during which various protocol models were proposed, such as TP/IX (RFC 1475), PIP (RFC 1621) and TUBA (TCP and UDP with Bigger Addresses, RFC 1347).

The assignment of the new protocol as IPv6 was uncertain until due diligence revealed that IPv6 had not yet been used previously. Other protocol proposals named *IPv9* and *IPv8* briefly surfaced, but had no affiliation with any international standards body, and have had no support.

On April 1, 1994, the IETF published an April Fool's Day joke about IPv9.

Reliability

The design of the Internet protocols is based on the end-to-end principle. The network infrastructure is considered inherently unreliable at any single network element or transmission medium and is dynamic in terms of availability of links and nodes. No central monitoring or performance measurement facility exists that tracks or maintains the state of the network. For the benefit of reducing network complexity, the intelligence in the network is purposely located in the end nodes.

As a consequence of this design, the Internet Protocol only provides best-effort delivery and its service is characterized as unreliable. In network architectural language, it is a connectionless protocol, in contrast to connection-oriented communication. Various error conditions may occur, such as data corruption, packet loss, duplication and out-of-order delivery. Because routing is dynamic, meaning every packet is treated independently, and because the network maintains no state based on the path of prior packets, different packets may be routed to the same destination via different paths, resulting in out-of-order sequencing at the receiver.

IPv4 provides safeguards to ensure that the IP packet header is error-free. A routing node calculates a checksum for a packet. If the checksum is bad, the routing node discards the packet. Although the Internet Control Message Protocol (ICMP) allows such notification, the routing node is not required to notify either end node of these errors. By contrast, in order to increase performance, and since current link layer technology is assumed to provide sufficient error detection, the IPv6 header has no checksum to protect it.

All error conditions in the network must be detected and compensated by the end nodes of a transmission. The upper layer protocols of the internet protocol suite are responsible for resolving reliability issues. For example, a host may buffer network data to ensure correct ordering before the data is delivered to an application.

Link Capacity and Capability

The dynamic nature of the Internet and the diversity of its components provide no guarantee that any particular path is actually capable of, or suitable for, performing the data transmission requested, even if the path is available and reliable. One of the technical constraints is the size of data packets allowed on a given link. An application must assure that it uses proper transmission characteristics. Some of this responsibility lies also in the upper layer protocols. Facilities exist to examine the maximum transmission unit (MTU) size of the local link and Path MTU Discovery can be used for the entire projected path to the destination. The IPv4 internetworking layer has the capability to automatically fragment the original datagram into smaller units for transmission. In this case, IP provides re-ordering of fragments delivered out of order.

The Transmission Control Protocol (TCP) is an example of a protocol that adjusts its segment size to be smaller than the MTU. The User Datagram Protocol (UDP) and the Internet Control Message Protocol (ICMP) disregard MTU size, thereby forcing IP to fragment oversized datagrams.

An IPv6 network does not perform fragmentation or reassembly, and as per the end-to-end principle, requires end stations and higher-layer protocols to avoid exceeding the network's MTU.

Security

During the design phase of the ARPANET and the early Internet, the security aspects and needs of a public, international network could not be adequately anticipated. Consequently, many Internet protocols exhibited vulnerabilities highlighted by network attacks and later security assessments. In 2008, a thorough security assessment and proposed mitigation of problems was published. The Internet Engineering Task Force (IETF) has been pursuing further studies.

Abstraction layers of Internet Protocol Suite

Application Layer

An application layer is an abstraction layer that specifies the shared protocols and interface methods used by hosts in a communications network. The application layer abstraction is used in both of the standard models of computer networking: the Internet Protocol Suite (TCP/IP) and the Open Systems Interconnection model (OSI model).

Although both models use the same term for their respective highest level layer, the detailed definitions and purposes are different.

In TCP/IP, the application layer contains the communications protocols and interface methods used in process-to-process communications across an Internet Protocol (IP) computer network. The application layer only standardizes communication and depends upon the underlying transport layer protocols to establish host-to-host data transfer channels and manage the data exchange in a client-server or peer-to-peer networking model. Though the TCP/IP application layer does not describe specific rules or data formats that applications must consider when communicating, the original specification (in RFC 1123) does rely on and recommend the robustness principle for application design.

In the OSI model, the definition of the application layer is narrower in scope. The OSI model defines the application layer as the user interface responsible for displaying received information to the user. In contrast, the Internet Protocol model does not concern itself with such detail. OSI also explicitly distinguishes additional functionality below the application layer, but above the transport layer at two additional levels: the session layer, and the presentation layer. OSI specifies a strict modular separation of functionality at these layers and provides protocol implementations for each layer.

Application Layer Protocols

(Session Layer under OSI model) The IETF definition document for the application layer in the Internet Protocol Suite is RFC 1123. It provided an initial set of protocols that covered the major aspects of functionality of the early Internet.

- Remote login to hosts: Telnet

- File transfer: File Transfer Protocol (FTP), Trivial File Transfer Protocol (TFTP)

- Electronic mail transport: Simple Mail Transfer Protocol (SMTP)

- Networking support: Domain Name System (DNS)

- Host initialization: BOOTP

- Remote host management: Simple Network Management Protocol (SNMP), Common Management Information Protocol over TCP (CMOT)

Other Protocol Examples

- 9P, Plan 9 from Bell Labs distributed file system protocol

- AFP, Apple Filing Protocol
- APPC, Advanced Program-to-Program Communication
- AMQP, Advanced Message Queuing Protocol
- Atom Publishing Protocol
- BEEP, Block Extensible Exchange Protocol
- Bitcoin
- BitTorrent
- CFDP, Coherent File Distribution Protocol
- CoAP, Constrained Application Protocol
- DDS, Data Distribution Service
- DeviceNet
- eDonkey
- ENRP, Endpoint Handlespace Redundancy Protocol
- FastTrack (KaZaa, Grokster, iMesh)
- Finger, User Information Protocol
- Freenet
- FTAM, File Transfer Access and Management
- Gopher, Gopher protocol
- HL7, Health Level Seven
- HTTP, HyperText Transfer Protocol
- H.323, Packet-Based Multimedia Communications System
- IRCP, Internet Relay Chat Protocol
- Kademlia
- KAP, Anonymous File Transfer over UDP/IP (KickAss Protocol)
- LDAP, Lightweight Directory Access Protocol
- LPD, Line Printer Daemon Protocol

- MIME (S-MIME), Multipurpose Internet Mail Extensions and Secure MIME
- Modbus
- MQTT Protocol
- Netconf
- NFS, Network File System
- NIS, Network Information Service
- NNTP, Network News Transfer Protocol
- NTCIP, National Transportation Communications for Intelligent Transportation System Protocol
- NTP, Network Time Protocol
- OSCAR, AOL Instant Messenger Protocol
- PNRP, Peer Name Resolution Protocol
- RDP, Remote Desktop Protocol
- RELP, Reliable Event Logging Protocol
- RIP, Routing Information Protocol
- Rlogin, Remote Login in UNIX Systems
- RPC, Remote Procedure Call
- RTMP, Real Time Messaging Protocol
- RTP, Real-time Transport Protocol
- RTPS, Real Time Publish Subscribe
- RTSP, Real Time Streaming Protocol
- SAP, Session Announcement Protocol
- SDP, Session Description Protocol
- SIP, Session Initiation Protocol
- SLP, Service Location Protocol
- SMB, Server Message Block
- SMTP, Simple Mail Transfer Protocol

- SNTP, Simple Network Time Protocol

- SSH, Secure Shell

- SSMS, Secure SMS Messaging Protocol

- TCAP, Transaction Capabilities Application Part

- TDS, Tabular Data Stream

- Tor (anonymity network)

- Tox

- TSP, Time Stamp Protocol

- VTP, Virtual Terminal Protocol

- Whois (and RWhois), Remote Directory Access Protocol

- WebDAV

- X.400, Message Handling Service Protocol

- X.500, Directory Access Protocol (DAP)

- XMPP, Extensible Messaging and Presence Protocol

Transport Layer

In computer networking, the transport layer is a conceptual division of methods in the layered architecture of protocols in the network stack in the Internet Protocol Suite and the Open Systems Interconnection (OSI). The protocols of the layer provide host-to-host communication services for applications. It provides services such as connection-oriented data stream support, reliability, flow control, and multiplexing.

The details of implementation and semantics of the Transport Layer of the TCP/IP model (RFC 1122), which is the foundation of the Internet, and the Open Systems Interconnection (OSI) model of general networking, are different. In the OSI model the transport layer is most often referred to as Layer 4 or L4, while numbered layers are not used in TCP/IP.

The best-known transport protocol of TCP/IP is the Transmission Control Protocol (TCP), and lent its name to the title of the entire suite. It is used for connection-oriented transmissions, whereas the connectionless User Datagram Protocol (UDP) is used for simpler messaging transmissions. TCP is the more complex protocol, due to its stateful design incorporating reliable transmission and data stream services. Other prominent protocols in this group are the Datagram Congestion Control Protocol (DCCP) and the Stream Control Transmission Protocol (SCTP).

Services

Transport layer services are conveyed to an application via a programming interface to the transport layer protocols. The services may include the following features:

- Connection-oriented communication: It is normally easier for an application to interpret a connection as a data stream rather than having to deal with the underlying connection-less models, such as the datagram model of the User Datagram Protocol (UDP) and of the Internet Protocol (IP).

- Same order delivery: The network layer doesn't generally guarantee that packets of data will arrive in the same order that they were sent, but often this is a desirable feature. This is usually done through the use of segment numbering, with the receiver passing them to the application in order. This can cause head-of-line blocking.

- Reliability: Packets may be lost during transport due to network congestion and errors. By means of an error detection code, such as a checksum, the transport protocol may check that the data is not corrupted, and verify correct receipt by sending an ACK or NACK message to the sender. Automatic repeat request schemes may be used to retransmit lost or corrupted data.

- Flow control: The rate of data transmission between two nodes must sometimes be managed to prevent a fast sender from transmitting more data than can be supported by the receiving data buffer, causing a buffer overrun. This can also be used to improve efficiency by reducing buffer underrun.

- Congestion avoidance: Congestion control can control traffic entry into a telecommunications network, so as to avoid congestive collapse by attempting to avoid oversubscription of any of the processing or link capabilities of the intermediate nodes and networks and taking resource reducing steps, such as reducing the rate of sending packets. For example, automatic repeat requests may keep the network in a congested state; this situation can be avoided by adding congestion avoidance to the flow control, including slow-start. This keeps the bandwidth consumption at a low level in the beginning of the transmission, or after packet retransmission.

- Multiplexing: Ports can provide multiple endpoints on a single node. For example, the name on a postal address is a kind of multiplexing, and distinguishes between different recipients of the same location. Computer applications will each listen for information on their own ports, which enables the use of more than one network service at the same time. It is part of the transport layer in the TCP/IP model, but of the session layer in the OSI model.

Analysis

The transport layer is responsible for delivering data to the appropriate application process on the host computers. This involves statistical multiplexing of data from different application processes, i.e. forming data packets, and adding source and destination port numbers in the header of each transport layer data packet. Together with the source and destination IP address, the port numbers constitutes a network socket, i.e. an identification address of the process-to-process communication. In the OSI model, this function is supported by the session layer.

Some transport layer protocols, for example TCP, but not UDP, support virtual circuits, i.e. provide connection oriented communication over an underlying packet oriented datagram network. A byte-stream is delivered while hiding the packet mode communication for the application processes. This involves connection establishment, dividing of the data stream into packets called segments, segment numbering and reordering of out-of order data.

Finally, some transport layer protocols, for example TCP, but not UDP, provide end-to-end reliable communication, i.e. error recovery by means of error detecting code and automatic repeat request (ARQ) protocol. The ARQ protocol also provides flow control, which may be combined with congestion avoidance.

UDP is a very simple protocol, and does not provide virtual circuits, nor reliable communication, delegating these functions to the application program. UDP packets are called datagrams, rather than segments.

TCP is used for many protocols, including HTTP web browsing and email transfer. UDP may be used for multicasting and broadcasting, since retransmissions are not possible to a large amount of hosts. UDP typically gives higher throughput and shorter latency, and is therefore often used for real-time multimedia communication where packet loss occasionally can be accepted, for example IP-TV and IP-telephony, and for online computer games.

Many non-IP-based networks, such as X.25, Frame Relay and ATM, implement the connection-oriented communication at the network or data link layer rather than the transport layer. In X.25, in telephone network modems and in wireless communication systems, reliable node-to-node communication is implemented at lower protocol layers.

The OSI connection-mode transport layer protocol specification defines five classes of transport protocols: *TP0*, providing the least error recovery, to *TP4*, which is designed for less reliable networks.

Protocols

This list shows some protocols that are commonly placed in the transport layers of the

Internet protocol suite, the OSI protocol suite, NetWare's IPX/SPX, AppleTalk, and Fibre Channel.

- ATP, AppleTalk Transaction Protocol
- CUDP, Cyclic UDP
- DCCP, Datagram Congestion Control Protocol
- FCP, Fibre Channel Protocol
- IL, IL Protocol
- MPTCP, Multipath TCP
- RDP, Reliable Datagram Protocol
- RUDP, Reliable User Datagram Protocol
- SCTP, Stream Control Transmission Protocol
- SPX, Sequenced Packet Exchange
- SST, Structured Stream Transport
- TCP, Transmission Control Protocol
- UDP, User Datagram Protocol
- UDP-Lite
- μTP, Micro Transport Protocol

Comparison of Transport Layer Protocols

Feature Name	UDP	UDP-Lite	TCP	Multipath TCP	SCTP	DCCP	RUDP
Packet header size	8 bytes	8 bytes	20–60 bytes	50–90 bytes	12 bytes	12 or 16 bytes	6+ bytes
Transport layer packet entity	Datagram	Datagram	Segment	Segment	Datagram	Datagram	Datagram
Connection oriented	No	No	Yes	Yes	Yes	Yes	Yes
Reliable transport	No	No	Yes	Yes	Yes	No	Yes
Unreliable transport	Yes	Yes	No	No	Yes	Yes	Yes
Preserve message boundary	Yes	Yes	No	No	Yes	Yes	Yes

Ordered delivery	No	No	Yes	Yes	Yes	No	Yes
Unordered delivery	Yes	Yes	No	No	Yes	Yes	Yes
Data checksum	Optional	Yes	Yes	Yes	Yes	Yes	Optional
Checksum size (bits)	16	16	16	16	32	16	16
Partial checksum	No	Yes	No	No	No	Yes	No
Path MTU	No	No	Yes	Yes	Yes	Yes	Unsure
Flow control	No	No	Yes	Yes	Yes	No	Yes
Congestion control	No	No	Yes	Yes	Yes	Yes	Unsure
Explicit Congestion Notification	No	No	Yes	Yes	Yes	Yes	
Multiple streams	No	No	No	Yes	Yes	No	No
Multi-homing	No	No	No	Yes	Yes	No	No
Bundling / Nagle	No	No	Yes	Yes	Yes	No	Unsure

Comparison of OSI Transport Protocols

ISO/IEC 8073/ITU-T Recommendation X.224, "Information Technology - Open Systems Interconnection - Protocol for providing the connection-mode transport service", defines five classes of connection-mode transport protocols designated class 0 (TP0) to class 4 (TP4). Class 0 contains no error recovery, and was designed for use on network layers that provide error-free connections. Class 4 is closest to TCP, although TCP contains functions, such as the graceful close, which OSI assigns to the session layer. All OSI connection-mode protocol classes provide expedited data and preservation of record boundaries. Detailed characteristics of the classes are shown in the following table:

Service	TP0	TP1	TP2	TP3	TP4
Connection oriented network	Yes	Yes	Yes	Yes	Yes
Connectionless network	No	No	No	No	Yes
Concatenation and separation	No	Yes	Yes	Yes	Yes
Segmentation and reassembly	Yes	Yes	Yes	Yes	Yes
Error Recovery	No	Yes	No	Yes	Yes
Reinitiate connection (if an excessive number of PDUs are unacknowledged)	No	Yes	No	Yes	No
multiplexing and demultiplexing over a single virtual circuit	No	No	Yes	Yes	Yes
Explicit flow control	No	No	Yes	Yes	Yes
Retransmission on timeout	No	No	No	No	Yes
Reliable Transport Service	No	Yes	No	Yes	Yes

There is also a connectionless transport protocol, specified by ISO/IEC 8602/ITU-T Recommendation X.234.

Link Layer

In computer networking, the link layer is the lowest layer in the Internet Protocol Suite, commonly known as *TCP/IP*, the networking architecture of the Internet. It is described in RFC 1122 and RFC 1123. The link layer is the group of methods and communications protocols that only operate on the link that a host is physically connected to. The link is the physical and logical network component used to interconnect hosts or nodes in the network and a link protocol is a suite of methods and standards that operate only between adjacent network nodes of a local area network segment or a wide area network connection.

Despite the different semantics of layering in TCP/IP and OSI, the link layer is sometimes described as a combination of the data link layer (layer 2) and the physical layer (layer 1) in the OSI model. However, the layers of TCP/IP are descriptions of operating scopes (application, host-to-host, network, link) and not detailed *prescriptions* of operating procedures, data semantics, or networking technologies.

RFC 1122 exemplifies that local area network protocols such as Ethernet and IEEE 802, and framing protocols such as Point-to-Point Protocol (PPP) belong to the link layer.

Definition in Standards and Textbooks

Local area networking standards such as Ethernet and IEEE 802 specifications use terminology from the seven-layer OSI model rather than the TCP/IP model. The TCP/IP model in general does not consider physical specifications, rather it assumes a working network infrastructure that can deliver media level frames on the link. Therefore, RFC 1122 and RFC 1123, the definition of the TCP/IP model, do not discuss hardware issues and physical data transmission and set no standards for those aspects. Some textbook authors have supported the interpretation that physical data transmission aspects are part of the link layer. Others assumed that physical data transmission standards are not considered communication protocols, and are not part of the TCP/IP model. These authors assume a hardware layer or physical layer below the link layer, and several of them adopt the OSI term data link layer instead of link layer in a modified description of layering. In the predecessor to the TCP/IP model, the *ARPAnet Reference Model* (RFC 908, 1982), aspects of the link layer are referred to by several poorly defined terms, such as *network-access layer, network-access protocol*, as well as *network layer*, while the next higher layer is called *internetwork layer*. In some modern text books, *network-interface layer, host-to-network layer* and *network-access layer* occur as synonyms either to the link layer or the data link layer, often including the physical layer.

Link Layer Protocols

The link layer in the TCP/IP model is a descriptive realm of networking protocols that operate only on the local network segment (link) that a host is connected to. Such protocol packets are not routed to other networks.

The core protocols specified by the Internet Engineering Task Force (IETF) in this layer are the Address Resolution Protocol (ARP), the Reverse Address Resolution Protocol (RARP), and the Neighbor Discovery Protocol (NDP), which is a facility delivering similar functionality as ARP for IPv6. Since the advent of IPv6, Open Shortest Path First (OSPF) is considered to operate on the link level as well, although the IPv4 version of the protocol was considered at the Internet layer.

IS-IS (RFC 1142) is another link-state routing protocol that fits into this layer when considering TCP/IP model, however it was developed within the OSI reference stack, where it is a Layer 2 protocol. It is not an Internet standard.

Relation to OSI Model

The link layer of the TCP/IP model is often compared directly with the combination of the data link layer and the physical layer in the Open Systems Interconnection (OSI) protocol stack. Although they are congruent to some degree in technical coverage of protocols, they are not identical. The link layer in TCP/IP is still wider in scope and in principle a different concept and terminology of classification. This may be observed when certain protocols, such as the Address Resolution Protocol (ARP), which is confined to the link layer in the TCP/IP model, is often said to fit between OSI's data link layer and the network layer. In general, direct or strict comparisons should be avoided, because the layering in TCP/IP is not a principal design criterion and in general is considered to be "harmful" (RFC 3439).

Another term sometimes encountered, *network access layer*, tries to suggest the closeness of this layer to the physical network. However, this use is misleading and non-standard, since the link layer implies functions that are wider in scope than just network access. Important link layer protocols are used to probe the topology of the local network, discover routers and neighboring hosts, i.e. functions that go well beyond network access.

IETF Standards

- RFC 1122, "Requirements for Internet Hosts -- Communication layers," IETF, R. Braden (Editor), October 1989

- RFC 1123, "Requirements for Internet Hosts -- Application and Support," IETF, R. Braden (Editor), October 1989

- RFC 893, "Trailer Encapsulations," S. Leffler and M. Karels, April 1984

- RFC 826, "An Ethernet Address Resolution Protocol," D. Plummer, November 1982

- RFC 894, "A Standard for the Transmission of IP Datagrams over Ethernet Networks," C. Hornig, April 1984

- RFC 1042, "A Standard for the Transmission of IP Datagrams over IEEE 802 Networks," J. Postel and J. Reynolds, February 1988

- RFC 2740, "OSPF for IPv6", R. Coltun, et al., December 1999

Internet Layer

The internet layer is a group of internetworking methods, protocols, and specifications in the Internet protocol suite that are used to transport datagrams (packets) from the originating host across network boundaries, if necessary, to the destination host specified by a network address (IP address) which is defined for this purpose by the Internet Protocol (IP). The internet layer derives its name from its function of forming an internet (uncapitalized), or facilitating internetworking, which is the concept of connecting multiple networks with each other through gateways.

Internet-layer protocols use IP-based packets. The internet layer does not include the protocols that define communication between local (on-link) network nodes which fulfill the purpose of maintaining link states between the local nodes, such as the local network topology, and that usually use protocols that are based on the framing of packets specific to the link types. Such protocols belong to the link layer.

A common design aspect in the internet layer is the robustness principle: "Be liberal in what you accept, and conservative in what you send" as a misbehaving host can deny Internet service to many other users.

Purpose

The internet layer has three basic functions:

- For outgoing packets, select the next-hop host (gateway) and transmit the packet to this host by passing it to the appropriate link layer implementation;

- For incoming packets, capture packets and pass the packet payload up to the appropriate transport layer protocol, if appropriate.

- Provide error detection and diagnostic capability.

In Version 4 of the Internet Protocol (IPv4), during both transmit and receive operations, IP is capable of automatic or intentional fragmentation or defragmentation of packets, based, for example, on the maximum transmission unit (MTU) of link elements. However, this feature has been dropped in IPv6, as the communications end points, the hosts, now have to perform path MTU discovery and assure that end-to-end transmissions don't exceed the maximum discovered.

In its operation, the internet layer is not responsible for reliable transmission. It provides only an *unreliable* service, and "best effort" delivery. This means that the network makes no guarantees about packets' proper arrival. This was an important design principle and change from the previous protocols used on the early AR-PANET. Since packet delivery across diverse networks is an inherently unreliable and failure-prone operation, the burden of providing reliability was placed with the end points of a communication path, i.e., the hosts, rather than on the network. This is one of the reasons of the resiliency of the Internet against individual link failures and its proven scalability.

The function of providing reliability of service is the duty of higher level protocols, such as the Transmission Control Protocol (TCP) in the transport layer.

In IPv4 (not IPv6), a checksum is used to protect the header of each datagram. The checksum ensures that the information in a received header is accurate, however, IP does not attempt to detect errors that may have occurred to the data in each packet.

Core Protocols

The primary protocols in the internet layer are the Internet Protocol (IP). It is implemented in two versions, IPv4 and IPv6. The Internet Control Message Protocol (ICMP) is primarily used for error and diagnostic functions. Different implementations exist for IPv4 and IPv6. The Internet Group Management Protocol (IGMP) is used by IPv4 hosts and adjacent multicast routers to establish multicast group memberships.

Security

Internet Protocol Security (IPsec) is a suite of protocols for securing Internet Protocol (IP) communications by authenticating and encrypting each IP packet in a data stream. IPsec also includes protocols for cryptographic key establishment. IPsec was originally designed as a base specification in IPv6 in 1995, and later adapted to IPv4, with which it has found widespread use in securing virtual private networks.

Relation to OSI Model

The internet layer of the TCP/IP model is often compared directly with the network layer (layer 3) in the Open Systems Interconnection (OSI) protocol stack. Although they have some overlap, these layering models represent different classification methods. In particular, the allowed characteristics of protocols (e.g., whether they are connection-oriented or connection-less) placed in these layers are different between the models. OSI's network layer is a *catch-all* layer for all protocols that facilitate network functionality. The internet layer, on the other hand, is specifically a suite of protocols that facilitate internetworking using the Internet Protocol.

Because of this, the OSI network layer is often described to include protocols such as the Address Resolution Protocol (ARP) which was placed in link layer by the original TCP/IP architects.

Strict comparison between the TCP/IP model and the OSI model should be avoided. Layering in TCP/IP is not a principal design criterion and is in general considered to be *harmful*.

Despite clear primary references and normative standards documents, the internet layer is often improperly called *network layer*, in analogy to the OSI model.

IETF Standards

- RFC 791, Internet Protocol (IP), J. Postel, September 1981

- RFC 792, Internet Control Message Protocol (ICMP), J. Postel, September 1981

- RFC 815: IP Datagram Reassembly Algorithms, D. Clark, July 1982

- RFC 816: Fault Isolation and Recovery, D. Clark, July 1982

- RFC 879, The TCP Maximum Segment Size and Related Topics, J. Postel, November 1983

- RFC 950, Internet Standard Subnetting Procedure, J. Mogul and J. Postel, August 1985

- RFC 1108: Internet Protocol Security Options, B. Schofield, October 1989

- RFC 1112, Host Extensions for IP Multicasting, S. Deering, August 1989

- RFC 1122, Requirements for Internet Hosts—Communication Layers, IETF, R. Braden (Editor), October 1989

- RFC 1123, Requirements for Internet Hosts—Application and Support, IETF, R. Braden (Editor), October 1989

- RFC 3439, Some Internet Architectural Guidelines and Philosophy, R. Bush, D. Meyer, December 2002

References

- Dye, Mark; McDonald, Rick; Rufi, Antoon (29 October 2007). "Network Fundamentals, CCNA Exploration Companion Guide". Cisco Press. ISBN 9780132877435. Retrieved 12 September 2016 – via Google Books.

- Comer, Douglas (1 January 2006). "Internetworking with TCP/IP: Principles, protocols, and architecture". Prentice Hall. ISBN 0-13-187671-6. Retrieved 12 September 2016

- Kozierok, Charles M. (1 January 2005). "The TCP/IP Guide: A Comprehensive, Illustrated Internet Protocols Reference". No Starch Press. ISBN 9781593270476. Retrieved 12 September 2016

- Stallings, William (1 January 2007). "Data and Computer Communications". Prentice Hall. ISBN 0-13-243310-9. Retrieved 12 September 2016.

- Tanenbaum, Andrew S. (1 January 2003). "Computer Networks". Prentice Hall PTR. ISBN 0-13-066102-3. Retrieved 12 September 2016.

- Wilde, Erik (2012) [1999]. Wilde's WWW: Technical Foundations of the World Wide Web. Springer Verlag. p. 26. doi:10.1007/978-3-642-95855-7. ISBN 978-3-642-95855-7.

- Comer, Douglas E. (2006). Internetworking with TCP/IP:Principles, Protocols, and Architecture. 1 (5th ed.). Prentice Hall. ISBN 0-13-187671-6.

- Richard W. Stevens (2006). November 2011 TCP/IP Illustrated. Vol. 1, The protocols Check |url= value (help). Addison-Wesley. pp. Chapter 20. ISBN 978-0-201-63346-7.

- Muhammad Adeel & Ahmad Ali Iqbal (2004). "TCP Congestion Window Optimization for CDMA2000 Packet Data Networks". International Conference on Information Technology (ITNG'07): 31–35. doi:10.1109/ITNG.2007.190. ISBN 978-0-7695-2776-5.

- Douglas E. Comer, Internetworking with TCP/IP: Principles, Protocols and Architecture, Pearson Prentice Hall 2005, ISBN 0-13-187671-6

- Postel, Jon, ed. (January 1980). Transmission Control Protocol. IETF. RFC 761. https://tools.ietf.org/html/rfc761. Retrieved June 9, 2014.

- Braden, R., ed. (October 1989). Requirements for Internet Hosts: Communication Layers. IETF. RFC 1122. https://tools.ietf.org/html/rfc1122. Retrieved June 9, 2014.

- Rose, M. (November 2001). On the Design of Application Protocols. IETF. RFC 3117. https://tools.ietf.org/html/rfc3117. Retrieved June 9, 2014.

Network Nodes: A Significant Aspect

Network nodes are either the sending, receiving or redirecting processes as well as devices of a computer network. The nature of the data and its reception and transmission differs in each aspect of network nodes. This chapter discusses the basic processes related to nodes and the hardware related to them.

Node (Networking)

In communication networks, a node is either a connection point, a redistribution point (e.g. data communications equipment), or a communication endpoint (e.g. data terminal equipment). The definition of a node depends on the network and protocol layer referred to. A physical network node is an active electronic device that is attached to a network, and is capable of creating, receiving, or transmitting information over a communications channel. A passive distribution point such as a distribution frame or patch panel is consequently not a node.

Computer Network Nodes

In data communication, a physical network node may either be a data communication equipment (DCE) such as a modem, hub, bridge or switch; or a data terminal equipment (DTE) such as a digital telephone handset, a printer or a host computer, for example a router, a workstation or a server.

If the network in question is a LAN or WAN, every LAN or WAN node (that are at least data link layer devices) must have a MAC address, typically one for each network interface controller it possesses. Examples are computers, packet switches, xDSL modems (with Ethernet interface) and wireless LAN access points. Note that a hub constitutes a physical network node, but does not constitute a LAN network node, since a hubbed network logically is a bus network. Analogously, a repeater or PSTN modem (with serial interface) is a physical network node but not a LAN node in this sense.

If the network in question is the Internet or an Intranet, many physical network nodes are host computers, also known as Internet nodes, identified by an IP address, and all hosts are physical network nodes. However, some datalink layer devices such as switches, bridges and WLAN access points do not have an IP host address (except sometimes for administrative purposes), and are not considered to be Internet nodes or hosts, but as physical network nodes and LAN nodes.

Telecommunication Network Nodes

In the fixed telephone network, a node may be a public or private telephone exchange, a remote concentrator or a computer providing some intelligent network service. In cellular communication, switching points and databases such as the Base station controller, Home Location Register, Gateway GPRS Support Node (GGSN) and Serving GPRS Support Node (SGSN) are examples of nodes. Cellular network base stations are not considered to be nodes in this context.

In cable television systems (CATV), this term has assumed a broader context and is generally associated with a fiber optic node. This can be defined as those homes or businesses within a specific geographic area that are served from a common fiber optic receiver. A fiber optic node is generally described in terms of the number of "homes passed" that are served by that specific fiber node.

Distributed System Nodes

If the network in question is a distributed system, the nodes are clients, servers or peers. A peer may sometimes serve as client, sometimes server. In a peer-to-peer or overlay network, nodes that actively route data for the other networked devices as well as themselves are called supernodes.

Distributed systems may sometimes use *virtual nodes* so that the system is not oblivious to the heterogeneity of the nodes. This issue is addressed with special algorithms, like consistent hashing, as it is the case in Amazon's.

End Node in Cloud Computing

Within a vast computer network, the individual computers on the periphery of the network, those that do not also connect other networks, and those that often connect transiently to one or more clouds are called end nodes. Typically, within the cloud computing construct, the individual user / customer computer that connects into one well-managed cloud is called an end node. Since these computers are a part of the network yet unmanaged by the cloud's host, they present significant risks to the entire cloud. This is called the End Node Problem. There are several means to remedy this problem but all require instilling trust in the end node computer.

Network Interface Controller

A network interface controller (NIC, also known as a network interface card, network adapter, LAN adapter or physical network interface, and by similar terms) is a computer hardware component that connects a computer to a computer network.

Early network interface controllers were commonly implemented on expansion cards that plugged into a computer bus. The low cost and ubiquity of the Ethernet standard means that most newer computers have a network interface built into the motherboard.

Modern network interface controllers offer advanced features such as interrupt and DMA interfaces to the host processors, support for multiple receive and transmit queues, partitioning into multiple logical interfaces, and on-controller network traffic processing such as the TCP offload engine.

Purpose

A Madge 4/16 Mbit/s Token Ring ISA-16 NIC

The network controller implements the electronic circuitry required to communicate using a specific physical layer and data link layer standard such as Ethernet, Fibre Channel, Wi-Fi or Token Ring. This provides a base for a full network protocol stack, allowing communication among small groups of computers on the same local area network (LAN) and large-scale network communications through routable protocols, such as Internet Protocol (IP).

The NIC allows computers to communicate over a computer network, either by using cables or wirelessly. The NIC is both a physical layer and data link layer device, as it provides physical access to a networking medium and, for IEEE 802 and similar networks, provides a low-level addressing system through the use of MAC addresses that are uniquely assigned to network interfaces.

Although other network technologies exist, IEEE 802 networks including the Ethernet variants have achieved near-ubiquity since the mid-1990s.

Implementation

Whereas network controllers used to operate on expansion cards that plugged into a computer bus, the low cost and ubiquity of the Ethernet standard means that most new computers have a network interface built into the motherboard. Newer server motherboards may even have dual network interfaces built-in. The Ethernet capabilities are either integrated into the motherboard chipset or implemented via a low-cost dedicated Ethernet chip, connected through the PCI (or the newer PCI Express) bus. A separate network card is not required unless additional interfaces are needed or some other type of network is used.

The NIC may use one or more of the following techniques to indicate the availability of packets to transfer:

- Polling is where the CPU examines the status of the peripheral under program control.

- Interrupt-driven I/O is where the peripheral alerts the CPU that it is ready to transfer data.

Also, NICs may use one or more of the following techniques to transfer packet data:

- Programmed input/output is where the CPU moves the data to or from the designated peripheral to memory.

- Direct memory access is where an intelligent peripheral assumes control of the system bus to access memory directly. This removes load from the CPU but requires more logic on the card. In addition, a packet buffer on the NIC may not be required and latency can be reduced.

An Ethernet network controller typically has an 8P8C socket where the network cable is connected. Older NICs also supplied BNC, or AUI connections. A few LEDs inform the user of whether the network is active, and whether or not data transmission occurs. Ethernet network controllers typically support 10 Mbit/s Ethernet, 100 Mbit/s Ethernet, and 1000 Mbit/s Ethernet varieties. Such controllers are designated as "10/100/1000", meaning that they can support a notional maximum transfer rate of 10, 100 or 1000 Mbit/s. 10 Gigabit Ethernet NICs are also available, and, as of November 2014, are beginning to be available on computer motherboards.

Performance and Advanced Functionality

Intel 82574L Gigabit Ethernet NIC, a PCI Express ×1 card, which provides two hardware receive queues

Multiqueue NICs provide multiple transmit and receive queues, allowing packets received by the NIC to be assigned to one of its receive queues. Each receive queue is assigned to a separate interrupt; by routing each of those interrupts to different CPUs/cores, processing of the interrupt requests triggered by the network traffic received by a single NIC can be distributed among multiple cores, bringing additional performance improvements in interrupt handling. Usually, a NIC distributes incoming traffic between the receive queues using a hash function, while separate interrupts can be routed to different CPUs/cores either automatically by the operating system, or manually by configuring the IRQ affinity.

The hardware-based distribution of the interrupts, described above, is referred to as *receive-side scaling* (RSS). Purely software implementations also exist, such as the receive packet steering (RPS) and receive flow steering (RFS). Further performance improvements can be achieved by routing the interrupt requests to the CPUs/cores executing the applications which are actually the ultimate destinations for network packets that generated the interrupts. That way, taking the application locality into account results in higher overall performance, reduced latency and better hardware utilization, resulting from the higher utilization of CPU caches and fewer required context switches. Examples of such implementations are the RFS and Intel *Flow Director*.

With multiqueue NICs, additional performance improvements can be achieved by distributing outgoing traffic among different transmit queues. By assigning different transmit queues to different CPUs/cores, various operating system's internal contentions can be avoided; this approach is usually referred to as *transmit packet steering* (XPS).

Some NICs support transmit and receive queues without kernel support allowing the NIC to execute even when the functionality of the operating system of a critical system has been severely compromised. Those NICs support:

1. Accessing local and remote memory without involving the remote CPU.

2. Accessing local and remote I/O devices without involving local/remote CPU. This capability is supported by device-to-device communication over the I/O bus, present in switched-based I/O interconnects.

3. Controlling access to local resources such as control registers and memory.

Some products feature *NIC partitioning* (NPAR, also known as *port partitioning*) that uses SR-IOV to divide a single 10 Gigabit Ethernet NIC into multiple discrete virtual NICs with dedicated bandwidth, which are presented to the firmware and operating system as separate PCI device functions. TCP offload engine is a technology used in some NICs to offload processing of the entire TCP/IP stack to the network controller. It is primarily used with high-speed network interfaces, such as Gigabit Ethernet and 10 Gigabit Ethernet, for which the processing overhead of the network stack becomes significant.

Some NICs offer integrated field-programmable gate arrays (FPGAs) for user-programmable processing of network traffic before it reaches the host computer, allowing for significantly reduced latencies in time-sensitive workloads. Moreover, some NICs offer complete low-latency TCP/IP stacks running on integrated FPGAs in combination with userspace libraries that intercept networking operations usually performed by the operating system kernel; Solarflare's open-source *OpenOnload* network stack that runs on Linux is an example. This kind of functionality is usually referred to as *user-level networking*.

Converged Network Adapter

A converged network adapter (CNA), also called a converged network interface controller (C-NIC), is a computer input/output device that combines the functionality of a host bus adapter (HBA) with a network interface controller (NIC). In other words, it "converges" access to, respectively, a storage area network and a general-purpose computer network.

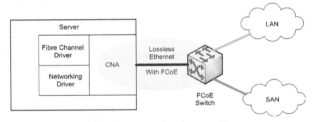

"Converged" network adapter diagram

Support

Some products were marketed around 2005 with the term C-NIC which combined iSCSI storage functionality with Gigabit Ethernet. Later products used the marketing term converged network adapter (CNA), combining Fibre Channel over Ethernet with 10 Gigabit Ethernet, for example.

Brocade

Brocade Communications Systems offers two types of CNAs, with PCI Express generation 2.0 interfaces. The only difference between the two models are the number of interfaces on the cards: one or two. The two port model will allow connection to two different switches to create a redundant configuration without having to use two PCI slots.

Broadcom

In 2009 Broadcom entered the CNA market. Broadcom offers their CNAs under their own brand name but also sell the application-specific integrated circuits and other related components to others. Their intended customers are the larger builders of server systems such as Dell and HP. These vendors can then include the ten Gigabit CNA with their servers: as embedded interface on the motherboard (LOM or LAN on Motherboard), via a mezzanine card in blade servers or as PCI extension-card.

Emulex

Emulex offers CNAs under the Emulex brand name as the OneConnect ten Gigabit series of dual port optical and copper adapters. They also OEM their adapters for Cisco, Dell, EMC, Fujitsu, HDS, HP, IBM and NetApp.

QLogic

QLogic offers CNAs via their QLogic 8200 & 8300 series Converged Network Adapters. They offer single and dual port PCI cards with copper or optical fibre interfaces. QLogic CNAs are available under the QLogic brandname and as OEM cards. The QME CNA and drivers were supported by Citrix, NetApp, EMC and IBM.

Hewlett-Packard

HP claims that their BL460c G7 was the first blade-server that offers FCoE via a *LOM* (Lan on Motherboard) instead of using a PCI-slot or mezzanine-card.

Dell

Dell uses the QLogic 8100 series in their PowerEdge servers. For the M-series, blade-servers for the M1000e enclosure a specially made dual-port mezzanine card QME8142 is designed. For the *normal* tower- and rackservers Dell offers an OEM version of the standard QME 8152.

Cisco

Cisco Systems offered Fibre Channel over Ethernet marketed as their Unified Computing System via number of their *Virtual Interface Cards* (VICs). These cards extends the functionality of traditional CNAs making it possible to create up to 256 virtual HBAs or NICs within one VIC.

Host Adapter

Fibre Channel host bus adapter (a 64-bit PCI-X card)

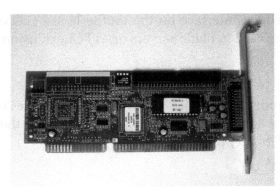

SCSI host bus adapter (a 16-bit ISA card)

In computer hardware, a host controller, host adapter, or host bus adapter (HBA) connects a computer, which acts as the host system, to other network and storage devices. The terms are primarily used to refer to devices for connecting SCSI, Fibre Channel and eSATA devices. However, devices for connecting to IDE, Ethernet, FireWire, USB and other systems may also be called host adapters.

The term network interface controller (NIC) is more often used for devices connecting to computer networks, while the term converged network adapter can be applied when protocols such as iSCSI or Fibre Channel over Ethernet allow storage and network functionality over the same physical connection. These can include TCP offload engines.

SCSI

A SCSI host adapter connects host system to boot from a SCSI device, but also facilitates configuration of the host adapter. Typically a device driver, linked to the operating system, controls the host adapter itself.

In a typical parallel SCSI subsystem, each device has assigned to it a unique numerical ID. As a rule, the host adapter appears as SCSI ID 7, which gives it the highest priority on the SCSI bus (priority descends as the SCSI ID descends; on a 16-bit or "wide" bus, ID 8 has the lowest priority, a feature that maintains compatibility with the priority scheme of the 8-bit or "narrow" bus).

The host adapter usually assumes the role of SCSI initiator, in that it issues commands to other SCSI devices.

A computer can contain more than one host adapter, which can greatly increase the number of SCSI devices available.

Major SCSI adapter manufacturers are HP, ATTO Technology, Promise Technology, Adaptec, and LSI Corporation. LSI, Adaptec, and ATTO offer PCIe SCSI adapters which fit in Apple Mac, on Intel PCs, and low-profile motherboards which lack SCSI support due to the inclusion of SAS and/or SATA connectivity.

Fibre Channel

The term *host bus adapter* (HBA) is most often used to refer to a Fibre Channel interface card. Fibre Channel HBAs are available for open systems, computer architectures, and buses, including PCI and SBus (obsolete today). Each HBA has a unique World Wide Name (WWN), which is similar to an Ethernet MAC address in that it uses an OUI assigned by the IEEE. However, WWNs are longer (8 bytes). There are two types of WWNs on a HBA; a node WWN (WWNN), which is shared by all ports on a host bus adapter, and a port WWN (WWPN), which is unique to each port. There are HBA models of different speeds: 1Gbit/s, 2Gbit/s, 4Gbit/s, 8Gbit/s, 10Gbit/s, 16Gbit/s and 20Gbit/s.

The major Fibre Channel HBA manufacturers are QLogic and Emulex. As of mid-2009, these vendors shared approximately 90% of the market. Other manufacturers include Agilent, ATTO, Brocade, and LSI Corporation.

HBA is also known to be interpreted as High Bandwidth Adapter in cases of Fibre Channel controllers.

InfiniBand

The term *host channel adapter* (HCA) is usually used to describe InfiniBand interface cards.

ATA

ATA host adapters are integrated into motherboards of most modern PCs. They are often improperly called *disk controllers*. The correct term for the component that allows a computer to talk to a peripheral bus is *host adapter*. A proper disk controller only allows a *disk* to talk to the same bus.

SAS and SATA

SAS or serial-attached SCSI is the current connectivity to replace the previous generation parallel-attached SCSI (PAS) devices. Ultra320 was the highest level of parallel SCSI available, but SAS has since replaced it as the highest-performing SCSI technology.

SATA is a similar technology from the aspect of connection options. HBAs can be created using a single connector to connect both SAS and SATA devices.

Major SAS/SATA adapter manufacturers are Promise Technologies, Adaptec, HP, QLogic, Areca, LSI and ATTO Technology.

eSATA

External Serial ATA disk enclosures and drives are increasingly common in the consumer computing market, but not all SATA-compatible motherboards and disk controllers include external SATA ports. As such, adapters to connect external SATA devices to ports on an internal SATA bus are commonly available.

Mainframe I/O Channels

In the mainframe field, the terms *host adapter* or *host bus adapter* were traditionally not used. A similar goal was achieved since the 1960s with a different technique: *I/O channel*, or simply *channel*, is a separate processor that can access main memory independently, in parallel with CPU (like later DMA in personal computer field), and that executes its own I/O-dedicated programs when pointed to such by the controlling CPU.

Protocols used by I/O channels to communicate with peripheral devices include ESCON and newer FICON.

Repeater

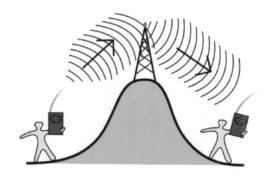

A radio repeater retransmits a radio signal.

In telecommunications, a repeater is an electronic device that receives a signal and retransmits it. Repeaters are used to extend transmissions so that the signal can cover longer distances or be received on the other side of an obstruction.

Some types of repeaters broadcast an identical signal, but alter its method of transmission, for example, on another frequency or baud rate.

There are several different types of repeaters; a telephone repeater is an amplifier in a telephone line, an optical repeater is an optoelectronic circuit that amplifies the light beam in an optical fiber cable; and a radio repeater is a radio receiver and transmitter that retransmits a radio signal.

A broadcast relay station is a repeater used in broadcast radio and television.

Overview

When an information-bearing signal passes through a communication channel, it is progressively degraded due to loss of power. For example, when a telephone call passes through a wire telephone line, some of the power in the electric current which represents the audio signal is dissipated as heat in the resistance of the copper wire. The longer the wire is, the more power is lost, and the smaller the amplitude of the signal at the far end. So with a long enough wire the call will not be audible at the other end. Similarly, the farther from a radio station a receiver is, the weaker the radio signal, and the poorer the reception. A repeater is an electronic device in a communication channel that increases the power of a signal and retransmits it, allowing it to travel further. Since it amplifies the signal, it requires a source of electric power.

The term "repeater" originated with telegraphy in the 19th century, and referred to an electromechanical device (a relay) used to regenerate telegraph signals. Use of the term has continued in telephony and data communications.

In computer networking, because repeaters work with the actual physical signal, and do not attempt to interpret the data being transmitted, they operate on the physical layer, the first layer of the OSI model.

Types

Telephone Repeater

This is used to increase the range of telephone signals in a telephone line. They are most frequently used in trunklines that carry long distance calls. In an analog telephone line consisting of a pair of wires, it consists of an amplifier circuit made of transistors which use power from a DC current source to increase the power of the alternating current audio signal on the line. Since the telephone is a duplex (bidirectional) communication system, the wire pair carries two audio signals, one going in each direction. So telephone repeaters have to be bilateral, amplifying the signal in both directions without causing feedback, which complicates their design considerably. Telephone repeaters were the first type of repeater and were some of the first applications of amplification. The development of telephone repeaters between 1900 and 1915 made long distance phone service possible. However most telecommunications cables are now fiber optic cables which use optical repeaters (below).

- Submarine cable repeater

This is a type of telephone repeater used in underwater submarine telecommunications cables.

Optical Communications Repeater

This is used to increase the range of signals in a fiber optic cable. Digital information travels through a fiber optic cable in the form of short pulses of light. The light is made up of particles called photons, which can be absorbed or scattered in the fiber. An optical communications repeater usually consists of a phototransistor which converts the light pulses to an electrical signal, an amplifier to increase the power of the signal, an electronic filter which reshapes the pulses, and a laser which converts the electrical signal to light again and sends it out the other fiber. However, optical amplifiers are being developed for repeaters to amplify the light itself without the need of converting it to an electric signal first. Some repeaters have been powered by light energy transmitted down the fiber with the signal.

Radio Repeater

This is used to extend the range of coverage of a radio signal. A radio repeater usually consists of a radio receiver connected to a radio transmitter. The received signal is amplified and retransmitted, often on another frequency, to provide coverage beyond the obstruction. Usage of a duplexer can allow the repeater to use one antenna for both receive and transmit at the same time.

- Broadcast relay station, rebroadcastor or translator: This is a repeater used to extend the coverage of a radio or television broadcasting station. It consists of a secondary radio or television transmitter. The signal from the main transmitter often comes over leased telephone lines or by microwave relay.

- Microwave relay: This is a specialized point-to-point telecommunications link, consisting of a microwave receiver that receives information over a beam of microwaves from another relay station in line-of-sight distance, and a microwave transmitter which passes the information on to the next station over another beam of microwaves. Networks of microwave relay stations transmit telephone calls, television programs, and computer data from one city to another over continent-wide areas.

- Passive repeater: This is a microwave relay that simply consists of a flat metal surface to reflect the microwave beam in another direction. It is used to get microwave relay signals over hills and mountains when it is not necessary to amplify the signal.

- Cellular repeater: This is a radio repeater for boosting cell phone reception in a limited area. The device functions like a small cellular base station, with a directional antenna to receive the signal from the nearest cell tower, an amplifier, and a local antenna to rebroadcast the signal to nearby cell phones. It is often used in downtown office buildings.

- • Digipeater: A repeater node in a packet radio network. It performs a store and forward function, passing on packets of information from one node to another.

Data Handling

Repeaters can be divided into two types depending on the type of data they handle:

Analog Repeater

This type is used in channels that transmit data in the form of an analog signal in which the voltage or current is proportional to the amplitude of the signal, as in an audio signal. They are also used in trunklines that transmit multiple signals using frequency division multiplexing (FDM). Analog repeaters are composed of a linear amplifier, and may include electronic filters to compensate for frequency and phase distortion in the line.

Digital Repeater

The digipeater is used in channels that transmit data by binary digital signals, in which the data is in the form of pulses with only two possible values, representing the binary digits 1 and 0. A digital repeater amplifies the signal, and it also may retime, resynchronize, and reshape the pulses. A repeater that performs the retiming or resynchronizing functions may be called a regenerator.

Telephone Repeater

Before the invention of electronic amplifiers, mechanically coupled carbon microphones were used as amplifiers in telephone repeaters. After the turn of the century it was found that negative resistance mercury lamps could amplify, and they were used. The invention of audion tube repeaters around 1916 made transcontinental telephony practical. In the 1930s vacuum tube repeaters using hybrid coils became commonplace, allowing the use of thinner wires. In the 1950s negative impedance gain devices were more popular, and a transistorized version called the E6 repeater was the final major type used in the Bell System before the low cost of digital transmission made all voiceband repeaters obsolete. Frequency frogging repeaters were commonplace in frequency-division multiplexing systems from the middle to late 20th century...

Ethernet Hub

An Ethernet hub, active hub, network hub, repeater hub, multiport repeater, or simply hub is a network hardware device for connecting multiple Ethernet devices together and making them act as a single network segment. It has multiple input/output (I/O) ports, in which a signal introduced at the input of any port appears at the output of every port except the original incoming. A hub works at the physical layer (layer 1) of the OSI model. Repeater hubs also participate in collision detection, forwarding a jam signal to all ports if it detects a collision. In addition to standard 8P8C ("RJ45") ports, some hubs may also come with a BNC or Attachment Unit Interface (AUI) connector to allow connection to legacy 10BASE2 or 10BASE5 network segments.

4-port Ethernet hub

Hubs are now largely obsolete, having been replaced by network switches except in very old installations or specialized applications.

Technical Information

Physical Layer Function

A network hub is an unsophisticated device in comparison with a switch. As a *multiport repeater* it works by repeating bits (symbols) received from one of its ports to all other ports. It is aware of physical layer packets, that is it can detect their start (preamble), an idle line (interpacket gap) and sense a collision which it also propagates by sending a jam signal. A hub cannot further examine or manage any of the traffic that comes through it: any packet entering any port is rebroadcast on all other ports. A hub/repeater has no memory to store any data in – a packet must be transmitted while it is received or is lost when a collision occurs (the sender should detect this and retry the transmission). Due to this, hubs can only run in half duplex mode. Consequently, due to a larger collision domain, packet collisions are more frequent in networks connected using hubs than in networks connected using more sophisticated devices.

Connecting Multiple Hubs

The need for hosts to be able to detect collisions limits the number of hubs and the total size of a network built using hubs (a network built using switches does not have these limitations). For 10 Mbit/s networks built using repeater hubs, the 5-4-3 rule must be followed: up to five segments (four hubs) are allowed between any two end stations. For

10BASE-T networks, up to five segments and four repeaters are allowed between any two hosts. For 100 Mbit/s networks, the limit is reduced to 3 segments (2 Class II hubs) between any two end stations, and even that is only allowed if the hubs are of Class II. Some hubs have manufacturer specific stack ports allowing them to be combined in a way that allows more hubs than simple chaining through Ethernet cables, but even so, a large Fast Ethernet network is likely to require switches to avoid the chaining limits of hubs.

Additional Functions

Most hubs detect typical problems, such as excessive collisions and jabbering on individual ports, and *partition* the port, disconnecting it from the shared medium. Thus, hub-based twisted-pair Ethernet is generally more robust than coaxial cable-based Ethernet (e.g. 10BASE2), where a misbehaving device can adversely affect the entire collision domain. Even if not partitioned automatically, a hub simplifies troubleshooting because hubs remove the need to troubleshoot faults on a long cable with multiple taps; status lights on the hub can indicate the possible problem source or, as a last resort, devices can be disconnected from a hub one at a time much more easily than from a coaxial cable.

To pass data through the repeater in a usable fashion from one segment to the next, the framing and data rate must be the same on each segment. This means that a repeater cannot connect an 802.3 segment (Ethernet) and an 802.5 segment (Token Ring) or a 10 Mbit/s segment to 100 Mbit/s Ethernet.

Fast Ethernet Classes

100 Mbit/s hubs and repeaters come in two different speed grades: Class I delay the signal for a maximum of 140 bit times (enabling translation/recoding between 100Base-TX, 100Base-FX and 100Base-T4) and Class II hubs delay the signal for a maximum of 92 bit times (enabling installation of two hubs in a single collision domain).

Dual-speed Hub

In the early days of Fast Ethernet, Ethernet switches were relatively expensive devices. Hubs suffered from the problem that if there were any 10BASE-T devices connected then the whole network needed to run at 10 Mbit/s. Therefore, a compromise between a hub and a switch was developed, known as a dual-speed hub. These devices make use of an internal two-port switch, bridging the 10 Mbit/s and 100 Mbit/s segments. When a network device becomes active on any of the physical ports, the device attaches it to either the 10 Mbit/s segment or the 100 Mbit/s segment, as appropriate. This obviated the need for an all-or-nothing migration to Fast Ethernet networks. These devices are considered hubs because the traffic between devices connected at the same speed is not switched.

Gigabit Ethernet Hubs

Repeater hubs have been defined for Gigabit Ethernet but commercial products have failed to appear due to the industry's transition to switching.

Uses

Historically, the main reason for purchasing hubs rather than switches was their price. This motivator has largely been eliminated by reductions in the price of switches, but hubs can still be useful in special circumstances:

- For inserting a protocol analyzer into a network connection, a hub is an alternative to a network tap or port mirroring.

- A hub with both 10BASE-T ports and a 10BASE2 port can be used to connect a 10BASE2 segment to a modern Ethernet-over-twisted-pair network.

- A hub with both 10BASE-T ports and an AUI port can be used to connect a 10BASE5 segment to a modern network.

Bridging (Networking)

A bridge connecting two LAN segments

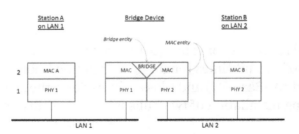

A high-level overview of network bridging, using the ISO/OSI layers and terminology

A network bridge is a computer networking device that creates a single aggregate network from multiple communication networks or network segments. This function is called network bridging. Bridging is distinct from routing, which allows multiple different networks to communicate independently while remaining separate. In the OSI model, bridging is performed in the first two layers, below the network layer (layer 3). If one or more segments of the bridged network are wireless, the device is known as a wireless bridge and the function as wireless bridging.

There are four types of network bridging technologies: simple bridging, multiport bridging, learning or transparent bridging, and source route bridging.

Simple Bridging

A simple bridge connects two network segments, typically by operating transparently and deciding on a packet-by-packet basis whether or not to forward from one network to the other. A store and forward technique is typically used so, during forwarding, the packet integrity is verified on the source network and CSMA/CD delays are accommodated on the destination network. Contrary to repeaters that simply extend the maximum span of a segment, bridges only forward packets that are required to cross the bridge. Additionally, bridges reduce collisions by partitioning the collision domain.

Multiport Bridging

A multiport bridge connects multiple networks and operates transparently to decide on a packet-by-packet basis whether and where to forward traffic. Like the simple bridge, a multiport bridge typically uses store and forward operation. The multiport bridge function serves as the basis for network switches.

Transparent Bridging

A transparent bridge uses a forwarding database to send frames across network segments. The forwarding database starts empty - entries in the database are built as the bridge receives frames. If an address entry is not found in the forwarding database, the frame is flooded to all other ports of the bridge, flooding the frame to all segments except the one from which it was received. By means of these flooded frames, the destination network will respond and a forwarding database entry will be created.

In the context of a two-port bridge, one can think of the forwarding database as a filtering database. A bridge reads a frame's destination address and decides to either forward or filter. If the bridge determines that the destination node is on another segment on the network, it forwards (retransmits) the frame to that segment. If the destination address belongs to the same segment as the source address, the bridge filters (discards) the frame. As nodes transmit data through the bridge, the bridge establishes a filtering database of known MAC addresses and their locations on the network. The bridge uses its filtering database to determine whether a packet should be forwarded or filtered.

Transparent bridging can also operate over devices with more than two ports. As an example, consider a bridge connected to three hosts, A, B, and C. The bridge has three ports. A is connected to bridge port 1, B is connected to bridge port 2, C is connected to bridge port 3. A sends a frame addressed to B to the bridge. The bridge examines the source address of the frame and creates an address and port number entry for A in its forwarding table. The bridge examines the destination address of the frame and does not find it in its forwarding table so it floods it to all other ports: 2 and 3. The frame is received by hosts B and C. Host C examines the destination address and ignores the frame. Host B recognizes a destination address match and generates a response to A.

On the return path, the bridge adds an address and port number entry for B to its forwarding table. The bridge already has A's address in its forwarding table so it forwards the response only to port 1. Host C or any other hosts on port 3 are not burdened with the response. Two-way communication is now possible between A and B without any further flooding in network.

Both source and destination addresses are used in this algorithm: source addresses are recorded in entries in the table, while destination addresses are looked up in the table and matched to the proper segment to send the frame to.

Digital Equipment Corporation (DEC) originally developed the technology in the 1980s.

Network Switch

Avaya ERS 2550T-PWR, a 50-port Ethernet switch

A network switch (also called switching hub, bridging hub, officially MAC bridge) is a computer networking device that connects devices together on a computer network, by using packet switching to receive, process and forward data to the destination device. Unlike less advanced network hubs, a network switch forwards data only to one or multiple devices that need to receive it, rather than broadcasting the same data out of each of its ports.

A network switch is a multiport network bridge that uses hardware addresses to process and forward data at the data link layer (layer 2) of the OSI model. Some switches can also process data at the network layer (layer 3) by additionally incorporating routing functionality that most commonly uses IP addresses to perform packet forwarding; such switches are commonly known as layer-3 switches or multilayer switches.

The first Ethernet switch was introduced by Kalpana in 1990.

Beside most commonly used Ethernet switches, they exist for various types of networks, including Fibre Channel, Asynchronous Transfer Mode, and InfiniBand.

Overview

A switch is a device in a computer network that electrically and logically connects together other devices. Multiple data cables are plugged into a switch to enable communication between different networked devices. Switches manage the flow of data across a network by transmitting a received network packet only to the one or more devices for which the packet is intended. Each networked device connected to a switch can be identified by its network address, allowing the switch to regulate the flow of traffic. This maximizes the security and efficiency of the network.

Cisco small business SG300-28 28-port Gigabit Ethernet rackmount switch and its internals

When a repeater hub is replaced with an Ethernet switch, the single large collision domain used by the hub is split up into smaller ones, reducing or eliminating the possibility and scope of collisions and, as a result, increasing the potential throughput. Because broadcasts are still being forwarded to all connected devices, the newly formed network segment continues to be a broadcast domain.

A switch is more intelligent than a repeater hub, which simply retransmits packets out of every port of the hub excepting the port on which the packet was received, unable to distinguish different recipients, and achieving an overall lower network efficiency.

Network Design

An Ethernet switch operates at the data link layer (layer 2) of the OSI model to create a separate collision domain for each switch port. Each device connected to a switch port can transfer data to any of the other ones at a time, and the transmissions will not interfere – with the limitation that, in half duplex mode, each switch port can only *either* receive from *or* transmit to its connected device at a certain time. In full duplex mode, each switch port can simultaneously transmit *and* receive, assuming the connected device also supports full duplex mode.

In the case of using a repeater hub, only a single transmission could take place at a time for all ports combined, so they would all share the bandwidth and run in half duplex. Necessary arbitration would also result in collisions, requiring retransmissions.

Applications

The network switch plays an integral role in most modern Ethernet local area networks (LANs). Mid-to-large sized LANs contain a number of linked managed switches. Small office/home office (SOHO) applications typically use a single switch, or an all-purpose converged device such as a residential gateway to access small office/home broadband services such as DSL or cable Internet. In most of these cases, the end-user device contains a router and components that interface to the particular physical broadband technology. User devices may also include a telephone interface for Voice over IP (VoIP) protocol.

Microsegmentation

Segmentation involves the use of a bridge or a switch (or a router) to split a larger collision domain into smaller ones in order to reduce collision probability, and to improve overall network throughput. In the extreme case (i.e. microsegmentation), each device is located on a dedicated switch port. In contrast to an Ethernet hub, there is a separate collision domain on each of the switch ports. This allows computers to have dedicated bandwidth on point-to-point connections to the network and also to run in full-duplex without collisions. Full-duplex mode has only one transmitter and one receiver per "collision domain", making collisions impossible.

Role of Switches in a Network

Switches may operate at one or more layers of the OSI model, including the data link and network layers. A device that operates simultaneously at more than one of these layers is known as a *multilayer switch*.

In switches intended for commercial use, built-in or modular interfaces make it possible to connect different types of networks, including Ethernet, Fibre Channel, RapidIO, ATM, ITU-T G.hn and 802.11. This connectivity can be at any of the layers mentioned. While the layer-2 functionality is adequate for bandwidth-shifting within one technology, interconnecting technologies such as Ethernet and token ring is performed easier at layer 3 or via routing. Devices that interconnect at the layer 3 are traditionally called routers, so layer 3 switches can also be regarded as relatively primitive and specialized routers.

Where there is a need for a great deal of analysis of network performance and security, switches may be connected between WAN routers as places for analytic modules.

Some vendors provide firewall, network intrusion detection, and performance analysis modules that can plug into switch ports. Some of these functions may be on combined modules.

In other cases, the switch is used to create a mirror image of data that can go to an external device. Since most switch port mirroring provides only one mirrored stream, network hubs can be useful for fanning out data to several read-only analyzers, such as intrusion detection systems and packet sniffers.

Layer-specific Functionality

While switches may learn about topologies at many layers, and forward at one or more layers, they do tend to have common features. Other than for high-performance applications, modern commercial switches use primarily Ethernet interfaces.

At any layer, a modern switch may implement power over Ethernet (PoE), which avoids the need for attached devices, such as a VoIP phone or wireless access point, to have a separate power supply. Since switches can have redundant power circuits connected to uninterruptible power supplies, the connected device can continue operating even when regular office power fails.

A modular network switch with three network modules (a total of 24 Ethernet and 14 Fast Ethernet ports) and one power supply.

Layer 1 (Hubs Vs. Higher-layer Switches)

A network hub, or a repeater, is a simple network device that does not manage any of the traffic coming through it. Any packet entering a port is flooded out or "repeated" on every other port, except for the port of entry. Since every packet is repeated on every other port, packet collisions affect the entire network, limiting its overall capacity.

A network switch creates the layer 1 end-to-end connection only virtually, while originally it was mandatory. The bridging function of a switch uses information taken from layer 2 to select for each packet the particular port(s) it has to be forwarded to, removing the requirement that every node is presented with all traffic. As a result, the connection lines are not "switched" literally, instead they only appear that way on the packet level.

There are specialized applications in which a network hub can be useful, such as copying traffic to multiple network sensors. High-end network switches usually have a feature called port mirroring that provides the same functionality.

By the early 2000s, there was little price difference between a hub and a low-end switch.

Layer 2

A network bridge, operating at the data link layer, may interconnect a small number of devices in a home or the office. This is a trivial case of bridging, in which the bridge learns the MAC address of each connected device.

Classic bridges may also interconnect using a spanning tree protocol that disables links so that the resulting local area network is a tree without loops. In contrast to routers, spanning tree bridges must have topologies with only one active path between two points. The older IEEE 802.1D spanning tree protocol could be quite slow, with forwarding stopping for 30 seconds while the spanning tree reconverged. A Rapid Spanning Tree Protocol was introduced as IEEE 802.1w. The newest standard Shortest path bridging (IEEE 802.1aq) is the next logical progression and incorporates all the older Spanning Tree Protocols (IEEE 802.1D STP, IEEE 802.1w RSTP, IEEE 802.1s MSTP) that blocked traffic on all but one alternative path. IEEE 802.1aq (Shortest Path Bridging SPB) allows all paths to be active with multiple equal cost paths, provides much larger layer 2 topologies (up to 16 million compared to the 4096 VLANs limit), faster convergence, and improves the use of the mesh topologies through increased bandwidth and redundancy between all devices by allowing traffic to load share across all paths of a mesh network.

While *layer 2 switch* remains more of a marketing term than a technical term, the products that were introduced as "switches" tended to use microsegmentation and full duplex to prevent collisions among devices connected to Ethernet. By using an internal forwarding plane much faster than any interface, they give the impression of simultaneous paths among multiple devices. 'Non-blocking' devices use a forwarding plane or equivalent method fast enough to allow full duplex traffic for each port simultaneously.

Once a bridge learns the addresses of its connected nodes, it forwards data link layer frames using a layer 2 forwarding method. There are four forwarding methods a bridge can use, of which the second through fourth method were performance-increasing methods when used on "switch" products with the same input and output port bandwidths:

1. Store and forward: the switch buffers and verifies each frame before forwarding it; a frame is received in its entirety before it is forwarded.

2. Cut through: the switch starts forwarding after the frame's destination address is received. When the outgoing port is busy at the time, the switch falls back to store-and-forward operation. There is no error checking with this method.

3. Fragment free: a method that attempts to retain the benefits of both store and forward and cut through. Fragment free checks the first 64 bytes of the frame, where addressing information is stored. According to Ethernet specifications, collisions should be detected during the first 64 bytes of the frame, so frames that are in error because of a collision will not be forwarded. This way the frame will always reach its intended destination. Error checking of the actual data in the packet is left for the end device.

4. Adaptive switching: a method of automatically selecting between the other three modes.

While there are specialized applications, such as storage area networks, where the input and output interfaces are the same bandwidth, this is not always the case in general LAN applications. In LANs, a switch used for end user access typically concentrates lower bandwidth and uplinks into a higher bandwidth.

Layer 3

Within the confines of the Ethernet physical layer, a layer-3 switch can perform some or all of the functions normally performed by a router. The most common layer-3 capability is awareness of IP multicast through IGMP snooping. With this awareness, a layer-3 switch can increase efficiency by delivering the traffic of a multicast group only to ports where the attached device has signaled that it wants to listen to that group.

Layer 4

While the exact meaning of the term *layer-4 switch* is vendor-dependent, it almost always starts with a capability for network address translation, but then adds some type of load distribution based on TCP sessions.

The device may include a stateful firewall, a VPN concentrator, or be an IPSec security gateway.

Layer 7

Layer-7 switches may distribute the load based on uniform resource locators (URLs), or by using some installation-specific technique to recognize application-level transactions. A layer-7 switch may include a web cache and participate in a content delivery network (CDN).

Types of Switches

A rack-mounted 24-port 3Com switch

Form Factors

Switches are available in many form factors including: desktop units not mounted in an enclosure which are typically intended to be used in a home or office environment outside a wiring closet; rack-mounted switches for use in an equipment rack; large chassis units with swappable module cards; DIN rail mounted for use in industrial environments; and small installation switches, mounted into a cable duct, floor box or communications tower, as found, for example, in FTTO Infrastructures.

Configuration Options

- *Unmanaged* switches – these switches have no configuration interface or options. They are plug and play. They are typically the least expensive switches, and therefore often used in a small office/home office environment. Unmanaged switches can be desktop or rack mounted.

- *Managed* switches – these switches have one or more methods to modify the operation of the switch. Common management methods include: a command-line interface (CLI) accessed via serial console, telnet or Secure Shell, an embedded Simple Network Management Protocol (SNMP) agent allowing management from a remote console or management station, or a web interface for management from a web browser. Examples of configuration changes that one can do from a managed switch include: enabling features such as Spanning Tree Protocol or port mirroring, setting port bandwidth, creating or modifying virtual LANs (VLANs), etc. Two sub-classes of managed switches are marketed today:

- *Smart* (or intelligent) switches – these are managed switches with a limited set of management features. Likewise "web-managed" switches are switches which fall into a market niche between unmanaged and managed. For a price much lower than a fully managed switch they provide a web interface (and usually no CLI access) and allow configuration of basic settings, such as VLANs, port-bandwidth and duplex.

- *Enterprise managed* (or fully managed) switches – these have a full set of management features, including CLI, SNMP agent, and web interface. They may have additional features to manipulate configurations, such as the ability to display, modify, backup and restore configurations. Compared with smart switches, enterprise switches have more features that can be customized or optimized, and are generally more expensive than smart switches. Enterprise switches are typically found in networks with larger number of switches and connections, where centralized management is a significant savings in administrative time and effort. A stackable switch is a version of enterprise-managed switch.

Typical Switch Management Features

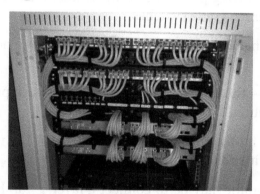

A couple of managed D-Link Gigabit Ethernet rackmount switches, connected to the Ethernetports on a few patch panels using Category 6 patch cables (all equipment is installed in a standard 19-inch rack)

- Turn particular port range on or off

- Link bandwidth and duplex settings

- Priority settings for ports

- IP management by IP clustering

- MAC filtering and other types of "port security" features which prevent MAC flooding

- Use of Spanning Tree Protocol (STP) and Shortest Path Bridging (SPB) technologies

- Simple Network Management Protocol (SNMP) monitoring of device and link health

- Port mirroring (also known as: port monitoring, spanning port, SPAN port, roving analysis port or link mode port)

- Link aggregation (also known as *bonding*, *trunking* or *teaming*) allows the use of multiple ports for the same connection achieving higher data transfer rates

- VLAN settings. Creating VLANs can serve security and performance goals by reducing the size of the broadcast domain

- 802.1X network access control

- IGMP snooping

Traffic Monitoring on a Switched Network

Unless port mirroring or other methods such as RMON, SMON or sFlow are implemented in a switch, it is difficult to monitor traffic that is bridged using a switch because only the sending and receiving ports can see the traffic. These monitoring features are rarely present on consumer-grade switches.

Two popular methods that are specifically designed to allow a network analyst to monitor traffic are:

- Port mirroring – the switch sends a copy of network packets to a monitoring network connection.

- SMON – "Switch Monitoring" is described by RFC 2613 and is a protocol for controlling facilities such as port mirroring.

Another method to monitor may be to connect a layer-1 hub between the monitored device and its switch port. This will induce minor delay, but will provide multiple interfaces that can be used to monitor the individual switch port.

References

- Sungook, Hong (2001). Wireless: From Marconi's Black-Box to the Audion. MIT Press. p. 165. ISBN 0262082985.

- Dong, Jielin. Network Dictionary. Javvin Technologies Inc. p. 23. ISBN 9781602670006. Retrieved 25 June 2016.

- "Cray makes its ethernet switches responsive to net conditions". IDG Network World Inc. 1 July 1996. Retrieved 25 June 2016.

- Jim O'Reilly (2014-01-22). "Will 2014 Be The Year Of 10 Gigabit Ethernet?". Network Computing. Retrieved 2015-04-29.

- "Breaking Speed Limits with ASRock X99 WS-E/10G and Intel 10G BASE-T LANs". asrock.com. 24 November 2014. Retrieved 19 May 2015.

- "Introduction to Intel Ethernet Flow Director and Memcached Performance" (PDF). Intel. October 14, 2014. Retrieved October 11, 2015.

- Patrick Kutch; Brian Johnson; Greg Rose (September 2011). "An Introduction to Intel Flexible Port Partitioning Using SR-IOV Technology" (PDF). Intel. Retrieved September 24, 2015.

- Joe Efferson; Ted Gary; Bob Nevins (February 2002). "Token-Ring to Ethernet Migration" (PDF). IBM. p. 13. Retrieved 2015-08-11.

- Thayumanavan Sridhar (September 1998). "The Internet Protocol Journal - Volume 1, No. 2: Layer 2 and Layer 3 Switch Evolution". Cisco Systems. Retrieved 2015-08-11.

- "Intel 82574 Gigabit Ethernet Controller Family Datasheet" (PDF). Intel. June 2014. p. 1. Retrieved November 16, 2014.

- Tom Herbert; Willem de Bruijn (May 9, 2014). "Linux kernel documentation: Documentation/networking/scaling.txt". kernel.org. Retrieved November 16, 2014.

- "Enhancing Scalability Through Network Interface Card Partitioning" (PDF). Dell. April 2011. Retrieved May 12, 2014.

- Timothy Prickett Morgan (2012-02-08). "Solarflare turns network adapters into servers: When a CPU just isn't fast enough". The Register. Retrieved 2014-05-08.

- Steve Pope; David Riddoch (2008-03-21). "OpenOnload: A user-level network stack" (PDF). openonload.org. Retrieved 2014-05-08.

- "Local Area Networks: Internetworking". manipalitdubai.com. Archived from the original (PPT) on 2014-05-13. Retrieved 2012-12-02.

- Thayumanavan Sridhar (September 1998). "Layer 2 and Layer 3 Switch Evolution". cisco.com. The Internet Protocol Journal. Cisco Systems. Retrieved 2014-08-05.

Routing: A Comprehensive Study

Routing can be defined as the hardware and software that enable the transmission and distribution of data. It is a networking device that allows for the connection of a device to a network by navigating through various existing networks. The themes in this chapter describe the concepts, processes and technology that is used in routing.

Routing

Routing is the process of selecting best paths in a network. Routing is performed for many kinds of networks, including the public switched telephone network (circuit switching), electronic data networks (such as the Internet), and transportation networks. This article is concerned primarily with routing in electronic data networks using packet switching technology.

In packet switching networks, routing directs packet forwarding (the transit of logically addressed network packets from their source toward their ultimate destination) through intermediate nodes. Intermediate nodes are typically network hardware devices such as routers, bridges, gateways, firewalls, or switches. General-purpose computers can also forward packets and perform routing, though they are not specialized hardware and may suffer from limited performance. The routing process usually directs forwarding on the basis of routing tables, which maintain a record of the routes to various network destinations. Thus, constructing routing tables, which are held in the router's memory, is very important for efficient routing. Most routing algorithms use only one network path at a time. Multipath routing techniques enable the use of multiple alternative paths.

Routing, in a more narrow sense of the term, is often contrasted with bridging in its assumption that network addresses are structured and that similar addresses imply proximity within the network. Structured addresses allow a single routing table entry to represent the route to a group of devices. In large networks, structured addressing (routing, in the narrow sense) outperforms unstructured addressing (bridging). Routing has become the dominant form of addressing on the Internet. Bridging is still widely used within localized environments.

Delivery Schemes

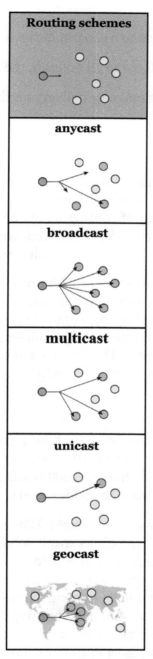

Routing schemes differ in how they deliver messages:

- unicast delivers a message to a single specific node

- anycast delivers a message to anyone out of a group of nodes, typically the one nearest to the source

- multicast delivers a message to a group of nodes that have expressed interest in receiving the message

- geocast delivers a message to a geographic area

- broadcast delivers a message to all nodes in the network

Unicast is the dominant form of message delivery on the Internet. This article focuses on unicast routing algorithms.

Topology Distribution

In static routing (or non-dynamic routing), small networks may use manually config-ured routing tables. Larger networks have complex topologies that can change rapidly, making the manual construction of routing tables unfeasible. Nevertheless, most of the public switched telephone network (PSTN) uses pre-computed routing tables, with fallback routes if the most direct route becomes blocked.

Dynamic routing attempts to solve this problem by constructing routing tables auto-matically, based on information carried by routing protocols, allowing the network to act nearly autonomously in avoiding network failures and blockages. Dynamic rout-ing dominates the Internet. Examples of dynamic-routing protocols and algorithms include Routing Information Protocol (RIP), Open Shortest Path First (OSPF) and En-hanced Interior Gateway Routing Protocol (EIGRP).

Distance Vector Algorithms

Distance vector algorithms use the Bellman–Ford algorithm. This approach assigns a *cost* number to each of the links between each node in the network. Nodes send infor-mation from point A to point B via the path that results in the lowest *total cost* (i.e. the sum of the costs of the links between the nodes used).

The algorithm operates in a very simple manner. When a node first starts, it only knows of its immediate neighbours, and the direct cost involved in reaching them. (This infor-mation — the list of destinations, the total cost to each, and the *next hop* to send data to get there — makes up the routing table, or *distance table*.) Each node, on a regular basis, sends to each neighbour node its own current assessment of the total cost to get to all the destinations it knows of. The neighbouring nodes examine this information and compare it to what they already 'know'; anything that represents an improvement on what they already have, they insert in their own routing table(s). Over time, all the nodes in the network discover the best next hop for all destinations, and the best total cost.

When one network node goes down, any nodes that used it as their next hop discard the entry, and create new routing-table information. These nodes convey the updated routing information to all adjacent nodes, which in turn repeat the process. Eventually all the nodes in the network receive the updates, and discover new paths to all the destinations they can still "reach".

Link-state Algorithms

When applying link-state algorithms, a graphical map of the network is the fundamental data used for each node. To produce its map, each node floods the entire network with information about the other nodes it can connect to. Each node then independently assembles this information into a map. Using this map, each router independently determines the least-cost path from itself to every other node using a standard shortest paths algorithm such as Dijkstra's algorithm. The result is a tree graph rooted at the current node, such that the path through the tree from the root to any other node is the least-cost path to that node. This tree then serves to construct the routing table, which specifies the best next hop to get from the current node to any other node.

Optimised Link State Routing algorithm

A link-state routing algorithm optimised for mobile ad hoc networks is the *Optimised Link State Routing Protocol (OLSR)*. OLSR is proactive; it uses Hello and Topology Control (TC) messages to discover and disseminate link state information through the mobile ad hoc network. Using Hello messages, each node discovers 2-hop neighbor information and elects a set of *multipoint relays* (MPRs). MPRs distinguish OLSR from other link state routing protocols.

Path Vector Protocol

Distance vector and link state routing are both intra-domain routing protocols. They are used inside an autonomous system, but not between autonomous systems. Both of these routing protocols become intractable in large networks and cannot be used in Inter-domain routing. Distance vector routing is subject to instability if there are more than a few hops in the domain. Link state routing needs huge amount of resources to calculate routing tables. It also creates heavy traffic due to flooding.

Path vector routing is used for inter-domain routing. It is similar to distance vector routing. Path vector routing assumes that one node (there can be many) in each autonomous system acts on behalf of the entire autonomous system. This node is called the *speaker node*. The speaker node creates a routing table and advertises it to neighboring speaker nodes in neighboring autonomous systems. The idea is the same as distance vector routing except that only speaker nodes in each autonomous system can communicate with each other. The speaker node advertises the path, not the metric, of the nodes in its autonomous system or other autonomous systems. Path vector routing is discussed in RFC 1322; the path vector routing algorithm is somewhat similar to the distance vector algorithm in the sense that each border router advertises the destinations it can reach to its neighboring router. However, instead of advertising networks in terms of a destination and the distance to that destination, networks are advertised as destination addresses and path descriptions to reach those destinations. A route is defined as a pairing between a destination and the attributes of the path to that destination, thus the name, path vector routing, where the routers receive a vector that contains paths to a set of destinations. The path, expressed in terms of the domains (or confederations) traversed so far, is carried in a special path attribute that records the sequence of routing domains through which the reachability information has passed.

Path Selection

Path selection involves applying a routing metric to multiple routes to select (or predict) the best route.

In computer networking, the metric is computed by a routing algorithm, and can cover information such as bandwidth, network delay, hop count, path cost, load, MTU (maximum transmission unit), reliability, and communication cost. The routing table stores only the best possible routes, while link-state or topological databases may store all other information as well.

In case of overlapping or equal routes, algorithms consider the following elements to decide which routes to install into the routing table (sorted by priority):

1. *Prefix-Length*: where longer subnet masks are preferred (independent of whether it is within a routing protocol or over different routing protocol)

2. *Metric*: where a lower metric/cost is preferred (only valid within one and the same routing protocol)

3. *Administrative distance*: where a route learned from a more reliable routing protocol is preferred (only valid between different routing protocols)

Because a routing metric is specific to a given routing protocol, multi-protocol routers must use some external heuristic to select between routes learned from different routing protocols. Cisco routers, for example, attribute a value known as the administrative distance to each route, where smaller administrative distances indicate routes learned from a supposedly more reliable protocol.

A local network administrator, in special cases, can set up host-specific routes to a particular device that provides more control over network usage, permits testing, and better overall security. This is useful for debugging network connections or routing tables.

In some small systems, a single central device decides ahead of time the complete path of every packet. In some other small systems, whichever edge device injects a packet into the network decides ahead of time the complete path of that particular packet. In both of these systems, that route-planning device needs to know a lot of information about what devices are connected to the network and how they are connected to each other. Once it has this information, it can use an algorithm such as A* search algorithm to find the best path.

In high-speed systems, there are so many packets transmitted every second that it is infeasible for a single device to calculate the complete path for each and every packet. Early high-speed systems dealt with this by setting up a circuit switching relay channel once for the first packet between some source and some destination; later packets between that same source and that same destination continue to follow the same path without recalculating until the channel teardown. Later high-speed systems inject packets into the network without any one device ever calculating a complete path for that packet—multiple agents.

In large systems, there are so many connections between devices, and those connections change so frequently, that it is infeasible for any one device to even know how all the devices are connected to each other, much less calculate a complete path through them. Such systems generally use next-hop routing.

Most systems use a deterministic dynamic routing algorithm: When a device chooses a path to a particular final destination, that device always chooses the same path to that destination until it receives information that makes it think some other path is better. A few routing algorithms do not use a deterministic algorithm to find the "best" link for a packet to get from its original source to its final destination. Instead, to avoid congestion in switched systems or network hot spots in packet systems, a few algorithms use a randomized algorithm—Valiant's paradigm—that routes a path to a randomly picked intermediate destination, and from there to its true final destination. In many early telephone switches, a randomizer was often used to select the start of a path through a multistage switching fabric.

Multiple Agents

In some networks, routing is complicated by the fact that no single entity is responsible for selecting paths; instead, multiple entities are involved in selecting paths or even parts of a single path. Complications or inefficiency can result if these entities choose paths to optimize their own objectives, which may conflict with the objectives of other participants.

A classic example involves traffic in a road system, in which each driver picks a path that minimizes their travel time. With such routing, the equilibrium routes can be longer than optimal for all drivers. In particular, Braess' paradox shows that adding a new road can *lengthen* travel times for all drivers.

In another model, for example, used for routing automated guided vehicles (AGVs) on a terminal, reservations are made for each vehicle to prevent simultaneous use of the same part of an infrastructure. This approach is also referred to as context-aware routing.

The Internet is partitioned into autonomous systems (ASs) such as internet service providers (ISPs), each of which controls routes involving its network, at multiple levels. First, AS-level paths are selected via the BGP protocol, which produces a sequence of ASs through which packets flow. Each AS may have multiple paths, offered by neighboring ASs, from which to choose. Its decision often involves business relationships with these neighboring ASs, which may be unrelated to path quality or latency. Second, once an AS-level path has been selected, there are often multiple corresponding router-level paths, in part because two ISPs may be connected in multiple locations. In choosing the single router-level path, it is common practice for each ISP to employ hot-potato routing: sending traffic along the path that minimizes the distance through the ISP's own network—even if that path lengthens the total distance to the destination.

Consider two ISPs, A and B. Each has a presence in New York, connected by a fast link with latency 5 ms—and each has a presence in London connected by a 5 ms link. Suppose both ISPs have trans-Atlantic links that connect their two networks, but A's link has latency 100 ms and B's has latency 120 ms. When routing a message from a source in A's London network to a destination in B's New York network, A may choose to immediately send the message to B in London. This saves A the work of sending it along an expensive trans-Atlantic link, but causes the message to experience latency 125 ms when the other route would have been 20 ms faster.

A 2003 measurement study of Internet routes found that, between pairs of neighboring ISPs, more than 30% of paths have inflated latency due to hot-potato routing, with 5% of paths being delayed by at least 12 ms. Inflation due to AS-level path selection, while substantial, was attributed primarily to BGP's lack of a mechanism to directly optimize for latency, rather than to selfish routing policies. It was also suggested that, were an appropriate mechanism in place, ISPs would be willing to cooperate to reduce latency rather than use hot-potato routing.

Such a mechanism was later published by the same authors, first for the case of two ISPs and then for the global case.

Route Analytics

As the Internet and IP networks become mission critical business tools, there has been increased interest in techniques and methods to monitor the routing posture of networks. Incorrect routing or routing issues cause undesirable performance degradation, flapping and/or downtime. Monitoring routing in a network is achieved using route analytics tools and techniques.

Router (Computing)

A Cisco ASM/2-32EM router deployed at CERN in 1987

A router is a networking device that forwards data packets between computer networks. Routers perform the traffic directing functions on the Internet. A data packet is typically forwarded from one router to another through the networks that constitute the internetwork until it reaches its destination node.

A router is connected to two or more data lines from different networks. When a data packet comes in on one of the lines, the router reads the address information in the packet to determine the ultimate destination. Then, using information in its routing table or routing policy, it directs the packet to the next network on its journey. This creates an overlay internetwork.

The most familiar type of routers are home and small office routers that simply pass IP packets between the home computers and the Internet. An example of a router would be the owner's cable or DSL router, which connects to the Internet through an Internet service provider (ISP). More sophisticated routers, such as enterprise routers, connect large business or ISP networks up to the powerful core routers that forward data at high speed along the optical fiber lines of the Internet backbone. Though routers are typically dedicated hardware devices, software-based routers also exist.

Applications

When multiple routers are used in interconnected networks, the routers can exchange information about destination addresses using a dynamic routing protocol. Each router builds up a routing table listing the preferred routes between any two systems on the interconnected networks.

A router has interfaces for different physical types of network connections, such as copper cables, fibre optic, or wireless transmission. It also contains firmware for different networking communications protocol standards. Each network interface uses this specialized computer software to enable data packets to be forwarded from one protocol transmission system to another.

Routers may also be used to connect two or more logical groups of computer devices known as subnets, each with a different network prefix. The network prefixes recorded in the routing table do not necessarily map directly to the physical interface connections.

A router has two stages of operation called planes:

- Control plane: A router maintains a routing table that lists which route should be used to forward a data packet, and through which physical interface connection. It does this using internal pre-configured directives, called static routes, or by learning routes using a dynamic routing protocol. Static and dynamic routes are stored in the Routing Information Base (RIB). The control-plane logic then strips non essential directives from the RIB and builds a Forwarding Information Base (FIB) to be used by the forwarding-plane.

- Forwarding plane: The router forwards data packets between incoming and outgoing interface connections. It routes them to the correct network type using information that the packet header contains. It uses data recorded in the routing table control plane.

Routers may provide connectivity within enterprises, between enterprises and the Internet, or between internet service providers' (ISPs) networks. The largest routers (such as the Cisco CRS-1 or Juniper T1600) interconnect the various ISPs, or may be used in large enterprise networks. Smaller routers usually provide connectivity for typical home and office networks. Other networking solutions may be provided by a backbone Wireless Distribution System (WDS), which avoids the costs of introducing networking cables into buildings.

All sizes of routers may be found inside enterprises. The most powerful routers are usually found in ISPs, academic and research facilities. Large businesses may also need more powerful routers to cope with ever increasing demands of intranet data traffic. A three-layer model is in common use, not all of which need be present in smaller networks.

Access

Access routers, including 'small office/home office' (SOHO) models, are located at customer sites such as branch offices that do not need hierarchical routing of their own. Typically, they are optimized for low cost. Some SOHO routers are capable of running alternative free Linux-based firmwares like Tomato, OpenWrt or DD-WRT.

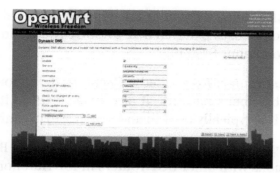

A screenshot of the LuCI web interface used by OpenWrt. This page configures Dynamic DNS.

Distribution

Distribution routers aggregate traffic from multiple access routers, either at the same site, or to collect the data streams from multiple sites to a major enterprise location. Distribution routers are often responsible for enforcing quality of service across a wide area network (WAN), so they may have considerable memory installed, multiple WAN interface connections, and substantial onboard data processing routines. They may also provide connectivity to groups of file servers or other external networks.

Security

External networks must be carefully considered as part of the overall security strategy. A router may include a firewall, VPN handling, and other security functions, or these may be handled by separate devices. Many companies produced security-oriented routers, including Cisco PIX series, Juniper NetScreen and WatchGuard. Routers also commonly perform network address translation, (which allows multiple devices on a network to share a single public IP address) and stateful packet inspection. Some experts argue that open source routers are more secure and reliable than closed source routers because open source routers allow mistakes to be quickly found and corrected.

Core

In enterprises, a core router may provide a "collapsed backbone" interconnecting the distribution tier routers from multiple buildings of a campus, or large enterprise locations. They tend to be optimized for high bandwidth, but lack some of the features of Edge Routers.

Internet Connectivity and Internal use

Routers intended for ISP and major enterprise connectivity usually exchange routing information using the Border Gateway Protocol (BGP). RFC 4098 standard defines the types of BGP routers according to their functions:

- *Edge router*: Also called a Provider Edge router, is placed at the edge of an ISP network. The router uses External BGP to EBGP routers in other ISPs, or a large enterprise Autonomous System.

- *Subscriber edge router*: Also called a Customer Edge router, is located at the edge of the subscriber's network, it also uses EBGP to its provider's Autonomous System. It is typically used in an (enterprise) organization.

- *Inter-provider border router*: Interconnecting ISPs, is a BGP router that maintains BGP sessions with other BGP routers in ISP Autonomous Systems.

- Core router: A *core router* resides within an Autonomous System as a back bone to carry traffic between edge routers.

- Within an ISP: In the ISP's Autonomous System, a router uses internal BGP to communicate with other ISP edge routers, other intranet core routers, or the ISP's intranet provider border routers.

- "Internet backbone:" The Internet no longer has a clearly identifiable backbone, unlike its predecessor networks. The major ISPs' system routers make up what could be considered to be the current Internet backbone core. ISPs operate all four types of the BGP routers described here. An ISP "core" router is used to interconnect its edge and border routers. Core routers may also have specialized functions in virtual private networks based on a combination of BGP and Multi-Protocol Label Switching protocols.

- Port forwarding: Routers are also used for port forwarding between private Internet connected servers.

- Voice/Data/Fax/Video Processing Routers: Commonly referred to as access servers or gateways, these devices are used to route and process voice, data, video and fax traffic on the Internet. Since 2005, most long-distance phone calls have been processed as IP traffic (VOIP) through a voice gateway. Use of access server type routers expanded with the advent of the Internet, first with dial-up access and another resurgence with voice phone service.

- Larger networks commonly use multilayer switches, with layer 3 devices being used to simply interconnect multiple subnets within the same security zone, and higher layer switches when filtering, translation, load balancing or other higher level functions are required, especially between zones.

Historical and Technical Information

The very first device that had fundamentally the same functionality as a router does today was the Interface Message Processor (IMP); IMPs were the devices that made up the ARPANET, the first TCP/IP network. The idea for a router (called "gateways" at the time) initially came about through an international group of computer networking researchers called the International Network Working Group (INWG). Set up in 1972 as an informal group to consider the technical issues involved in connecting different networks, later that year it became a subcommittee of the International Federation for Information Processing. These devices were different from most previous packet switching schemes in two ways. First, they connected dissimilar kinds of networks, such as serial lines and local area networks. Second, they were connectionless devices, which had no role in assuring that traffic was delivered reliably, leaving that entirely to the hosts.

Avaya ERS 8600 (2010)

The idea was explored in more detail, with the intention to produce a prototype system as part of two contemporaneous programs. One was the initial DARPA-initiated program, which created the TCP/IP architecture in use today. The other was a program at Xerox PARC to explore new networking technologies, which produced the PARC Universal Packet system; due to corporate intellectual property concerns it received little attention outside Xerox for years. Some time after early 1974, the first Xerox routers became operational. The first true IP router was developed by Virginia Strazisar at BBN, as part of that DARPA-initiated effort, during 1975-1976. By the end of 1976, three PDP-11-based routers were in service in the experimental prototype Internet.

The first multiprotocol routers were independently created by staff researchers at MIT and Stanford in 1981; the Stanford router was done by William Yeager, and the MIT one by Noel Chiappa; both were also based on PDP-11s. Virtually all networking now uses TCP/IP, but multiprotocol routers are still manufactured. They were important in the early stages of the growth of computer networking, when protocols other than TCP/IP were in use. Modern Internet routers that handle both IPv4 and IPv6 are multiprotocol, but are simpler devices than routers processing AppleTalk, DECnet, IP and Xerox protocols.

From the mid-1970s and in the 1980s, general-purpose mini-computers served as routers. Modern high-speed routers are highly specialized computers with extra hardware added to speed both common routing functions, such as packet forwarding, and specialised functions such as IPsec encryption. There is substantial use of Linux and Unix software based machines, running open source routing code, for research and other applications. Cisco's operating system was independently designed. Major router operating systems, such as those from Juniper Networks and Extreme Networks, are extensively modified versions of Unix software.

Forwarding

The main purpose of a router is to connect multiple networks and forward packets destined either for its own networks or other networks. A router is considered a layer-3 device because its primary forwarding decision is based on the information in the layer-3 IP packet, specifically the destination IP address. When a router receives a packet, it searches its routing table to find the best match between the destination IP address of the packet and one of the addresses in the routing table. Once a match is found, the packet is encapsulated in the layer-2 data link frame for the outgoing interface indicated in the table entry. A router typically does not look into the packet payload, but only at the layer-3 addresses to make a forwarding decision, plus optionally other information in the header for hints on, for example, quality of service (QoS). For pure IP forwarding, a router is designed to minimize the state information associated with individual packets. Once a packet is forwarded, the router does not retain any historical information about the packet.

The routing table itself can contain information derived from a variety of sources, such as a default or static routes that are configured manually, or dynamic routing protocols where the router learns routes from other routers. A default route is one that is used to route all traffic whose destination does not otherwise appear in the routing table; this is common – even necessary – in small networks, such as a home or small business where the default route simply sends all non-local traffic to the Internet service provider. The default route can be manually configured (as a static route), or learned by dynamic routing protocols, or be obtained by DHCP.

A router can run more than one routing protocol at a time, particularly if it serves as an autonomous system border router between parts of a network that run different routing protocols; if it does so, then redistribution may be used (usually selectively) to share information between the different protocols running on the same router.

Besides making a decision as to which interface a packet is forwarded to, which is handled primarily via the routing table, a router also has to manage congestion when packets arrive at a rate higher than the router can process. Three policies commonly used in the Internet are tail drop, random early detection (RED), and weighted random early detection (WRED). Tail drop is the simplest and most easily implemented; the router simply drops new incoming packets once the length of the queue exceeds the size of the buffers in the router. RED probabilistically drops datagrams early when the queue exceeds a pre-configured portion of the buffer, until a pre-determined max, when it becomes tail drop. WRED requires a weight on the average queue size to act upon when the traffic is about to exceed the pre-configured size, so that short bursts will not trigger random drops.

Another function a router performs is to decide which packet should be processed first when multiple queues exist. This is managed through QoS, which is critical when Voice over IP is deployed, so as not to introduce excessive latency.

Yet another function a router performs is called policy-based routing where special rules are constructed to override the rules derived from the routing table when a packet forwarding decision is made.

Router functions may be performed through the same internal paths that the packets travel inside the router. Some of the functions may be performed through an application-specific integrated circuit (ASIC) to avoid overhead of scheduling CPU time to process the packets. Others may have to be performed through the CPU as these packets need special attention that cannot be handled by an ASIC.

Multipath Routing

Multipath routing is the routing technique of using multiple alternative paths through a network, which can yield a variety of benefits such as fault tolerance, increased bandwidth, or improved security. The multiple paths computed might be overlapped, edge-disjointed or node-disjointed with each other. Extensive research has been done on multipath routing techniques, but multipath routing is not yet widely deployed in practice.

Multipath Routing in Wireless Networks

To improve performance or fault tolerance:

CMR (Concurrent Multipath Routing) is often taken to mean simultaneous management and utilization of multiple available paths for the transmission of streams of data emanating from an application or multiple applications. In this form, each stream is assigned a separate path, uniquely to the extent supported by the number of paths available. If there are more streams than available paths, some streams will share paths. This provides better utilization of available bandwidth by creating multiple active transmission queues. It also provides a measure of fault tolerance in that, should a path fail, only the traffic assigned to that path is affected, the other paths continuing to serve their stream flows; there is also, ideally, an alternative path immediately available upon which to continue or restart the interrupted stream.

This method provides better transmission performance and fault tolerance by providing:

- Simultaneous, parallel transport over multiple carriers.

- Load balancing over available assets.

- Avoidance of path discovery when reassigning an interrupted stream.

Shortcomings of this method are:

- Some applications may be slower in offering traffic to the transport layer, thus starving paths assigned to them, causing under-utilization.

- Moving to the alternative path will incur a potentially disruptive period during which the connection is re-established.

A more powerful form of CMR (true CMR) goes beyond merely presenting paths to applications to which they can bind. True CMR aggregates all available paths into a single, virtual path. All applications offer their packets to this virtual path, which is de-muxed at the Network Layer, the packets then being distributed to the actual paths via some method such as round-robin or weighted fair queuing. Should a link or relay node fail, thus invalidating one or more paths, succeeding packets are not directed to that (/ those) path(s). The stream continues uninterrupted, transparently to the application. This method provides significant performance benefits over the former:

- By continually offering packets to all paths, the paths are more fully utilized.

- No matter how many nodes (and thus paths) fail, so long as at least one path constituting the virtual path is still available, all sessions remain connected. This means that no streams need to be restarted from the beginning and no re-connection penalty is incurred.

It is noted that true CMR can, by its nature, cause out-of-order delivery (OOOD) of packets, which is severely debilitating for standard TCP. Standard TCP, however, has been exhaustively proven to be inappropriate for use in challenged wireless environments and must, in any case, be augmented by a facility, such as a TCP gateway, that is designed to meet the challenge. One such gateway tool is SCPS-TP, which, through its Selective Negative Acknowledgement (SNACK) capability, deals successfully with the OOOD problem.

Another important benefit of true CMR, desperately needed in wireless network communications, is its support for enhanced security. Simply put, for an exchange to be compromised, multiple of the routes it traverses must be compromised. The reader is referred to the references in the "To improve network security" section for discussion on this topic.

Capillary Routing

In networking and in graph theory, capillary routing, for a given network, is a multi-path solution between a pair of source and destination nodes. Unlike shortest-path routing or max-flow routing for any network topology only one capillary routing solution exists.

Capillary routing can be constructed by an iterative linear programming (LP) process transforming a single-path flow into a capillary route. First minimize the maximal value of the load of all links by minimizing an upper bound value applied to all links. The full mass of the flow will be split equally across the possible parallel routes. Find the bottleneck links of the first layer and fix their load at the found minimum. Minimize similarly the maximal load of all remaining links without the bottleneck links of the first layer. This second iteration further refines the path diversity. Find the bottleneck links of the second layer. Minimize the maximal load of all remaining links, but now without the bottlenecks of the second layer as well. Repeat this iteration until the entire communication footprint is enclosed in the bottlenecks of the constructed layers.

At each layer, after minimizing the maximal load of links, the bottlenecks of the layer are discovered in a bottleneck hunting loop. At each iteration of the hunting loop, we minimize the load of the traffic over all links having maximal load and being suspected as bottlenecks. Links not maintaining their load at the maximum are removed from the suspect list. The bottleneck hunting loop stops if there are no more links to remove.

The animated image shows capillary routing footprint between a pair of nodes in a mobile ad-hoc network.

Static Routing

Static routing is a form of routing that occurs when a router uses a manually-configured routing entry, rather than information from a dynamic routing traffic. In many cases, static routes are manually configured by a network administrator by adding in entries into a routing table, though this may not always be the case. Unlike dynamic routing, static routes are fixed and do not change if the network is changed or reconfigured. Static routing and dynamic routing are not mutually exclusive. Both dynamic routing and static routing are usually used on a router to maximise routing efficiency and to provide backups in the event that dynamic routing information fails to be exchanged. Static routing can also be used in stub networks, or to provide a gateway of last resort.

Uses

Static routing may have the following uses:

- Static routing can be used to define an exit point from a router when no other routes are available or necessary. This is called a default route.

- Static routing can be used for small networks that require only one or two routes. This is often more efficient since a link is not being wasted by exchanging dynamic routing information.

- Static routing is often used as a complement to dynamic routing to provide a failsafe backup in the event that a dynamic route is unavailable.

- Static routing is often used to help transfer routing information from one routing protocol to another (routing redistribution).

Disadvantages

Static routing can have some potential disadvantages:

- Human error: In many cases, static routes are manually configured. This increases the potential for input mistakes. Administrators can make mistakes and mistype in network information, or configure incorrect routing paths by mistake.

- Fault tolerance: Static routing is not fault tolerant. This means that when there is a change in the network or a failure occurs between two statically defined devices, traffic will not be re-routed. As a result, the network is unusable until the failure is repaired or the static route is manually reconfigured by an administrator.

- Administrative distance: Static routes typically take precedence over routes configured with a dynamic routing protocol. This means that static routes may prevent routing protocols from working as intended. A solution is to manually modify the administrative distance.

- Administrative overhead: Static routes must be configured on each router in the network(s). This configuration can take a long time if there are many routers. It also means that reconfiguration can be slow and inefficient. Dynamic routing on the other hand automatically propagates routing changes, reducing the need for manual reconfiguration.

Example

To route IP traffic destined for the network *10.10.20.0/24* via the next-hop router with the IPv4 address of *192.168.100.1*, the following configuration commands or steps can be used:-

Linux

In most Linux distributions, a static route can be added using the iproute2 command. The following is typed at a terminal:-

```
root@router:~# ip route add 10.10.20.0 via 192.168.100.1
```

Cisco

Enterprise-level Cisco routers are configurable using the Cisco IOS command line, rather than a web management interface.

Add a Static Route

The commands to add a static route are as follows:

Router> enable

Router# configure terminal

Router(config)# ip route 10.10.20.0 255.255.255.0 192.168.100.1

Network configurations are not restricted to a single static route per destination:

Router> enable

Router# configure terminal

Router(config)# ip route 197.164.73.0 255.255.255.0 197.164.72.2

Router(config)# ip route 197.164.74.0 255.255.255.0 197.164.72.2

Add Static Route by Specifying Exit Interface

Static routes can also be added by specifying the exit interface rather than the "next hop" IP address of the router.

Router(config)# ip route 10.10.20.0 255.255.255.0 Serial 0/0/0

Configuring Administrative Distance

The administrative distance can be manually (re)configured so that the static route can be configured as a backup route, to be used only if the dynamic route is unavailable.

Router(config)# ip route 10.10.20.0 255.255.255.0 exampleRoute 1 254

Setting the administrative distance to 254 will result in the route being used only as a backup.

Metrics (Networking)

Router metrics are metrics used by a router to make routing decisions. A *metric* is typically one of many fields in a routing table.

Metrics are used to determine whether one route should be chosen over another. The routing table stores possible routes, while link-state or topological databases may store all other information as well. For example, Routing Information Protocol uses hop-count (number of hops) to determine the best possible route. The route will go in the direction of the gateway with the lowest metric. The direction with the lowest metric can be a default gateway.

Router metrics can contain any number of values that help the router determine the best route among multiple routes to a destination. A router metric typically based on information like path length, bandwidth, load, hop count, path cost, delay, maximum transmission unit (MTU), reliability and communications cost.

Examples

A Metric can include:

- measuring link utilisation (using SNMP)
- number of hops (hop count)
- speed of the path
- packet loss (router congestion/conditions)
- latency (delay)
- path reliability
- path bandwidth
- throughput [SNMP - query routers]
- load
- MTU
- administrator configured value

In EIGRP, metrics is represented by an integer from 0 to 4,294,967,295 (The size of a 32-bit integer). In Microsoft Windows XP routing it ranges from 1 to 9999.

A Metric can be considered as:

- additive - the total cost of a path is the sum of the costs of individual links along the path,
- concave - the total cost of a path is the minimum of the costs of individual links along the path,
- multiplicative - the total cost of a path is the product of the costs of individual links along the path.

Service Level Metrics

Router metrics are metrics used by a router to make routing decisions. It is typically one of many fields in a routing table.

Router metrics can contain any number of values that help the router determine the best route among multiple routes to a destination. A router metric typically based on information like path length, bandwidth, load, hop count, path cost, delay, Maximum Transmission Unit (MTU), reliability and communications cost.

Availability

The availability of a computer network (or an individual service) may be expressed using the notation hh/d/ww. For a 24-hour service, seven days a week, available all year around, this would be expressed 24/7/52 (where the 52 stands for the number of weeks in a year). Service providers usually express that a service will be available for a *percentage* of this time.

To calculate the availability of a service expressed in this format, you need to do the following calculation:

98% availability on 24/7/52

1. Multiply 24 hours per day by 7 days per week by 52 weeks per year = 8736 hours per year

2. Find 98% of the hours per year = 8736 * 98 / 100 = 8561.28 hours guaranteed

You can then deduce how many full hours/days per year the service can be unavailable before the supplier is in breach of their Service Level Agreement. In this example, 8736 (hours) - 8561 (hours) = 175 hours (or around 7.3 days).

References

- Roberts, Lawrence (22 July 2003). "The Next Generation of IP - Flow Routing". Retrieved 22 February 2015.

- But see "Security Considerations Of NAT" (PDF). University of Michigan. Archived from the original (PDF) on October 18, 2014., which argues that NAT is not a security feature.

- Diane Teare (Mar 2013). Implementing Cisco IP Routing (ROUTE): Foundation Learning Guide. Cisco Press. pp. 330–334.

- Diane Teare (Mar 2013). "Chapter 5: Implementing Path Control". Implementing Cisco IP Routing (ROUTE): Foundation Learning Guide. Cisco Press. pp. 330–334.

- "Overview Of Key Routing Protocol Concepts: Architectures, Protocol Types, Algorithms and Metrics". Tcpipguide.com. Retrieved 15 January 2011.

- "Windows Small Business Server 2008: Router Setup". Microsoft Technet Nov 2010. Retrieved 15 January 2011.

Various Network Protocols

Fast local Internet protocol specifies security transparency and security and routing protocols helps in the communication of routers. The various network protocols discussed in this section are fast local Internet protocol, routing protocol, HTTPS, datagram congestion control protocol and point-to-point protocol.

Fast Local Internet Protocol

The Fast Local Internet Protocol (FLIP) is a suite of internet protocols, which provide Security transparency, security and network management. FLIP was designed at the Vrije Universiteit in Amsterdam to support remote procedure calling in the Amoeba distributed operating system. In the OSI model, FLIP occupies layer 3, thus replacing IP, but it also obviates the need for a transport-level protocol like TCP.

FLIP is a connectionless protocol designed to support transparency, group communication, secure communication and easy network management. The following FLIP properties helps to achieve the efficiency requirements:

- FLIP identifies entities called network service access points (NSAPs).

- FLIP uses a one way mapping between the "private" address, used to register an endpoint of a network connection, and the "public" address used to advertise the endpoint.

- FLIP routes messages based on NSAP.

- FLIP uses a bit in the message header to request transmission of sensitive messages across trusted networks.

Routing Protocol

A routing protocol specifies how routers communicate with each other, disseminating information that enables them to select routes between any two nodes on a computer network. Routing algorithms determine the specific choice of route. Each router has a priori knowledge only of networks attached to it directly. A routing protocol shares this information first among immediate neighbors, and then throughout the network. This way, routers gain knowledge of the topology of the network.

Although there are many types of routing protocols, three major classes are in widespread use on IP networks:

- Interior gateway protocols type 1, link-state routing protocols, such as OSPF and IS-IS

- Interior gateway protocols type 2, distance-vector routing protocols, such as Routing Information Protocol, RIPv2, IGRP.

- Exterior gateway protocols are routing protocols used on the Internet for exchanging routing information between Autonomous Systems, such as Border Gateway Protocol (BGP), Path Vector Routing Protocol.

Exterior gateway protocols should not be confused with Exterior Gateway Protocol (EGP), an obsolete routing protocol.

Many routing protocols are defined in documents called RFCs.

Some versions of the Open System Interconnection (OSI) networking model distinguish routing protocols in a special sublayer of the Network Layer (Layer 3).

The specific characteristics of routing protocols include the manner in which they avoid routing loops, the manner in which they select preferred routes, using information about hop costs, the time they require to reach routing convergence, their scalability, and other factors.

OSI Layer Designation

Routing protocols, according to the OSI routing framework, are layer management protocols for the network layer, regardless of their transport mechanism:

- IS-IS runs on the data link layer (Layer 2)

- Open Shortest Path First (OSPF) is encapsulated in IP, but runs only on the IPv4 subnet, while the IPv6 version runs on the link using only link-local addressing.

- IGRP, and EIGRP are directly encapsulated in IP. EIGRP uses its own reliable transmission mechanism, while IGRP assumed an unreliable transport.

- RIP runs over UDP

- BGP runs over TCP

Interior Gateway Protocols

Interior gateway protocols (IGPs) exchange routing information within a single routing domain. Examples of IGPs include:

- Open Shortest Path First (OSPF)

- Routing Information Protocol (RIP)

- Intermediate System to Intermediate System (IS-IS)

- Enhanced Interior Gateway Routing Protocol (EIGRP)

Exterior Gateway Protocols

Exterior gateway protocols exchange routing information between autonomous systems. Examples include:

- Exterior Gateway Protocol (EGP)

- Border Gateway Protocol (BGP)

Routing Software

Many software implementations exist for most of the common routing protocols. Examples of open-source applications are Bird Internet routing daemon, Quagga, GNU Zebra, OpenBGPD, OpenOSPFD, and XORP.

Routed Protocols

Some network certification courses distinguish between routing protocols and *routed* protocols. A routed protocol is used to deliver application traffic. It provides appropriate addressing information in its Internet Layer (Network Layer) addressing to allow a packet to be forwarded from one network to another.

Examples of routed protocols are the Internet Protocol (IP) and Internetwork Packet Exchange (IPX).

HTTPS

HTTPS (also called HTTP over TLS, HTTP over SSL, and HTTP Secure) is a protocol for secure communication over a computer network which is widely used on the Internet. HTTPS consists of communication over Hypertext Transfer Protocol (HTTP) within a connection encrypted by Transport Layer Security or its predecessor, Secure Sockets Layer. The main motivation for HTTPS is authentication of the visited website and protection of the privacy and integrity of the exchanged data.

In its popular deployment on the internet, HTTPS provides authentication of the website and associated web server with which one is communicating, which protects against man-in-the-middle attacks. Additionally, it provides bidirectional encryption of communications between a client and server, which protects against eavesdropping and tampering with or forging the contents of the communication. In practice, this provides a reasonable guarantee that one is communicating with precisely the website that one intended to communicate with (as opposed to an impostor), as well as ensuring that the contents of communications between the user and site cannot be read or forged by any third party.

Historically, HTTPS connections were primarily used for payment transactions on the World Wide Web, e-mail and for sensitive transactions in corporate information systems. In the late 2000s and early 2010s, HTTPS began to see widespread use for protecting page authenticity on all types of websites, securing accounts and keeping user communications, identity and web browsing private.

Overview

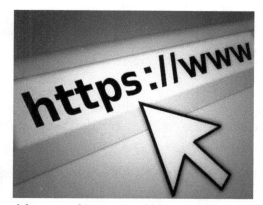

Logo of the networking protocol https and the www letters

The *HTTPS* uniform resource identifier (URI) scheme has identical syntax to the standard HTTP scheme, aside from its scheme token. However, HTTPS signals the browser to use an added encryption layer of SSL/TLS to protect the traffic. SSL/TLS is especially suited for HTTP, since it can provide some protection even if only one side of the communication is authenticated. This is the case with HTTP transactions over the Internet, where typically only the server is authenticated (by the client examining the server's certificate).

HTTPS creates a secure channel over an insecure network. This ensures reasonable protection from eavesdroppers and man-in-the-middle attacks, provided that adequate cipher suites are used and that the server certificate is verified and trusted.

Because HTTPS piggybacks HTTP entirely on top of TLS, the entirety of the underlying HTTP protocol can be encrypted. This includes the request URL (which particular web page was requested), query parameters, headers, and cookies (which often contain identity information about the user). However, because host (website) addresses and port numbers are necessarily part of the underlying TCP/IP protocols, HTTPS cannot protect their disclosure. In practice this means that even on a correctly configured web server, eavesdroppers can infer the IP address and port number of the web server (sometimes even the domain name e.g. www.example.org, but not the rest of the URL) that one is communicating with, as well as the amount (data transferred) and duration (length of session) of the communication, though not the content of the communication.

Web browsers know how to trust HTTPS websites based on certificate authorities that come pre-installed in their software. Certificate authorities (such as Symantec, Comodo, GoDaddy and GlobalSign) are in this way being trusted by web browser creators to provide valid certificates. Therefore, a user should trust an HTTPS connection to a website if and only if all of the following are true:

- The user trusts that the browser software correctly implements HTTPS with correctly pre-installed certificate authorities.

- The user trusts the certificate authority to vouch only for legitimate websites.

- The website provides a valid certificate, which means it was signed by a trusted authority.

- The certificate correctly identifies the website (e.g., when the browser visits "https://example.com", the received certificate is properly for "example.com" and not some other entity).

- The user trusts that the protocol's encryption layer (SSL/TLS) is sufficiently secure against eavesdroppers.

HTTPS is especially important over insecure networks (such as public Wi-Fi access points), as anyone on the same local network can packet-sniff and discover sensitive information not protected by HTTPS. Additionally, many free to use and even paid for WLAN networks engage in packet injection in order to serve their own ads on webpages. However, this can be exploited maliciously in many ways, such as injecting malware onto webpages and stealing users' private information.

HTTPS is also very important for connections over the Tor anonymity network, as malicious Tor nodes can damage or alter the contents passing through them in an insecure fashion and inject malware into the connection. This is one reason why the Electronic Frontier Foundation and the Tor project started the development of HTTPS Everywhere, which is included in the Tor Browser Bundle.

As more information is revealed about global mass surveillance and criminals stealing personal information, the use of HTTPS security on all websites is becoming increasingly important regardless of the type of Internet connection being used. While meta-data about individual pages that a user visits is not sensitive, when combined together, they can reveal a lot about the user and compromise the user's privacy.

Deploying HTTPS also allows the use of HTTP/2 (or its predecessor, the now-depre-cated protocol SPDY), that are new generations of HTTP, designed to reduce page load times and latency.

It is recommended to use HTTP Strict Transport Security (HSTS) with HTTPS to pro-tect users from man-in-the-middle attacks, especially SSL stripping.

HTTPS should not be confused with the little-used Secure HTTP (S-HTTP) specified in RFC 2660.

Usage in Websites

As of June 2016, 10.2% of Alexa top 1,000,000 websites use HTTPS as default, 43.1% of the Internet's 141,387 most popular websites have a secure implementation of HTTPS, and 45% of page loads (measured by Firefox Telemetry) use HTTPS.

Browser Integration

Most browsers display a warning if they receive an invalid certificate. Older brows-ers, when connecting to a site with an invalid certificate, would present the user with a dialog box asking whether they wanted to continue. Newer browsers display a warning across the entire window. Newer browsers also prominently display the site's security information in the address bar. Extended validation certificates turn the address bar green in newer browsers. Most browsers also display a warning to the user when visiting a site that contains a mixture of encrypted and unencrypted content.

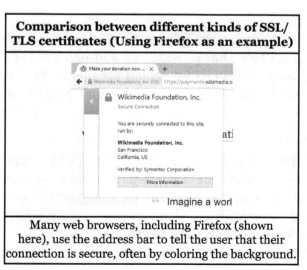

Many web browsers, including Firefox (shown here), use the address bar to tell the user that their connection is secure, often by coloring the background.

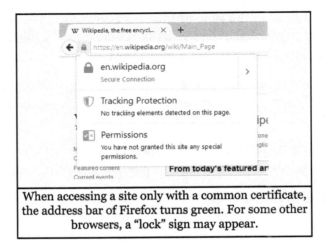

When accessing a site only with a common certificate, the address bar of Firefox turns green. For some other browsers, a "lock" sign may appear.

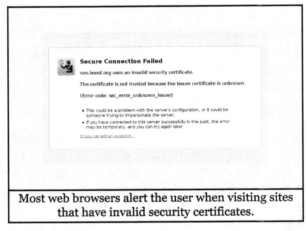

Most web browsers alert the user when visiting sites that have invalid security certificates.

Firefox uses HTTPS for Google searches as of version 14, to "shield our users from network infrastructure that may be gathering data about the users or modifying/censoring their search results".

The Electronic Frontier Foundation, opining that "In an ideal world, every web request could be defaulted to HTTPS", has provided an add-on called HTTPS Everywhere for Mozilla Firefox that enables HTTPS by default for hundreds of frequently used websites. A beta version of this plugin is also available for Google Chrome and Chromium.

Security

The security of HTTPS is that of the underlying TLS, which typically uses long-term public and private keys to generate a short-term session key, which is then used to encrypt the data flow between client and server. X.509 certificates are used to authenticate the server (and sometimes the client as well). As a consequence, certificate authorities and public key certificates are necessary to verify the relation between the certificate and its owner, as well as to generate, sign, and administer the validity of certificates. While this can be more beneficial than verifying the identities via a web of trust, the 2013 mass surveillance disclosures drew attention to certificate authorities as a potential weak point allowing man-in-the-middle attacks. An important property in this context is forward secrecy, which ensures that encrypted communications recorded in the past cannot be retrieved and decrypted should long-term secret keys or passwords be compromised in the future. Not all web servers provide forward secrecy.

A site must be completely hosted over HTTPS, without having part of its contents loaded over HTTP – for example, having scripts loaded insecurely – or the user will be vulnerable to some attacks and surveillance. Also having only a certain page that contains sensitive information (such as a log-in page) of a website loaded over HTTPS, while having the rest of the website loaded over plain HTTP, will expose the user to attacks. On a site that has sensitive information somewhere on it, every time that site is accessed with HTTP instead of HTTPS, the user and the session will get exposed. Similarly, cookies on a site served through HTTPS have to have the secure attribute enabled.

Technical

Difference from HTTP

HTTPS URLs begin with "https://" and use port 443 by default, whereas HTTP URLs begin with "http://" and use port 80 by default.

HTTP is not encrypted and is vulnerable to man-in-the-middle and eavesdropping attacks, which can let attackers gain access to website accounts and sensitive information, and modify webpages to inject malware or advertisements. HTTPS is designed to withstand such attacks and is considered secure against them (with the exception of older, deprecated versions of SSL).

Network Layers

HTTP operates at the highest layer of the TCP/IP model, the Application layer; as does the TLS security protocol (operating as a lower sublayer of the same layer), which encrypts an HTTP message prior to transmission and decrypts a message upon arrival. Strictly speaking, HTTPS is not a separate protocol, but refers to use of ordinary HTTP over an encrypted SSL/TLS connection.

Everything in the HTTPS message is encrypted, including the headers, and the request/response load. With the exception of the possible CCA cryptographic attack described in the limitations section below, the attacker can only know that a connection is taking place between the two parties and their domain names and IP addresses.

Server Setup

To prepare a web server to accept HTTPS connections, the administrator must create a public key certificate for the web server. This certificate must be signed by a trusted certificate authority for the web browser to accept it without warning. The authority certifies that the certificate holder is the operator of the web server that presents it. Web browsers are generally distributed with a list of signing certificates of major certificate authorities so that they can verify certificates signed by them.

Acquiring Certificates

Authoritatively signed certificates may be free or cost between 8 USD and 70 USD per year (in 2012–2014).

Organizations may also run their own certificate authority, particularly if they are responsible for setting up browsers to access their own sites (for example, sites on a company intranet, or major universities). They can easily add copies of their own signing certificate to the trusted certificates distributed with the browser.

There also exists a peer-to-peer certificate authority, CACert. However, it is not included in the trusted root certificates of many popular browsers (e.g. Firefox, Chrome, Internet Explorer), which may cause warning messages to be displayed to end users.

Let's Encrypt, launched in April 2016, provides free and automated SSL/TLS certificates to websites. According to the Electronic Frontier Foundation, "Let's Encrypt" will make switching from HTTP to HTTPS "as easy as issuing one command, or clicking one button."

Use as Access Control

The system can also be used for client authentication in order to limit access to a web server to authorized users. To do this, the site administrator typically creates a certificate for each user, a certificate that is loaded into their browser. Normally, that contains the name and e-mail address of the authorized user and is automatically checked by the server on each reconnect to verify the user's identity, potentially without even entering a password.

In Case of Compromised Secret (Private) Key

An important property in this context is perfect forward secrecy (PFS). Possessing one of the long-term asymmetric secret keys used to establish an HTTPS session should not make it easier to derive the short-term session key to then decrypt the conversation, even at a later time. Diffie–Hellman key exchange (DHE) and Elliptic curve Diffie–Hellman key exchange (ECDHE) are in 2013 the only ones known to have that property. Only 30% of Firefox, Opera, and Chromium Browser sessions use it, and nearly 0% of Apple's Safari and Microsoft Internet Explorer sessions. Among the larger internet providers, only Google supports PFS since 2011 (State of September 2013).

A certificate may be revoked before it expires, for example because the secrecy of the private key has been compromised. Newer versions of popular browsers such as Firefox, Opera, and Internet Explorer on Windows Vista implement the Online Certificate Status Protocol (OCSP) to verify that this is not the case. The browser sends the certificate's serial number to the certificate authority or its delegate via OCSP and the authority responds, telling the browser whether or not the certificate is still valid.

Limitations

SSL/TLS comes in two options, simple and mutual. The mutual version is more secure, but requires the user to install a personal client certificate into their web browser in order to authenticate themselves.

Whether the strategy is simple or mutual, the level of protection strongly depends on the correctness of the implementation of the web browser and the server software and the actual cryptographic algorithms supported.

SSL/TLS does not prevent the entire site from being indexed using a web crawler, and in some cases the URI of the encrypted resource can be inferred by knowing only the intercepted request/response size. This allows an attacker to have access to the plaintext (the publicly available static content), and the encrypted text (the encrypted version of the static content), permitting a cryptographic attack.

Because TLS operates below HTTP and has no knowledge of higher-level protocols, TLS servers can only strictly present one certificate for a particular IP/port combination. This means that, in most cases, it is not feasible to use name-based virtual hosting with HTTPS. A solution called Server Name Indication (SNI) exists, which sends the hostname to the server before encrypting the connection, although many older browsers do not support this extension. Support for SNI is available since Firefox 2, Opera 8, Safari 2.1, Google Chrome 6, and Internet Explorer 7 on Windows Vista.

From an architectural point of view:

1. An SSL/TLS connection is managed by the first front machine that initiates the TLS connection. If, for any reasons (routing, traffic optimization, etc.), this front machine is not the application server and it has to decipher data, solutions have to be found to propagate user authentication information or certificate to the application server, which needs to know who is going to be connected.

2. For SSL/TLS with mutual authentication, the SSL/TLS session is managed by the first server that initiates the connection. In situations where encryption has to be propagated along chained servers, session timeOut management becomes extremely tricky to implement.

3. With mutual SSL/TLS, security is maximal, but on the client-side, there is no

way to properly end the SSL/TLS connection and disconnect the user except by waiting for the server session to expire or closing all related client applications.

A sophisticated type of man-in-the-middle attack called SSL stripping was presented at the Blackhat Conference 2009. This type of attack defeats the security provided by HTTPS by changing the https: link into an http: link, taking advantage of the fact that few Internet users actually type "https" into their browser interface: they get to a secure site by clicking on a link, and thus are fooled into thinking that they are using HTTPS when in fact they are using HTTP. The attacker then communicates in clear with the client. This prompted the development of a countermeasure in HTTP called HTTP Strict Transport Security.

HTTPS has been shown vulnerable to a range of traffic analysis attacks. Traffic analysis attacks are a type of side-channel attack that relies on variations in the timing and size of traffic in order to infer properties about the encrypted traffic itself. Traffic analysis is possible because SSL/TLS encryption changes the contents of traffic, but has minimal impact on the size and timing of traffic. In May 2010, a research paper by researchers from Microsoft Research and Indiana University discovered that detailed sensitive user data can be inferred from side channels such as packet sizes. More specifically, the researchers found that an eavesdropper can infer the illnesses/medications/surgeries of the user, his/her family income and investment secrets, despite HTTPS protection in several high-profile, top-of-the-line web applications in healthcare, taxation, investment and web search. Although this work demonstrated vulnerability of HTTPS to traffic analysis, the approach presented by the authors required manual analysis and focused specifically on web applications protected by HTTPS.

In June 2014, a team of researchers at UC Berkeley and Intel led by Brad Miller demonstrated a generalized approach to HTTPS traffic analysis based on machine learning. The researchers demonstrated that the attack applied to a range of websites, including Mayo Clinic, Planned Parenthood and Youtube. The attack assumes that the attacker is able to visit the same webpages as the victim to gather network traffic which serves as training data. The attacker is then able to identify similarities in the packet sizes and orderings between the victim traffic and the training data traffic which frequently allow the attacker to infer the exact page the victim is visiting. For example, this attack could be used to determine whether a user browsing the Planned Parenthood website is looking for information about preventative health screening or an abortion. Note that the attack can not be used to discover user specific values embedded in a webpage. For example, many banks offer web interfaces which allow users to view account balances. While the attacker would be able to discover that the user was viewing an account balance page, they would be unable to learn the user's exact account balance or account number.

History

Netscape Communications created HTTPS in 1994 for its Netscape Navigator web browser. Originally, HTTPS was used with the SSL protocol. As SSL evolved into Transport Layer Security (TLS), the current version of HTTPS was formally specified by RFC 2818 in May 2000.

Datagram Congestion Control Protocol

The Datagram Congestion Control Protocol (DCCP) is a message-oriented transport layer protocol. DCCP implements reliable connection setup, teardown, Explicit Congestion Notification (ECN), congestion control, and feature negotiation. DCCP was published as RFC 4340, a proposed standard, by the IETF in March, 2006. RFC 4336 provides an introduction.

DCCP provides a way to gain access to congestion control mechanisms without having to implement them at the application layer. It allows for flow-based semantics like in Transmission Control Protocol (TCP), but does not provide reliable in-order delivery. Sequenced delivery within multiple streams as in the Stream Control Transmission Protocol (SCTP) is not available in DCCP.

DCCP is useful for applications with timing constraints on the delivery of data. Such applications include streaming media, multiplayer online games and Internet telephony. The primary feature of these applications is that old messages quickly become stale so that getting new messages is preferred to resending lost messages. Currently such applications have often either settled for TCP or used User Datagram Protocol (UDP) and implemented their own congestion control mechanisms, or have no congestion control at all.

While being useful for these applications, DCCP can also be positioned as a general congestion control mechanism for UDP-based applications, by adding, as needed, a mechanism for reliable and/or in-order delivery on the top of UDP/DCCP. In this context, DCCP allows the use of different, but generally TCP-friendly congestion control mechanisms.

A DCCP connection contains acknowledgment traffic as well as data traffic. Acknowledgments inform a sender whether its packets have arrived, and whether they were marked by Explicit Congestion Notification (ECN). Acknowledgements are transmitted as reliably as the congestion control mechanism in use requires, possibly completely reliably.

DCCP has the option for very long (48-bit) sequence numbers corresponding to a packet ID, rather than a byte ID as in TCP. The long length of the sequence numbers is intended to guard against *some blind attacks, such as the injection of DCCP-Resets into the connection.*

Implementations

The following operating systems implement DCCP:

- FreeBSD, version 5.1 as patch

- Linux since version 2.6.14

Userspace library:

- DCCP-TP implementation is optimized for portability, but has had no changes since June 2008.

- GoDCCP purpose of this implementation is to provide a standardized, portable NAT-friendly framework for peer-to-peer communications with flexible congestion control, depending on application.

Packet Structure

The DCCP generic header takes different forms depending on the value of X, the Extended Sequence Numbers bit. If X is one, the Sequence Number field is 48 bits long, and the generic header takes 16 bytes, as follows.

If X is zero, only the low 24 bits of the Sequence Number are transmitted, and the generic header is 12 bytes long.

Source port (16 bits)

Identifies the sending port

Destination port (16 bits)

Identifies the receiving port

Data Offset

(8 bits): The offset from the start of the packet's DCCP header to the start of its application data area, in 32-bit words.

CCVal (4 bits)

Used by the HC-Sender CCID

Checksum Coverage (CsCov) (4 bits)

Checksum Coverage determines the parts of the packet that are covered by the Checksum field.

Checksum (16 bits)

The Internet checksum of the packet's DCCP header (including options), a network-layer pseudoheader, and, depending on Checksum Coverage, all, some, or none of the application data

Reserved (Res) (3 bits)

Senders MUST set this field to all zeroes on generated packets, and receivers MUST ignore its value

Type (4 bits)

The Type field specifies the type of the packet

Extended Sequence Numbers (X) (1 bit)

Set to one to indicate the use of an extended generic header with 48-bit Sequence and Acknowledgement Numbers

Sequence Number (48 or 24 bits)

Identifies the packet uniquely in the sequence of all packets the source sent on this connection

Point-to-Point Protocol

In computer networking, Point-to-Point Protocol (PPP) is a data link (layer 2) protocol used to establish a direct connection between two nodes. It can provide connection authentication, transmission encryption (using ECP, RFC 1968), and compression.

PPP is used over many types of physical networks including serial cable, phone line, trunk line, cellular telephone, specialized radio links, and fiber optic links such as SONET. PPP is also used over Internet access connections. Internet service providers (ISPs) have used PPP for customer dial-up access to the Internet, since IP packets cannot be transmitted over a modem line on their own, without some data link protocol.

Two derivatives of PPP, Point-to-Point Protocol over Ethernet (PPPoE) and Point-to-Point Protocol over ATM (PPPoA), are used most commonly by Internet Service Providers (ISPs) to establish a Digital Subscriber Line (DSL) Internet service connection with customers.

PPP is commonly used as a data link layer protocol for connection over synchronous and asynchronous circuits, where it has largely superseded the older Serial Line Internet Protocol (SLIP) and telephone company mandated standards (such as Link Access Protocol, Balanced (LAPB) in the X.25 protocol suite). The only requirement for PPP is that the circuit provided be duplex. PPP was designed to work with numerous network layer protocols, including Internet Protocol (IP), TRILL, Novell's Internetwork Packet Exchange (IPX), NBF, DECnet and AppleTalk.

Description

PPP was designed somewhat after the original HDLC specifications. The designers of PPP included many additional features that had been seen only in proprietary data-link protocols up to that time.

RFC 2516 describes Point-to-Point Protocol over Ethernet (PPPoE) as a method for transmitting PPP over Ethernet that is sometimes used with DSL. RFC 2364 describes Point-to-Point Protocol over ATM (PPPoA) as a method for transmitting PPP over ATM Adaptation Layer 5 (AAL5), which is also a common alternative to PPPoE used with DSL.

PPP is a layered protocol that has three components:

- An encapsulation component that is used to transmit datagrams over the specified physical layer.

- A Link Control Protocol (LCP) to establish, configure, and test the link as well as negotiate capabilities.

- One or more Network Control Protocols (NCP) used to negotiate optional configuration parameters and facilities for the network layer. There is one NCP for each higher-layer protocol supported by PPP.

PPP is specified in RFC 1661.

Automatic Self Configuration

Link Control Protocol (LCP) initiates and terminates connections gracefully, allowing hosts to negotiate connection options. It is an integral part of PPP, and is defined in the same standard specification. LCP provides automatic configuration of the interfaces at each end (such as setting datagram size, escaped characters, and magic numbers) and for selecting optional authentication. The LCP protocol runs on top of PPP (with PPP protocol number 0xC021) and therefore a basic PPP connection has to be established before LCP is able to configure it.

RFC 1994 describes Challenge-handshake authentication protocol (CHAP), which is preferred for establishing dial-up connections with ISPs. Although deprecated, Password authentication protocol (PAP) is still sometimes used.

Another option for authentication over PPP is Extensible Authentication Protocol (EAP) described in RFC 2284.

After the link has been established, additional network (layer 3) configuration may take place. Most commonly, the Internet Protocol Control Protocol (IPCP) is used, although Internetwork Packet Exchange Control Protocol (IPXCP) and AppleTalk Control Protocol (ATCP) were once very popular.Internet Protocol Version 6 Control Protocol (IPv6CP) will see extended use in the future, when IPv6 replaces IPv4 as the dominant layer-3 protocol.

Multiple Network Layer Protocols

PPP architecture			
			IP
LCP	CHAP PAP EAP	IPCP	
PPP encapsulation			
HDLC-like Framing		PPPoE	PPPoA
	POS		
RS-232	SONET/SDH	Ethernet	ATM

PPP permits multiple network layer protocols to operate on the same communication link. For every network layer protocol used, a separate Network Control Protocol (NCP) is provided in order to encapsulate and negotiate options for the multiple network layer protocols. It negotiates network-layer information, e.g. network address or compression options, after the connection has been established.

For example, Internet Protocol (IP) uses the IP Control Protocol (IPCP), and Internetwork Packet Exchange (IPX) uses the Novell IPX Control Protocol (IPX/SPX). NCPs include fields containing standardized codes to indicate the network layer protocol type that the PPP connection encapsulates.

The following NCPs may be used with PPP:

- the Internet Protocol Control Protocol (IPCP) for the Internet Protocol, protocol code number 0x8021, RFC 1332

- the OSI Network Layer Control Protocol (OSINLCP) for the various OSI network layer protocols, protocol code number 0x8023, RFC 1377

- the AppleTalk Control Protocol (ATCP) for AppleTalk, protocol code number 0x8029, RFC 1378

- the Internetwork Packet Exchange Control Protocol (IPXCP) for the Internet Packet Exchange, protocol code number 0x802B, RFC 1552

- the DECnet Phase IV Control Protocol (DNCP) for DNA Phase IV Routing protocol (DECnet Phase IV), protocol code number 0x8027, RFC 1762

- the NetBIOS Frames Control Protocol (NBFCP) for NetBIOS Frames protocol (or NetBEUI as it was called before that), protocol code number 0x803F, RFC 2097

- the IPv6 Control Protocol (IPV6CP) for IPv6, protocol code number 0x8057, RFC 5072

Looped Link Detection

PPP detects looped links using a feature involving magic numbers. When the node sends PPP LCP messages, these messages may include a magic number. If a line is looped, the node receives an LCP message with its own magic number, instead of getting a message with the peer's magic number.

PPP Configuration Options

The previous section introduced the use of LCP options to meet specific WAN connection requirements. PPP may include the following LCP options:

- Authentication - Peer routers exchange authentication messages. Two authentication choices are Password Authentication Protocol (PAP) and Challenge Handshake Authentication Protocol (CHAP). Authentication is explained in the next section.

- Compression - Increases the effective throughput on PPP connections by reducing the amount of data in the frame that must travel across the link. The protocol decompresses the frame at its destination.

- Error detection - Identifies fault conditions. The Quality and Magic Number options help ensure a reliable, loop-free data link. The Magic Number field helps in detecting links that are in a looped-back condition. Until the Magic-Number Configuration Option has been successfully negotiated, the Magic-Number must be transmitted as zero. Magic numbers are generated randomly at each end of the connection.

- Multilink - Provides load balancing several interfaces used by PPP through Multilink PPP.

PPP Frame

Structure of a PPP Frame

PPP frames are variants of HDLC frames:

Name	Number of bytes	Description
Flag	1	0x7E, the beginning of a PPP frame
Address	1	0xFF, standard broadcast address
Control	1	0x03, unnumbered data

Protocol	2	PPP ID of embedded data
Information	variable (0 or more)	datagram
Padding	variable (0 or more)	optional padding
Frame Check Sequence	2	frame checksum
Flag	1	0x7E, omitted for successive PPP packets

If both peers agree to Address field and Control field compression during LCP, then those fields are omitted. Likewise if both peers agree to Protocol field compression, then the 0x00 byte can be omitted.

The Protocol field indicates the type of payload packet: 0xC021 for LCP, 0x80xy for various NCPs, 0x0021 for IP, 0x0029 AppleTalk, 0x002B for IPX, 0x003D for Multilink, 0x003F for NetBIOS, 0x00FD for MPPC and MPPE, etc. PPP is limited, and cannot contain general Layer 3 data, unlike EtherType.

The Information field contains the PPP payload; it has a variable length with a negotiated maximum called the Maximum Transmission Unit. By default, the maximum is 1500 octets. It might be padded on transmission; if the information for a particular protocol can be padded, that protocol must allow information to be distinguished from padding.

Encapsulation

PPP frames are encapsulated in a lower-layer protocol that provides framing and may provide other functions such as a checksum to detect transmission errors. PPP on serial links is usually encapsulated in a framing similar to HDLC, described by IETF RFC 1662.

Name	Number of bytes	Description
Flag	1	indicates frame's begin or end
Address	1	broadcast address
Control	1	control byte
Protocol	1 or 2 or 3	l in information field
Information	variable (0 or more)	datagram
Padding	variable (0 or more)	optional padding
FCS	2 (or 4)	error check

The Flag field is present when PPP with HDLC-like framing is used.

The Address and Control fields always have the value hex FF (for "all stations") and hex 03 (for "unnumbered information"), and can be omitted whenever PPP LCP Address-and-Control-Field-Compression (ACFC) is negotiated.

The frame check sequence (FCS) field is used for determining whether an individual frame has an error. It contains a checksum computed over the frame to provide basic protection against errors in transmission. This is a CRC code similar to the one used for other layer two protocol error protection schemes such as the one used in Ethernet. According to RFC 1662, it can be either 16 bits (2 bytes) or 32 bits (4 bytes) in size (default is 16 bits - Polynomial $x^{16} + x^{12} + x^5 + 1$).

The FCS is calculated over the Address, Control, Protocol, Information and Padding fields after the message has been encapsulated.

PPP Line Activation and Phases

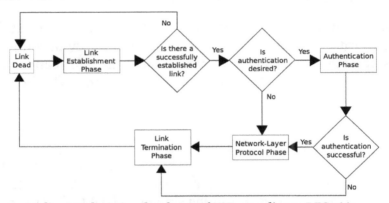

A diagram depicting the phases of PPP according to RFC 1661.

The phases of the Point to Point Protocol according to RFC 1661 are listed below:

Link Dead

> This phase occurs when the link fails, or one side has been told to disconnect (e.g. a user has finished his or her dialup connection.)

Link Establishment Phase

> This phase is where Link Control Protocol negotiation is attempted. If successful, control goes either to the authentication phase or the Network-Layer Protocol phase, depending on whether authentication is desired.

Authentication Phase

> This phase is optional. It allows the sides to authenticate each other before a connection is established. If successful, control goes to the network-layer protocol phase.

Network-Layer Protocol Phase

> This phase is where each desired protocols' Network Control Protocols are invoked. For example, IPCP is used in establishing IP service over the line. Data transport for all protocols which are successfully started with their network control protocols also occurs in this phase. Closing down of network protocols also occur in this phase.

Link Termination Phase

> This phase closes down this connection. This can happen if there is an authentication failure, if there are so many checksum errors that the two parties decide to tear down the link automatically, if the link suddenly fails, or if the user decides to hang up a connection.

PPP Over Several Links

Multilink PPP

Multilink PPP (also referred to as MLPPP, MP, MPPP, MLP, or Multilink) provides a method for spreading traffic across multiple distinct PPP connections. It is defined in RFC 1990. It can be used, for example, to connect a home computer to an Internet Service Provider using two traditional 56k modems, or to connect a company through two leased lines.

On a single PPP line frames cannot arrive out of order, but this is possible when the frames are divided among multiple PPP connections. Therefore, Multilink PPP must number the fragments so they can be put in the right order again when they arrive.

Multilink PPP is an example of a link aggregation technology. Cisco IOS Release 11.1 and later supports Multilink PPP.

Multiclass PPP

With PPP, one cannot establish several simultaneous distinct PPP connections over a single link.

That's not possible with Multilink PPP either. Multilink PPP uses contiguous numbers for all the fragments of a packet, and as a consequence it is not possible to suspend the sending of a sequence of fragments of one packet in order to send another packet. This prevents from running Multilink PPP multiple times on the same links.

Multiclass PPP is a kind of Multilink PPP where each "class" of traffic uses a separate sequence number space and reassembly buffer. Multiclass PPP is defined in RFC 2686.

PPP and Tunnels

Simplified OSI protocol stack for an example SSH+PPP tunnel						
Application	FTP	SMTP	HTTP	...	DNS	...
Transport	TCP				UDP	
Network	IP					
Data Link	PPP					
Application	SSH					
Transport	TCP					
Network	IP					
Data Link	Ethernet				ATM	
Physical	Cables, Hubs, and so on					

Derived Protocols

PPTP (Point-to-Point Tunneling Protocol) is a form of PPP between two hosts via GRE using encryption (MPPE) and compression (MPPC).

PPP as a Layer 2 Protocol Between Both Ends of a Tunnel

Many protocols can be used to tunnel data over IP networks. Some of them, like SSL, SSH, or L2TP create virtual network interfaces and give the impression of a direct physical connections between the tunnel endpoints. On a Linux host for example, these interfaces would be called tun0.

As there are only two endpoints on a tunnel, the tunnel is a point-to-point connection and PPP is a natural choice as a data link layer protocol between the virtual network interfaces. PPP can assign IP addresses to these virtual interfaces, and these IP addresses can be used, for example, to route between the networks on both sides of the tunnel.

IPsec in tunneling mode does not create virtual physical interfaces at the end of the tunnel, since the tunnel is handled directly by the TCP/IP stack. L2TP can be used to provide these interfaces, this technique is called L2TP/IPsec. In this case too, PPP provides IP addresses to the extremities of the tunnel.

References

- Aas, Josh (22 June 2016). "Progress Towards 100% HTTPS, June 2016". Lets Encrypt. Retrieved 23 July 2016.

- Catalin Cimpanu. "Let's Encrypt Launched Today, Currently Protects 3.8 Million Domains". Softpedia News. Retrieved April 12, 2016.

- "Manage client certificates on Chrome devices - Chrome for business and education Help". support.google.com. Retrieved 2016-10-13.

- Kerner, Sean Michael (November 18, 2014). "Let's Encrypt Effort Aims to Improve Internet Security". eWeek.com. Quinstreet Enterprise. Retrieved February 27, 2015.

- Eckersley, Peter (November 18, 2014). "Launching in 2015: A Certificate Authority to Encrypt the Entire Web". Electronic Frontier Foundation. Retrieved February 27, 2015.

- Konigsburg, Eitan; Pant, Rajiv; Kvochko, Elena (November 13, 2014). "Embracing HTTPS". The New York Times. Retrieved February 27, 2015.

- Gallagher, Kevin (September 12, 2014). "Fifteen Months After the NSA Revelations, Why Aren't More News Organizations Using HTTPS?". Freedom of the Press Foundation. Retrieved February 27, 2015.

- Grigorik, Ilya; Far, Pierre (June 26, 2014). "Google I/O 2014 - HTTPS Everywhere". Google Developers. Retrieved February 27, 2015.

- Network Working Group (May 2000). "HTTP Over TLS". The Internet Engineering Task Force. Retrieved February 27, 2015.

- "Statistical Tricks Extract Sensitive Data from Encrypted Communications". MIT Technology Review. 2014-06-19.

Essential Aspects of Computer Networks

Network sockets are endpoints that connect computer networks whereas encapsulation is a process of designing modular communications. Other aspects of computer networking are circuit switching and routing. The following chapter unfolds its crucial aspects in a critical yet systematic manner.

Encapsulation (Networking)

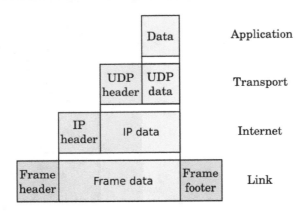

Encapsulation of user data in the Unix-style UDP stack, in which each new layer includes the data from the previous layer, but without being able to identify which part of the data is the header or trailer from the previous layer. This effectively hides (encapsulates) the information from lower layers.

In computer networking, encapsulation is a method of designing modular communication protocols in which logically separate functions in the network are abstracted from their underlying structures by inclusion or information hiding within higher level objects.

The physical layer is responsible for physical transmission of the data. Link encapsulation allows local area networking and Internet Protocol (IP) provides global addressing of individual computers; Transmission Control Protocol (TCP) adds application or process selection, i.e., the port specifies the service such as a Web or TFTP server.

During encapsulation, each layer builds a protocol data unit (PDU) by adding a header (and sometimes trailer) containing control information to the PDU from the layer above. For example, in the Internet protocol suite, the contents of a web page are encapsulated with an HTTP header, then by a TCP header, an IP header, and, finally, by a frame header and trailer. The frame is forwarded to the destination node as a stream of bits, where it is decapsulated (or de-encapsulated) into the respective PDUs and interpreted at each layer by the receiving node.

The result of encapsulation is that each lower layer provides a service to the layer or layers above it, while at the same time each layer communicates with its corresponding layer on the receiving node. These are known as adjacent-layer interaction and same-layer interaction, respectively.

In discussions of encapsulation, the more abstract layer is often called the upper layer protocol while the more specific layer is called the lower layer protocol. Sometimes, however, the terms upper layer protocols and lower layer protocols are used to describe the layers above and below IP, respectively.

Encapsulation is a characteristic feature of most networking models, including both the OSI model and TCP/IP suite of protocols.

Network Socket

A network socket is an endpoint of a connection in a computer network. In Internet Protocol (IP) networks, these are often called Internet sockets. It is handle (abstract reference) that a program can pass to the networking application programming interface (API) to use the connection for receiving and sending data. Sockets are often represented internally as integers.

A socket API is an application programming interface, usually provided by the operating system, that allows application programs to control and use network sockets. Internet socket APIs are usually based on the Berkeley sockets standard. In the Berkeley sockets standard, sockets are a form of file descriptor (a *file* handle), due to the Unix philosophy that "everything is a file", and the analogies between sockets and files. Both have functions to read, write, open, and close. In practice the differences mean the analogy is strained, and one instead uses different interfaces (send and receive) on a socket. In inter-process communication, each end generally has its own socket, but these may use different APIs: they are abstracted by the network protocol.

A socket address is the combination of an IP address and a port number, much like one end of a telephone connection is the combination of a phone number and a particular extension. Sockets need not have an address, for example, for only sending data, but if a program *binds* a socket to an address, the socket can be used to receive data sent to that address. Based on this address, Internet sockets deliver incoming data packets to the appropriate application process or thread.

Definition

An Internet socket is characterized by at least the following:

- local socket address, consisting of the local IP address and a port number

- protocol: A transport protocol, e.g., TCP, UDP, raw IP. This means that TCP port 53 and UDP port 53 are distinct sockets.

A socket that has been connected to another socket, e.g., during the establishment of a TCP connection, also has a remote socket address.

Within the operating system and the application that created a socket, a socket is referred to by a unique integer value called a *socket descriptor*. The operating system forwards the payload of incoming IP packets to the corresponding application by extracting the socket address information from the IP and transport protocol headers and stripping the headers from the application data.

In IETF Request for Comments, Internet Standards, in many textbooks, as well as in this article, the term *socket* refers to an entity that is uniquely identified by the socket number. In other textbooks, the term *socket* refers to a local socket address, i.e. a "combination of an IP address and a port number". In the original definition of *socket* given in RFC 147, as it was related to the ARPA network in 1971, *"the socket is specified as a 32 bit number with even sockets identifying receiving sockets and odd sockets identifying sending sockets."* Today, however, socket communications are bidirectional.

On Unix-like operating systems and Microsoft Windows, the command line tools netstat and *ss* are used to list established sockets and related information.

Example

This example, modeled according to the Berkeley socket interface, sends the string "Hello, world!" via TCP to port 80 of the host with address 1.2.3.4. It illustrates the creation of a socket (getSocket), connecting it to the remote host, sending the string, and finally closing the socket:

Socket socket = getSocket(type = "TCP")

connect(socket, address = "1.2.3.4", port = "80")

send(socket, "Hello, world!")

close(socket)

Types

Several types of Internet socket are available:

- Datagram sockets, also known as connectionless sockets, which use User Datagram Protocol (UDP).

- Stream sockets, also known as connection-oriented sockets, which use Transmission Control Protocol (TCP), Stream Control Transmission Protocol (SCTP) or Datagram Congestion Control Protocol (DCCP).

- Raw sockets (or *Raw IP sockets*), typically available in routers and other network equipment. Here the transport layer is bypassed, and the packet headers are made accessible to the application.

Other socket types are implemented over other transport protocols, such as Systems Network Architecture (SNA). Unix domain sockets (UDS), for internal inter-process communication.

Socket States in the Client-server Model

Computer processes that provide application services are referred to as servers, and create sockets on start up that are in *listening state*. These sockets are waiting for initiatives from client programs.

A TCP server may serve several clients concurrently, by creating a child process for each client and establishing a TCP connection between the child process and the client. Unique *dedicated sockets* are created for each connection. These are in *established* state when a socket-to-socket virtual connection or virtual circuit (VC), also known as a TCP session, is established with the remote socket, providing a duplex byte stream.

A server may create several concurrently established TCP sockets with the same local port number and local IP address, each mapped to its own server-child process, serving its own client process. They are treated as different sockets by the operating system, since the remote socket address (the client IP address and/or port number) are different; i.e. since they have different socket pair tuples.

A UDP socket cannot be in an established state, since UDP is connectionless. Therefore, netstat does not show the state of a UDP socket. A UDP server does not create new child processes for every concurrently served client, but the same process handles incoming data packets from all remote clients sequentially through the same socket. It implies that UDP sockets are not identified by the remote address, but only by the local address, although each message has an associated remote address.

Socket Pairs

Communicating local and remote sockets are called socket pairs. Each socket pair is described by a unique 4-tuple consisting of source and destination IP addresses and port numbers, i.e. of local and remote socket addresses. As seen in the discussion above, in the TCP case, each unique socket pair 4-tuple is assigned a socket number, while in the UDP case, each unique local socket address is assigned a socket number.

Implementations

Sockets are usually implemented by an application programming interface (API) library. Most implementations are based on Berkeley sockets, for example Winsock introduced in 1991. Other API implementations exist, such as the STREAMS-based Transport Layer Interface (TLI).

Development of application programs that utilize this API is called socket programming or network programming.

In 1983, Berkeley sockets, also known as the BSD socket API, originated with the 4.2BSD Unix operating system (released in 1983) as an API. Only in 1989, however, could UC Berkeley release versions of its operating system and networking library free from the licensing constraints of AT&T's copyright-protected Unix.

In 1987, the Transport Layer Interface (TLI) was the networking application programming interface provided by AT&T UNIX System V Release 3 (SVR3). and continued into Release 4 (SVR4).

Other early implementations were written for TOPS-20, MVS, VM, IBM-DOS (PCIP).

Sockets in Network Equipment

The socket is primarily a concept used in the Transport Layer of the Internet model. Networking equipment such as routers and switches do not require implementations of the Transport Layer, as they operate on the Link Layer level (switches) or at the Internet Layer (routers). However, stateful network firewalls, network address translators, and proxy servers keep track of active socket pairs. Also in fair queuing, layer 3 switching and quality of service (QoS) support in routers, packet flows may be identified by extracting information about the socket pairs. Raw sockets are typically available in network equipment and are used for routing protocols such as IGRP and OSPF, and in Internet Control Message Protocol (ICMP).

Circuit Switching

Circuit switching is a method of implementing a telecommunications network in which two network nodes establish a dedicated communications channel (circuit) through the network before the nodes may communicate. The circuit guarantees the full bandwidth of the channel and remains connected for the duration of the communication session. The circuit functions as if the nodes were physically connected as with an electrical circuit.

The defining example of a circuit-switched network is the early analog telephone network. When a call is made from one telephone to another, switches within the telephone exchanges create a continuous wire circuit between the two telephones, for as long as the call lasts.

Circuit switching contrasts with packet switching which divides the data to be transmitted into packets transmitted through the network independently. In packet switching, instead of being dedicated to one communication session at a time, network links are shared by packets from multiple competing communication sessions, resulting in the loss of the quality of service guarantees that are provided by circuit switching.

In circuit switching, the bit delay is constant during a connection, as opposed to packet switching, where packet queues may cause varying and potentially indefinitely long packet transfer delays. No circuit can be degraded by competing users because it is protected from use by other callers until the circuit is released and a new connection is set up. Even if no actual communication is taking place, the channel remains reserved and protected from competing users.

Virtual circuit switching is a packet switching technology that emulates circuit switching, in the sense that the connection is established before any packets are transferred, and packets are delivered in order.

While circuit switching is commonly used for connecting voice circuits, the concept of a dedicated path persisting between two communicating parties or nodes can be extended to signal content other than voice. Its advantage is that it provides for continuous transfer without the overhead associated with packets making maximal use of available bandwidth for that communication. Its disadvantage is that it can be relatively inefficient because unused capacity guaranteed to a connection cannot be used by other connections on the same network.

The Call

For call setup and control (and other administrative purposes), it is possible to use a separate dedicated signalling channel from the end node to the network. ISDN is one such service that uses a separate signalling channel while plain old telephone service (POTS) does not.

The method of establishing the connection and monitoring its progress and termination through the network may also utilize a separate control channel as in the case of links between telephone exchanges which use CCS7 packet-switched signalling protocol to communicate the call setup and control information and use TDM to transport the actual circuit data.

Early telephone exchanges are a suitable example of circuit switching. The subscriber would ask the operator to connect to another subscriber, whether on the same exchange or via an inter-exchange link and another operator. In any case, the end result was a physical electrical connection between the two subscribers' telephones for the duration of the call. The copper wire used for the connection could not be used to carry other calls at the same time, even if the subscribers were in fact not talking and the line was silent.

Compared With Datagram Packet Switching

Circuit switching contrasts with packet switching which divides the data to be transmitted into small units, called packets, transmitted through the network independently. Packet switching shares available network bandwidth between multiple communication sessions.

Multiplexing multiple telecommunications connections over the same physical conductor has been possible for a long time, but nonetheless each channel on the multiplexed link was either dedicated to one call at a time, or it was idle between calls.

In circuit switching, a route and its associated bandwidth is reserved from source to destination, making circuit switching relatively inefficient since capacity is reserved whether or not the connection is in continuous use.

In contrast, packet switching is the process of segmenting data to be transmitted into several smaller packets. Each packet is labeled with its destination and a sequence number for ordering related packets, precluding the need for a dedicated path to help the packet find its way to its destination. Each packet is dispatched independently and each may be routed via a different path. At the destination, the original message is re-ordered based on the packet number to reproduce the original message. As a result, datagram packet switching networks do not require a circuit to be established and allow many pairs of nodes to communicate concurrently over the same channel.

Examples of Circuit-switched Networks

- Public switched telephone network (PSTN)

- B channel of ISDN

- Circuit Switched Data (CSD) and High-Speed Circuit-Switched Data (HSCSD) service in cellular systems such as GSM

- Datakit

- X.21 (Used in the German DATEX-L and Scandinavian DATEX circuit switched data network)

- Optical mesh network

Network Service

In computer networking, a network service is an application running at the network application layer and above, that provides data storage, manipulation, presentation, communication or other capability which is often implemented using a client-server or peer-to-peer architecture based on application layer network protocols.

Each service is usually provided by a server component running on one or more computers (often a dedicated server computer offering multiple services) and accessed via a network by client components running on other devices. However, the client and server components can both be run on the same machine.

Clients and servers will often have a user interface, and sometimes other hardware associated with them.

Examples

Examples are the Domain Name System (DNS) which translates domain names to Internet protocol (IP) addresses and the Dynamic Host Configuration Protocol (DHCP) to assign networking configuration information to network hosts. Authentication servers identify and authenticate users, provide user account profiles, and may log usage statistics.

E-mail, printing and distributed (network) file system services are common services on local area networks. They require users to have permissions to access the shared resources.

Other Network Services Include:

- Directory services
- e-Mail
- File sharing
- Instant messaging
- Online game
- Printing
- File server
- Voice over IP
- Video on demand
- Video telephony

- World Wide Web

- Simple Network Management Protocol

- Time service

- Wireless sensor network

Application Layer

In computer network programming, the application layer is an abstraction layer reserved for communications protocols and methods designed for process-to-process communications across an Internet Protocol (IP) computer network. Application layer protocols use the underlying transport layer protocols to establish host-to-host connections for network services.

TCP-IP Network Services

Port Numbers

Many Internet Protocol-based services are associated with a particular well-known port number which is standardized by the Internet technical governance.

For example, World-Wide-Web servers operate on port 80, and email relay servers usually listen on port 25.

TCP Versus UDP

Different services use different packet transmission techniques.

In general, packets that must get through in the correct order, without loss, use TCP, whereas real time services where later packets are more important than older packets use UDP.

For example, file transfer requires complete accuracy and so is normally done using TCP, and audio conferencing is frequently done via UDP, where momentary glitches may not be noticed.

UDP lacks built-in network congestion avoidance and the protocols that use it must be extremely carefully designed to prevent network collapse.

Network Congestion

Network congestion in data networking and queueing theory is the reduced quality of service that occurs when a network node is carrying more data than it can handle. Typical effects include queueing delay, packet loss or the blocking of new connections. A consequence of congestion is that an incremental increase in offered load leads either only to a small increase or even a decrease in network throughput.

Network protocols that use aggressive retransmissions to compensate for packet loss due to congestion can increase congestion, even after the initial load has been reduced to a level that would not normally have induced network congestion. Such networks exhibit two stable states under the same level of load. The stable state with low throughput is known as *congestive collapse.*

Networks use congestion control and congestion avoidance techniques to try to avoid collapse. These include: exponential backoff in protocols such as 802.11 CSMA/CA and the original Ethernet, window reduction in TCP, and fair queueing in devices such as routers. Another method is to implement priority schemes, transmitting some packets with higher priority than others. A third avoidance method is the explicit allocation of network resources to specific flows. One example of this is the use of Contention-Free Transmission Opportunities (CFTXOPs) in the ITU-T G.hn standard, which provides high-speed (up to 1 Gbit/s) local area networking over varying wires (power lines, phone lines and coaxial cables).

Network Capacity

Network resources are limited, including router processing time and link throughput.

For example:

- A wireless LAN is easily filled by a single personal computer

- Even on fast computer networks (e.g. Gigabit Ethernet), the backbone can easily be congested by a few servers and client PCs.

- The aggregate transmission from P2P networks have no problem filling an uplink or some other network bottleneck.

- Denial-of-service attacks by botnets are capable of filling even the largest Internet backbone network links, generating large-scale network congestion

- In telephone networks (particularly mobile phones), a mass call event can overwhelm digital telephone circuits

Congestive Collapse

Congestive collapse (or congestion collapse) is the condition in which congestion prevents or limits useful communication. Congestion collapse generally occurs at "choke points" in the network, where incoming traffic exceeds outgoing bandwidth. Connection points between a local area network and a wide area network are common choke points.

When a network is in this condition, it settles into a stable state where traffic demand is high but little useful throughput is available, packet delay and loss and quality of service is extremely poor.

Congestion collapse was identified as a possible problem by 1984, for example in RFC 896. It was first observed on the early Internet in October 1986, when the NSFnet phase-I backbone dropped three orders of magnitude from its capacity of 32 kbit/s to 40 bit/s, which continued until end nodes started implementing Van Jacobson's congestion control between 1987 and 1988.

When more packets were sent than could be handled by intermediate routers, the intermediate routers discarded many packets, expecting the end points of the network to retransmit the information. However, early TCP implementations had poor retransmission behavior. When this packet loss occurred, the endpoints sent extra packets that repeated the information lost, doubling the incoming rate.

Congestion Control

Congestion control modulates traffic entry into a telecommunications network in order to avoid congestive collapse resulting from oversubscription. This is typically accomplished by reducing the rate of packets and it should not be confused with flow control, which prevents the sender from overwhelming the receiver.

Theory of Congestion Control

The theory on congestion control was pioneered by Frank Kelly, who applied microeconomic theory and convex optimization theory to describe how individuals controlling their own rates can interact to achieve an "optimal" network-wide rate allocation.

Examples of "optimal" rate allocation are max-min fair allocation and Kelly's suggestion of proportionally fair allocation, although many others are possible.

Let x_i be the rate of flow i , c_l be the capacity of link l, and r_{li} be 1 if flow i uses link l and 0 otherwise. Let x, c and R be the corresponding vectors and matrix. Let $U(x)$ be an increasing, strictly concave function, called the utility, which measures how much benefit a user obtains by transmitting at rate x. The optimal rate allocation then satisfies

$$\max_x \sum_i U(x_i)$$

such that $Rx \leq c$

The Lagrange dual of this problem decouples, so that each flow sets its own rate, based only on a "price" signalled by the network. Each link capacity imposes a constraint, which gives rise to a Lagrange multiplier, p_l. The sum of these multipliers, $y_i = \sum_l p_l r_{li}$, is the price to which the flow responds.

Congestion control then becomes a distributed optimisation algorithm. Many current congestion control algorithms can be modelled in this framework, with p_l being either the loss probability or the queueing delay at link l.

A major weakness is that it assigns the same price to all flows, while sliding window flow control causes "burstiness" that causes different flows to observe different loss or delay at a given link.

Classification of Congestion Control Algorithms

Among the ways to classify congestion control algorithms are:

- By type and amount of feedback received from the network: Loss; delay; single-bit or multi-bit explicit signals

- By incremental deployability: Only sender needs modification; sender and receiver need modification; only router needs modification; sender, receiver and routers need modification.

- By performance aspect: high bandwidth-delay product networks; lossy links; fairness; advantage to short flows; variable-rate links

- By fairness criterion: max-min, proportional, "minimum potential delay"

Mitigation

A few mechanisms have been invented to prevent network congestion or to deal with a network collapse:

- Network scheduler – active queue management (that is, the arbitrary reorder or drop of network packets under overload)

- Explicit Congestion Notification – an extension to IP and TCP communications protocols that adds a flow control mechanism

- TCP congestion control – various implementations of efforts to deal with network congestion

The correct endpoint behavior is usually to repeat dropped information, but progressively slow the repetition rate. Provided all endpoints do this, the congestion lifts and the network resumes normal behavior. Other strategies such as slow-start ensure that new connections don't overwhelm the router before congestion detection initiates.

The most common router congestion avoidance mechanisms are fair queuing and other scheduling algorithms, and random early detection, or RED, where packets are randomly dropped, proactively triggering the endpoints to slow transmission before congestion collapse occurs. Fair queuing is most useful in routers at choke-points with a small number of connections passing through them. Larger routers must rely on RED.

Some end-to-end protocols behave better under congested conditions. TCP is perhaps the best behaved. The first TCP implementations to handle congestion were developed in 1984, but Van Jacobson's inclusion of an open source solution in the Berkeley Standard Distribution UNIX ("BSD") in 1988 first provided good behavior.

UDP does not control congestion. Protocols built atop UDP must handle congestion independently. Protocols that transmit at a fixed rate, independent of congestion, can be problematic. Real-time streaming protocols, including many Voice over IP protocols, have this property. Thus, special measures, such as quality-of-service routing, must be taken to keep packets from being dropped.

In general, congestion in pure datagram networks must be kept at the periphery of the network, where the above mechanisms can handle it. Congestion in the Internet backbone is problematic. Cheap fiber-optic lines have reduced costs in the Internet backbone allowing it to be provisioned with enough bandwidth to keep congestion at the periphery.

Practical Network Congestion Avoidance

Connection-oriented protocols, such as the widely used TCP protocol, generally watch for packet errors, losses, or delays to adjust the transmit speed. Various network congestion avoidance processes, support different trade-offs.

TCP/IP Congestion Avoidance

The TCP congestion avoidance algorithm is the primary basis for congestion control in the Internet.

Problems occur when concurrent TCP flows experience port queue buffer tail-drops, defeating TCP's automatic congestion avoidance. All flows that experience port queue buffer tail-drop begin a TCP retrain at the same moment – this is called TCP global synchronization.

Active Queue Management

Active queue management (AQM) is the reorder or drop of network packets inside a transmit buffer that is associated with a network interface controller (NIC). This task is performed by the network scheduler.

Random Early Detection

One solution is to use random early detection (RED) on the network equipment's port queue buffer. On network equipment ports with more than one queue buffer, weighted random early detection (WRED) could be used if available.

RED indirectly signals to sender and receiver by deleting some packets, e.g. when the average queue buffer lengths are more than a threshold (e.g. 50%) and deletes linearly or cubically more packets, up to e.g. 100%. The average queue buffer lengths are computed over 1 second intervals.

Robust Random Early Detection (RRED)

The robust random early detection (RRED) algorithm was proposed to improve the TCP throughput against denial-of-service (DoS) attacks, particularly low-rate denial-of-service (LDoS) attacks. Experiments confirmed that RED-like algorithms were vulnerable under Low-rate Denial-of-Service (LDoS) attacks due to the oscillating TCP queue size caused by the attacks.

Flowbased-RED/WRED

Some network equipment is equipped with ports that can follow and measure each flow (flowbased-RED/WRED) and are thereby able to signal a too big bandwidth flow according to some quality of service policy. A policy could then divide the bandwidth among all flows by some criteria.

Explicit Congestion Notification

Another approach is to use IP Explicit Congestion Notification (ECN). ECN is used only when two hosts signal that they want to use it. With this method, a protocol bit is used to signal explicit congestion. This is better than the indirect packet delete congestion notification performed by the RED/WRED algorithms, but it requires explicit support by both hosts. ECN coauthor Sally Floyd published detailed information on ECN, including the version required for Cisco IOS.

When a router receives a packet marked as ECN-capable and anticipates (using RED) congestion, it sets the ECN flag, notifying the sender of congestion. The sender should respond by decreasing its transmission bandwidth, e.g., by decreasing the TCP window size (sending rate) or by other means.

Cisco AQM: Dynamic Buffer Limiting

Cisco Systems (Engine IV and V) has the capability to classify flows as aggressive (bad) or adaptive (good). It ensures that no flows fill the port queues. DBL can utilize IP ECN instead of packet-delete-signalling.

TCP Window Shaping

Congestion avoidance can be achieved efficiently by reducing traffic. When an application requests a large file, graphic or web page, it usually advertises a "window" of between 32K and 64K. This results in the server sending a full window of data (assuming the file is larger than the window). When many applications simultaneously request downloads, this data creates a congestion point at an upstream provider by flooding the queue. By using a device to reduce the window advertisement, the remote servers send less data, thus reducing the congestion. This technique can reduce network congestion by a factor of 40.

Backward ECN

Backward ECN (BECN) is another proposed congestion mechanism. It uses ICMP source quench messages as an IP signalling mechanism to implement a basic ECN mechanism for IP networks, keeping congestion notifications at the IP level and requiring no negotiation between network endpoints. Effective congestion notifications can be propagated to transport layer protocols, such as TCP and UDP, for the appropriate adjustments.

Side Effects of Congestive Collapse Avoidance

Radio Links

The protocols that avoid congestive collapse are often based on the idea that data loss is caused by congestion. This is true in nearly all cases; errors during transmission are rare. However, this causes WiFi, 3G or other networks with a radio layer to have poor throughput in some cases since wireless networks are susceptible to data loss due to interference. The TCP connections running over a radio based physical layer see the data loss and tend to erroneously believe that congestion is occurring.

Short-lived Connections

The slow-start protocol performs badly for short connections. Older web browsers created many short-lived connections and opened and closed the connection for each file. This kept most connections in the slow start mode, which slowed response times.

To avoid this problem, modern browsers either open multiple connections simultaneously or reuse one connection for all files requested from a particular server. Initial performance can be poor, and many connections never get out of the slow-start regime, significantly increasing latency.

Network Security

Network security consists of the policies and practices adopted to prevent and monitor unauthorized access, misuse, modification, or denial of a computer network and network-accessible resources. Network security involves the authorization of access to data in a network, which is controlled by the network administrator. Users choose or are assigned an ID and password or other authenticating information that allows them access to information and programs within their authority. Network security covers a variety of computer networks, both public and private, that are used in everyday jobs; conducting transactions and communications among businesses, government agencies and individuals. Networks can be private, such as within a company, and others which might be open to public access. Network security is involved in organizations, enterprises, and other types of institutions. It does as its title explains: It secures the network, as well as protecting and over ing operations being done. The most common and simple way of protecting a network resource is by assigning it a unique name and a corresponding password.

Network Security Concepts

Network security starts with authenticating, commonly with a username and a password. Since this requires just one detail authenticating the user name—i.e., the password—this is sometimes termed one-factor authentication. With two-factor authentication, something the user 'has' is also used (e.g., a security token or 'dongle', an ATM card, or a mobile phone); and with three-factor authentication, something the user 'is' also used (e.g., a fingerprint or retinal scan).

Once authenticated, a firewall enforces access policies such as what services are allowed to be accessed by the network users. Though effective to prevent unauthorized access, this component may fail to check potentially harmful content such as computer worms or Trojans being transmitted over the network. Anti-virus software or an intrusion prevention system (IPS) help detect and inhibit the action of such malware. An anomaly-based intrusion detection system may also monitor the network like wireshark traffic and may be logged for audit purposes and for later high-level analysis.

Communication between two hosts using a network may be encrypted to maintain privacy.

Honeypots, essentially decoy network-accessible resources, may be deployed in a network as surveillance and early-warning tools, as the honeypots are not normally accessed for legitimate purposes. Techniques used by the attackers that attempt to compromise these decoy resources are studied during and after an attack to keep an eye on new exploitation techniques. Such analysis may be used to further tighten security of the actual network being protected by the honeypot. A honeypot can also direct an attacker's attention away from legitimate servers. A honeypot encourages attackers to spend their time and energy on the decoy server while distracting their attention from the data on the real server. Similar to a honeypot, a honeynet is a network set up with intentional vulnerabilities. Its purpose is also to invite attacks so that the attacker's methods can be studied and that information can be used to increase network security. A honeynet typically contains one or more honeypots.

Security Management

Security management for networks is different for all kinds of situations. A home or small office may only require basic security while large businesses may require high-maintenance and advanced software and hardware to prevent malicious attacks from hacking and spamming.

Types of Attacks

Networks are subject to attacks from malicious sources. Attacks can be from two categories: "Passive" when a network intruder intercepts data traveling through the network, and "Active" in which an intruder initiates commands to disrupt the network's normal operation.

Types of attacks include:

- Passive
    - Network
        - Wiretapping
        - Port scanner
        - Idle scan
- Active
    - Denial-of-service attack
    - DNS spoofing
    - Man in the middle
    - ARP poisoning
    - VLAN hopping
    - Smurf attack
    - Buffer overflow
    - Heap overflow
    - Format string attack

- o SQL injection

- o Phishing

- o Cross-site scripting

- o CSRF

- o Cyber-attack

References

- Forouzan, Behrouz A. (2010). TCP/IP protocol suite (4th ed.). Boston: McGraw-Hill Higher Education. p. 23. ISBN 0073376043.

- Odom, Wendell (2013). Cisco CCENT/ CCNA ICND1 100-101 Official Cert Guide. Pearson Education. pp. Ch. 1. ISBN 978-1-58714-385-4.

- Cisco Networking Academy Program, CCNA 1 and 2 Companion Guide Revised Third Edition, P.480, ISBN 1-58713-150-1

- "Deploying IP and MPLS QoS for Multiservice Networks: Theory and Practice" by John Evans, Clarence Filsfils (Morgan Kaufmann, 2007, ISBN 0-12-370549-5)

- "How Encapsulation Works Within the TCP/IP Model". learn-networking.com. 2008-01-27. Retrieved 2013-11-22.

Evolution of Computer Networking

Computer networking has a history spanning to many decades. It began in the late 1950s and since then has made enormous progress. The history discussed in the following text is of great importance to broaden the existing knowledge on computer networking.

The history of the Internet begins with the development of electronic computers in the 1950s. Initial concepts of packet networking originated in several computer science laboratories in the United States, United Kingdom, and France. The US Department of Defense awarded contracts as early as the 1960s for packet network systems, including the development of the ARPANET. The first message was sent over the ARPANET from computer science Professor Leonard Kleinrock's laboratory at University of California, Los Angeles (UCLA) to the second network node at Stanford Research Institute (SRI).

Packet switching networks such as ARPANET, NPL network, CYCLADES, Merit Network, Tymnet, and Telenet, were developed in the late 1960s and early 1970s using a variety of communications protocols. Donald Davies first designed a packet-switched network at the National Physics Laboratory in the UK, which became a testbed for UK research for almost two decades. The ARPANET project led to the development of protocols for internetworking, in which multiple separate networks could be joined into a network of networks.

Access to the ARPANET was expanded in 1981 when the National Science Foundation (NSF) funded the Computer Science Network (CSNET). In 1982, the Internet protocol suite (TCP/IP) was introduced as the standard networking protocol on the ARPANET. In the early 1980s the NSF funded the establishment for national supercomputing centers at several universities, and provided interconnectivity in 1986 with the NSFNET project, which also created network access to the supercomputer sites in the United States from research and education organizations. Commercial Internet service providers (ISPs) began to emerge in the very late 1980s. The ARPANET was decommissioned in 1990. Limited private connections to parts of the Internet by officially commercial entities emerged in several American cities by late 1989 and 1990, and the NSFNET was decommissioned in 1995, removing the last restrictions on the use of the Internet to carry commercial traffic.

In the 1980s, research at CERN in Switzerland by British computer scientist Tim Berners-Lee resulted in the World Wide Web, linking hypertext documents into an information system, accessible from any node on the network. Since the mid-1990s, the Internet has had a revolutionary impact on culture, commerce, and technology, including the rise of near-instant communication by electronic mail, instant messaging, voice over Internet Protocol (VoIP) telephone calls, two-way interactive video calls, and the World Wide Web with its discussion forums, blogs, social networking, and online shopping sites. The research and education community continues to develop and use advanced networks such as NSF's very high speed Backbone Network Service (vBNS), Internet2, and National LambdaRail. Increasing amounts of data are transmitted at higher and higher speeds over fiber optic networks operating at 1-Gbit/s, 10-Gbit/s, or more. The Internet's takeover of the global communication landscape was almost instant in historical terms: it only communicated 1% of the information flowing through two-way telecommunications networks in the year 1993, already 51% by 2000, and more than 97% of the telecommunicated information by 2007. Today the Internet continues to grow, driven by ever greater amounts of online information, commerce, entertainment, and social networking.

Precursors

The concept of data communication – transmitting data between two different places through an electromagnetic medium such as radio or an electric wire – predates the introduction of the first computers. Such communication systems were typically limited to point to point communication between two end devices. Telegraph systems and telex machines can be considered early precursors of this kind of communication. The Telegraph in the late 19th century was the first fully digital communication system.

Fundamental theoretical work in data transmission and information theory was developed by Claude Shannon, Harry Nyquist, and Ralph Hartley in the early 20th century.

Early computers had a central processing unit and remote terminals. As the technology evolved, new systems were devised to allow communication over longer distances (for terminals) or with higher speed (for interconnection of local devices) that were necessary for the mainframe computer model. These technologies made it possible to exchange data (such as files) between remote computers. However, the point-to-point communication model was limited, as it did not allow for direct communication between any two arbitrary systems; a physical link was necessary. The technology was also considered unsafe for strategic and military use because there were no alternative paths for the communication in case of an enemy attack.

Development of Wide-area Networking

With limited exceptions, the earliest computers were connected directly to terminals used by individual users, typically in the same building or site. Such networks became known as local-area networks (LANs). Networking beyond this scope, known as wide-area networks (WANs), emerged during the 1950s and became established during the 1960s.

Inspiration

J. C. R. Licklider, Vice President at Bolt Beranek and Newman, Inc., proposed a global network in his January 1960 paper *Man-Computer Symbiosis*:

A network of such [computers], connected to one another by wide-band communication lines [which provided] the functions of present-day libraries together with anticipated advances in information storage and retrieval and [other] symbiotic functions

In August 1962, Licklider and Welden Clark published the paper "On-Line Man-Computer Communication" which was one of the first descriptions of a networked future.

In October 1962, Licklider was hired by Jack Ruina as director of the newly established Information Processing Techniques Office (IPTO) within DARPA, with a mandate to interconnect the United States Department of Defense's main computers at Cheyenne Mountain, the Pentagon, and SAC HQ. There he formed an informal group within DARPA to further computer research. He began by writing memos describing a distributed network to the IPTO staff, whom he called "Members and Affiliates of the Intergalactic Computer Network". As part of the information processing office's role, three network terminals had been installed: one for System Development Corporation in Santa Monica, one for Project Genie at University of California, Berkeley, and one for the Compatible Time-Sharing System project at Massachusetts Institute of Technology (MIT). Licklider's identified need for inter-networking would become obvious by the apparent waste of resources this caused.

For each of these three terminals, I had three different sets of user commands. So if I was talking online with someone at S.D.C. and I wanted to talk to someone I knew at Berkeley or M.I.T. about this, I had to get up from the S.D.C. terminal, go over and log into the other terminal and get in touch with them....

I said, oh man, it's obvious what to do: If you have these three terminals, there ought to be one terminal that goes anywhere you want to go where you have interactive computing. That idea is the ARPAnet.

Although he left the IPTO in 1964, five years before the ARPANET went live, it was his vision of universal networking that provided the impetus for his successors such as Lawrence Roberts and Robert Taylor to further the ARPANET development. Licklider later returned to lead the IPTO in 1973 for two years.

Development of Packet Switching

The issue of connecting separate physical networks to form one logical network was the first of many problems. In the 1960s, Paul Baran of the RAND Corporation produced a study of survivable networks for the U.S. military in the event of nuclear war. Information transmitted across Baran's network would be divided into what he called "message-blocks". Independently, Donald Davies (National Physical Laboratory, UK), proposed and was the first to put into practice a similar network based on what he called packet-switching, the term that would ultimately be adopted. Leonard Kleinrock (MIT) developed a mathematical theory behind this technology (without the packets). Packet-switching provides better bandwidth utilization and response times than the traditional circuit-switching technology used for telephony, particularly on resource-limited interconnection links.

Packet switching is a rapid store and forward networking design that divides messages up into arbitrary packets, with routing decisions made per-packet. Early networks used message switched systems that required rigid routing structures prone to single point of failure. This led Tommy Krash and Paul Baran's U.S. military-funded research to focus on using message-blocks to include network redundancy.

Networks that led to the Internet

ARPANET

Promoted to the head of the information processing office at Defense Advanced Research Projects Agency (DARPA), Robert Taylor intended to realize Licklider's ideas of an interconnected networking system. Bringing in Larry Roberts from MIT, he initiated a project to build such a network. The first ARPANET link was established between the University of California, Los Angeles (UCLA) and the Stanford Research Institute at 22:30 hours on October 29, 1969.

"We set up a telephone connection between us and the guys at SRI ...", Kleinrock ... said in an interview: "We typed the L and we asked on the phone,

> "Do you see the L?"
>
> "Yes, we see the L," came the response.
>
> We typed the O, and we asked, "Do you see the O."
>
> "Yes, we see the O."
>
> Then we typed the G, and the system crashed ...

Yet a revolution had begun" ....

By December 5, 1969, a 4-node network was connected by adding the University of Utah and the University of California, Santa Barbara. Building on ideas developed in ALOHAnet, the ARPANET grew rapidly. By 1981, the number of hosts had grown to 213, with a new host being added approximately every twenty days.

35 Years of the Internet, 1969–2004. Stamp of Azerbaijan, 2004.

ARPANET development was centered around the Request for Comments (RFC) process, still used today for proposing and distributing Internet Protocols and Systems. RFC 1, entitled "Host Software", was written by Steve Crocker from the University of California, Los Angeles, and published on April 7, 1969. These early years were documented in the 1972 film Computer Networks: The Heralds of Resource Sharing.

ARPANET became the technical core of what would become the Internet, and a primary tool in developing the technologies used. The early ARPANET used the Network Control Program (NCP, sometimes Network Control Protocol) rather than TCP/IP. On January 1, 1983, known as flag day, NCP on the ARPANET was replaced by the more flexible and powerful family of TCP/IP protocols, marking the start of the modern Internet.

International collaborations on ARPANET were sparse. For various political reasons, European developers were concerned with developing the X.25 networks. Notable exceptions were the *Norwegian Seismic Array* (NORSAR) in 1972, followed in 1973 by Sweden with satellite links to the Tanum Earth Station and Peter Kirstein's research group in the UK, initially at the Institute of Computer Science, London University and later at University College London.

NPL

In 1965, Donald Davies of the National Physical Laboratory (United Kingdom) proposed a national data network based on packet-switching. The proposal was not taken up nationally, but by 1970 he had designed and built the Mark I packet-switched network to meet the needs of the multidisciplinary laboratory and prove the technology under operational conditions. By 1976 12 computers and 75 terminal devices were attached and more were added until the network was replaced in 1986. NPL, followed by ARPANET, were the first two networks in the world to use packet switching.

Merit Network

The Merit Network was formed in 1966 as the Michigan Educational Research Information Triad to explore computer networking between three of Michigan's public universities as a means to help the state's educational and economic development. With initial support from the State of Michigan and the National Science Foundation (NSF), the packet-switched network was first demonstrated in December 1971 when an interactive host to host connection was made between the IBM mainframe computer systems at the University of Michigan in Ann Arbor and Wayne State University in Detroit. In October 1972 connections to the CDC mainframe at Michigan State University in East Lansing completed the triad. Over the next several years in addition to host to host interactive connections the network was enhanced to support terminal to host connections, host to host batch connections (remote job submission, remote printing, batch file transfer), interactive file transfer, gateways to the Tymnet and Telenet public data networks, X.25 host attachments, gateways to X.25 data networks, Ethernet attached hosts, and eventually TCP/IP and additional public universities in Michigan join the network. All of this set the stage for Merit's role in the NSFNET project starting in the mid-1980s.

CYCLADES

The CYCLADES packet switching network was a French research network designed and directed by Louis Pouzin. First demonstrated in 1973, it was developed to explore alternatives to the initial ARPANET design and to support network research generally. It was the first network to make the hosts responsible for the reliable delivery of data, rather than the network itself, using unreliable datagrams and associated end-to-end protocol mechanisms.

X.25 and Public Data Networks

1974 ABC interview with Arthur C. Clarke, in which he describes a future of ubiquitous networked personal computers.

Based on ARPA's research, packet switching network standards were developed by the International Telecommunication Union (ITU) in the form of X.25 and related standards. While using packet switching, X.25 is built on the concept of virtual circuits emulating traditional telephone connections. In 1974, X.25 formed the basis for the SERCnet network between British academic and research sites, which later became JANET. The initial ITU Standard on X.25 was approved in March 1976.

The British Post Office, Western Union International and Tymnet collaborated to create the first international packet switched network, referred to as the International Packet Switched Service (IPSS), in 1978. This network grew from Europe and the US to cover Canada, Hong Kong, and Australia by 1981. By the 1990s it provided a worldwide networking infrastructure.

Unlike ARPANET, X.25 was commonly available for business use. Telenet offered its Telemail electronic mail service, which was also targeted to enterprise use rather than the general email system of the ARPANET.

The first public dial-in networks used asynchronous TTY terminal protocols to reach a concentrator operated in the public network. Some networks, such as CompuServe, used X.25 to multiplex the terminal sessions into their packet-switched backbones, while others, such as Tymnet, used proprietary protocols. In 1979, CompuServe became the first service to offer electronic mail capabilities and technical support to personal computer users. The company broke new ground again in 1980 as the first to offer real-time chat with its CB Simulator. Other major dial-in networks were America Online (AOL) and Prodigy that also provided communications, content, and entertainment features. Many bulletin board system (BBS) networks also provided on-line access, such as FidoNet which was popular amongst hobbyist computer users, many of them hackers and amateur radio operators.

UUCP and Usenet

In 1979, two students at Duke University, Tom Truscott and Jim Ellis, originated the idea of using Bourne shell scripts to transfer news and messages on a serial line UUCP connection with nearby University of North Carolina at Chapel Hill. Following public release of the software in 1980, the mesh of UUCP hosts forwarding on the Usenet news rapidly expanded. UUCPnet, as it would later be named, also created gateways and links between FidoNet and dial-up BBS hosts. UUCP networks spread quickly due to the lower costs involved, ability to use existing leased lines, X.25 links or even ARPANET connections, and the lack of strict use policies compared to later networks like CSNET and Bitnet. All connects were local. By 1981 the number of UUCP hosts had grown to 550, nearly doubling to 940 in 1984. – Sublink Network, operating since 1987 and officially founded in Italy in 1989, based its interconnectivity upon UUCP to redistribute mail and news groups messages throughout its Italian nodes (about 100 at the time) owned both by private individuals and small companies. Sublink Network represented possibly one of the first examples of the Internet technology becoming progress through popular diffusion.

Merging the Networks and Creating the Internet (1973–95)

TCP/IP

With so many different network methods, something was needed to unify them. Robert

E. Kahn of DARPA and ARPANET recruited Vinton Cerf of Stanford University to work with him on the problem. By 1973, they had worked out a fundamental reformulation, where the differences between network protocols were hidden by using a common internetwork protocol, and instead of the network being responsible for reliability, as in the ARPANET, the hosts became responsible. Cerf credits Hubert Zimmermann, Gerard LeLann and Louis Pouzin (designer of the CYCLADES network) with important work on this design.

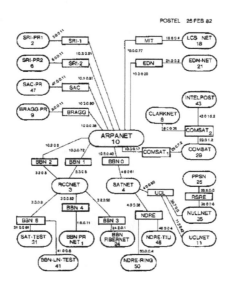

Map of the TCP/IP test network in February 1982

The specification of the resulting protocol, *RFC 675 – Specification of Internet Transmission Control Program*, by Vinton Cerf, Yogen Dalal and Carl Sunshine, Network Working Group, December 1974, contains the first attested use of the term *internet*, as a shorthand for *internetworking*; later RFCs repeat this use, so the word started out as an adjective rather than the noun it is today.

With the role of the network reduced to the bare minimum, it became possible to join almost any networks together, no matter what their characteristics were, thereby solving Kahn's initial problem. DARPA agreed to fund development of prototype software, and after several years of work, the first demonstration of a gateway between the Packet Radio network in the SF Bay area and the ARPANET was conducted by the Stanford Research Institute. On November 22, 1977 a three network demonstration was conducted including the ARPANET, the SRI's Packet Radio Van on the Packet Radio Network and the Atlantic Packet Satellite network.

Stemming from the first specifications of TCP in 1974, TCP/IP emerged in mid-late 1978 in nearly its final form, as used for the first decades of the Internet, known as "IPv4". (IPv4 eventually became superseded by its successor, called "IPv6", but this was largely due to the sheer number of devices being connected post-2005, which overwhelmed the numbers that IPv4 had been able to accommodate worldwide. However, due to IPv4's entrenched position by that time, the shift is still in its early stages as of 2015, and expected to take many years, decades, or perhaps longer, to complete).

The associated standards for IPv4 were published by 1981 as RFCs 791, 792 and 793, and adopted for use. DARPA sponsored or encouraged the development of TCP/IP implementations for many operating systems and then scheduled a migration of all hosts on all of its packet networks to TCP/IP. On January 1, 1983, known as flag day, TCP/IP protocols became the only approved protocol on the ARPANET, replacing the earlier NCP protocol.

From ARPANET to NSFNET

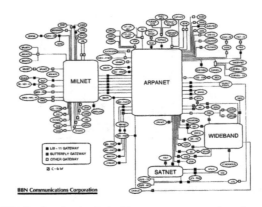

BBN Technologies TCP/IP Internet map of early 1986.

After the ARPANET had been up and running for several years, ARPA looked for another agency to hand off the network to; ARPA's primary mission was funding cutting edge research and development, not running a communications utility. Eventually, in July 1975, the network had been turned over to the Defense Communications Agency, also part of the Department of Defense. In 1983, the U.S. military portion of the ARPANET was broken off as a separate network, the MILNET. MILNET subsequently became the unclassified but military-only NIPRNET, in parallel with the SECRET-level SIPRNET and JWICS for TOP SECRET and above. NIPRNET does have controlled security gateways to the public Internet.

The networks based on the ARPANET were government funded and therefore restricted to noncommercial uses such as research; unrelated commercial use was strictly forbidden. This initially restricted connections to military sites and universities. During the 1980s, the connections expanded to more educational institutions, and even to a growing number of companies such as Digital Equipment Corporation and Hewlett-Packard, which were participating in research projects or providing services to those who were.

Several other branches of the U.S. government, the National Aeronautics and Space Administration (NASA), the National Science Foundation (NSF), and the Department of Energy (DOE) became heavily involved in Internet research and started development of a successor to ARPANET. In the mid-1980s, all three of these branches developed the first Wide Area Networks based on TCP/IP. NASA developed the NASA Science Network, NSF developed CSNET and DOE evolved the Energy Sciences Network or ESNet.

NSFNET T3 Network 1992

T3 NSFNET Backbone, c. 1992

NASA developed the TCP/IP based NASA Science Network (NSN) in the mid-1980s, connecting space scientists to data and information stored anywhere in the world. In 1989, the DECnet-based Space Physics Analysis Network (SPAN) and the TCP/IP-based NASA Science Network (NSN) were brought together at NASA Ames Research Center creating the first multiprotocol wide area network called the NASA Science Internet, or NSI. NSI was established to provide a totally integrated communications infrastructure to the NASA scientific community for the advancement of earth, space and life sciences. As a high-speed, multiprotocol, international network, NSI provided connectivity to over 20,000 scientists across all seven continents.

In 1981 NSF supported the development of the Computer Science Network (CSNET). CSNET connected with ARPANET using TCP/IP, and ran TCP/IP over X.25, but it also supported departments without sophisticated network connections, using automated dial-up mail exchange.

In 1986, the NSF created NSFNET, a 56 kbit/s backbone to support the NSF-sponsored supercomputing centers. The NSFNET also provided support for the creation of regional research and education networks in the United States, and for the connection of university and college campus networks to the regional networks. The use of NSFNET and the regional networks was not limited to supercomputer users and the 56 kbit/s network quickly became overloaded. NSFNET was upgraded to 1.5 Mbit/s in 1988 under a cooperative agreement with the Merit Network in partnership with IBM, MCI, and the State of Michigan. The existence of NSFNET and the creation of Federal Internet Exchanges (FIXes) allowed the ARPANET to be decommissioned in 1990.

NSFNET was expanded and upgraded to 45 Mbit/s in 1991, and was decommissioned in 1995 when it was replaced by backbones operated by several commercial Internet Service Providers.

Transition Towards the Internet

The term "internet" was adopted in the first RFC published on the TCP protocol (RFC 675: Internet Transmission Control Program, December 1974) as an abbreviation of the term *internetworking* and the two terms were used interchangeably. In general, an internet was any network using TCP/IP. It was around the time when ARPANET was interlinked with NSFNET in the late 1980s, that the term was used as the name of the network, Internet, being the large and global TCP/IP network.

As interest in networking grew and new applications for it were developed, the Internet's technologies spread throughout the rest of the world. The network-agnostic approach in TCP/IP meant that it was easy to use any existing network infrastructure, such as the IPSS X.25 network, to carry Internet traffic. In 1984, University College London replaced its transatlantic satellite links with TCP/IP over IPSS.

Many sites unable to link directly to the Internet created simple gateways for the transfer of electronic mail, the most important application of the time. Sites with only intermittent connections used UUCP or FidoNet and relied on the gateways between these networks and the Internet. Some gateway services went beyond simple mail peering, such as allowing access to File Transfer Protocol (FTP) sites via UUCP or mail.

Finally, routing technologies were developed for the Internet to remove the remaining centralized routing aspects. The Exterior Gateway Protocol (EGP) was replaced by a new protocol, the Border Gateway Protocol (BGP). This provided a meshed topology for the Internet and reduced the centric architecture which ARPANET had emphasized. In 1994, Classless Inter-Domain Routing (CIDR) was introduced to support better conservation of address space which allowed use of route aggregation to decrease the size of routing tables.

TCP/IP Goes Global (1980s)

CERN, the European Internet, the link to the Pacific and beyond

Between 1984 and 1988 CERN began installation and operation of TCP/IP to interconnect its major internal computer systems, workstations, PCs and an accelerator control system. CERN continued to operate a limited self-developed system (CERNET) internally and several incompatible (typically proprietary) network protocols externally. There was considerable resistance in Europe towards more widespread use of TCP/IP, and the CERN TCP/IP intranets remained isolated from the Internet until 1989.

In 1988, Daniel Karrenberg, from Centrum Wiskunde & Informatica (CWI) in Amsterdam, visited Ben Segal, CERN's TCP/IP Coordinator, looking for advice about the transition of the European side of the UUCP Usenet network (much of which ran over X.25 links) over to TCP/IP. In 1987, Ben Segal had met with Len Bosack from the then still small company Cisco about purchasing some TCP/IP routers for CERN, and was able to give Karrenberg advice and forward him on to Cisco for the appropriate hardware. This expanded the European portion of the Internet across the existing UUCP networks, and in 1989 CERN opened its first external TCP/IP connections. This coincided with the creation of Réseaux IP Européens (RIPE), initially a group of IP network administrators who met regularly to carry out coordination work together. Later, in 1992, RIPE was formally registered as a cooperative in Amsterdam.

At the same time as the rise of internetworking in Europe, ad hoc networking to ARPA and in-between Australian universities formed, based on various technologies such as X.25 and UUCPNet. These were limited in their connection to the global networks, due to the cost of making individual international UUCP dial-up or X.25 connections. In 1989, Australian universities joined the push towards using IP protocols to unify their networking infrastructures. AARNet was formed in 1989 by the Australian Vice-Chancellors' Committee and provided a dedicated IP based network for Australia.

The Internet began to penetrate Asia in the 1980s. In May 1982 South Korea became the second country to successfully set up TCP/IP IPv4 network. Japan, which had built the UUCP-based network JUNET in 1984, connected to NSFNET in 1989. It hosted the annual meeting of the Internet Society, INET'92, in Kobe. Singapore developed TECHNET in 1990, and Thailand gained a global Internet connection between Chulalongkorn University and UUNET in 1992.

The Early Global "Digital Divide" Emerges

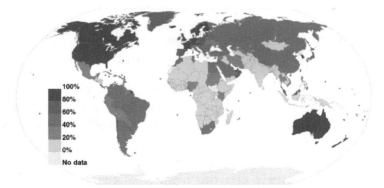

Internet users in 2012 as a percentage of a country's population

Source: International Telecommunications Union.

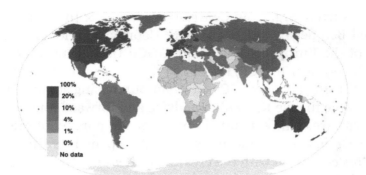

Fixed broadband Internet subscriptions in 2012 as a percentage of a country's population

Source: International Telecommunications Union.

Mobile broadband Internet subscriptions in 2012 as a percentage of a country's population

While developed countries with technological infrastructures were joining the Internet, developing countries began to experience a digital divide separating them from the Internet. On an essentially continental basis, they are building organizations for Internet resource administration and sharing operational experience, as more and more transmission facilities go into place.

Africa

At the beginning of the 1990s, African countries relied upon X.25 IPSS and 2400 baud modem UUCP links for international and internetwork computer communications.

In August 1995, InfoMail Uganda, Ltd., a privately held firm in Kampala now known as InfoCom, and NSN Network Services of Avon, Colorado, sold in 1997 and now known as Clear Channel Satellite, established Africa's first native TCP/IP high-speed satellite Internet services. The data connection was originally carried by a C-Band RSCC Russian satellite which connected InfoMail's Kampala offices directly to NSN's MAE-West point of presence using a private network from NSN's leased ground station in New Jersey. InfoCom's first satellite connection was just 64 kbit/s, serving a Sun host computer and twelve US Robotics dial-up modems.

In 1996, a USAID funded project, the Leland Initiative, started work on developing full Internet connectivity for the continent. Guinea, Mozambique, Madagascar and Rwanda gained satellite earth stations in 1997, followed by Ivory Coast and Benin in 1998.

Africa is building an Internet infrastructure. AfriNIC, headquartered in Mauritius, manages IP address allocation for the continent. As do the other Internet regions, there is an operational forum, the Internet Community of Operational Networking Specialists.

There are many programs to provide high-performance transmission plant, and the western and southern coasts have undersea optical cable. High-speed cables join North Africa and the Horn of Africa to intercontinental cable systems. Undersea cable development is slower for East Africa; the original joint effort between New Partnership for Africa's Development (NEPAD) and the East Africa Submarine System (Eassy) has broken off and may become two efforts.

Asia and Oceania

The Asia Pacific Network Information Centre (APNIC), headquartered in Australia, manages IP address allocation for the continent. APNIC sponsors an operational forum, the Asia-Pacific Regional Internet Conference on Operational Technologies (APRICOT).

In 1991, the People's Republic of China saw its first TCP/IP college network, Tsinghua University's TUNET. The PRC went on to make its first global Internet connection in 1994, between the Beijing Electro-Spectrometer Collaboration and Stanford University's Linear Accelerator Center. However, China went on to implement its own digital divide by implementing a country-wide content filter.

Latin America

As with the other regions, the Latin American and Caribbean Internet Addresses Registry (LACNIC) manages the IP address space and other resources for its area. LACNIC, headquartered in Uruguay, operates DNS root, reverse DNS, and other key services.

Rise of the Global Internet (Late 1980s/early 1990s Onward)

Initially, as with its predecessor networks, the system that would evolve into the Internet was primarily for government and government body use.

However, interest in commercial use of the Internet quickly became a commonly debated topic. Although commercial use was forbidden, the exact definition of commercial use was unclear and subjective. UUCPNet and the X.25 IPSS had no such restrictions, which would eventually see the official barring of UUCPNet use of ARPANET and NSFNET connections. (Some UUCP links still remained connecting to these networks however, as administrators cast a blind eye to their operation.)

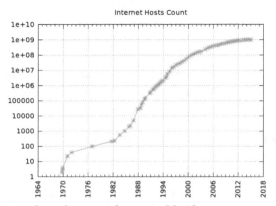

Number of Internet hosts worldwide: 1969–2012

As a result, during the late 1980s, the first Internet service provider (ISP) companies were formed. Companies like PSINet, UUNET, Netcom, and Portal Software were formed to provide service to the regional research networks and provide alternate network access, UUCP-based email and Usenet News to the public. The first commercial dialup ISP in the United States was The World, which opened in 1989.

In 1992, the U.S. Congress passed the Scientific and Advanced-Technology Act, 42 U.S.C. § 1862(g), which allowed NSF to support access by the research and education communities to computer networks which were not used exclusively for research and education purposes, thus permitting NSFNET to interconnect with commercial networks. This caused controversy within the research and education community, who were concerned commercial use of the network might lead to an Internet that was less responsive to their needs, and within the community of commercial network providers, who felt that government subsidies were giving an unfair advantage to some organizations.

By 1990, ARPANET's goals had been fulfilled and new networking technologies exceeded the original scope and the project came to a close. New network service providers including PSINet, Alternet, CERFNet, ANS CO+RE, and many others were offering network access to commercial customers. NSFNET was no longer the de facto backbone and exchange point of the Internet. The Commercial Internet eXchange (CIX), Metropolitan Area Exchanges (MAEs), and later Network Access Points (NAPs) were becoming the primary interconnections between many networks. The final restrictions on carrying commercial traffic ended on April 30, 1995 when the National Science Foundation ended its sponsorship of the NSFNET Backbone Service and the service ended. NSF provided initial support for the NAPs and interim support to help the regional research and education networks transition to commercial ISPs. NSF also sponsored the very high speed Backbone Network Service (vBNS) which continued to provide support for the supercomputing centers and research and education in the United States.

World Wide Web and introduction of browsers

The World Wide Web (sometimes abbreviated "www" or "W3") is an information space where documents and other web resources are identified by URIs, interlinked by hypertext links, and can be accessed via the Internet using a web browser and (more recently) web-based applications. It has become known simply as "the Web". As of the 2010s, the World Wide Web is the primary tool billions use to interact on the Internet, and it has changed people's lives immeasurably.

Precursors to the web browser emerged in the form of hyperlinked applications during the mid and late 1980s (the bare concept of hyperlinking had by then existed for some decades). Following these, Tim Berners-Lee is credited with inventing the World Wide Web in 1989 and developing in 1990 both the first web server, and the first web browser, called WorldWideWeb (no spaces) and later renamed Nexus. Many others were soon developed, with Marc Andreessen's 1993 Mosaic (later Netscape), being particularly easy to use and install, and often credited with sparking the internet boom of the 1990s. Today, the major web browsers are Firefox, Internet Explorer, Google Chrome, Opera and Safari.

A boost in web users was triggered in September 1993 by NCSA Mosaic, a graphical browser which eventually ran on several popular office and home computers. This was the first web browser aiming to bring multimedia content to non-technical users, and therefore included images and text on the same page, unlike previous browser designs; its founder, Marc Andreessen, also established the company that in 1994, released Netscape Navigator, which resulted in one of the early browser wars, when it ended up in a competition for dominance (which it lost) with Microsoft Windows' Internet Explorer. Commercial use restrictions were lifted in 1995. The online service America Online (AOL) offered their users a connection to the Internet via their own internal browser.

Use in Wider Society 1990s to Early 2000s (Web 1.0)

During the first decade or so of the public internet, the immense changes it would eventually enable in the 2000s were still nascent. In terms of providing context for this period, mobile cellular devices ("smartphones" and other cellular devices) which today provide near-universal access, were used for business and not a routine household item owned by parents and children worldwide. Social media in the modern sense had yet to come into existence, laptops were bulky and most households did not have computers. Data rates were slow and most people lacked means to video or digitize video so websites such as YouTube did not yet exist, media storage was transitioning slowly from analog tape to digital optical discs (DVD and to an extent still, floppy disc to CD). Enabling technologies used from the early 2000s such as PHP, modern Javascript and Java, technologies such as AJAX, HTML 4 (and its emphasis on CSS), and various software frameworks, which enabled and simplified speed of web development, largely awaited invention and their eventual widespread adoption.

The Internet was widely used for mailing lists, emails, e-commerce and early popular online shopping (Amazon and eBay for example), online forums and bulletin boards, and personal websites and blogs, and use was growing rapidly, but by more modern standards the systems used were static and lacked widespread social engagement. It awaited a number of events in the early 2000s to change from a communications technology to gradually develop into a key part of global society's infrastructure.

Typical design elements of these "Web 1.0" era websites included: Static pages instead of dynamic HTML; content served from filesystems instead of relational databases; pages built using Server Side Includes or CGI instead of a web application written in a dynamic programming language; HTML 3.2-era structures such as frames and tables to create page layouts; online guestbooks; overuse of GIF buttons and similar small graphics promoting particular items; and HTML forms sent via email. (Support for server side scripting was rare on shared servers so the usual feedback mechanism was via email, using mailto forms and their email program.

During the period 1997 to 2001, the first speculative investment bubble related to the Internet took place, in which "dot-com" companies (referring to the ".com" top level domain used by businesses) were propelled to exceedingly high valuations as investors rapidly stoked stock values, followed by a market crash; the first dot-com bubble. However this only temporarily slowed enthusiasm and growth, which quickly recovered and continued to grow.

The changes that would propel the Internet into its place as a social system took place during a relatively short period of no more than five years, starting from around 2004. They included:

- The call to "Web 2.0" in 2004 (first suggested in 1999),

- Accelerating adoption and commoditization among households of, and familiarity with, the necessary hardware (such as computers).

- Accelerating storage technology and data access speeds – hard drives emerged, took over from far smaller, slower floppy discs, and grew from megabytes to gigabytes (and by around 2010, terabytes), RAM from hundreds of kilobytes to gigabytes as typical amounts on a system, and Ethernet, the enabling technology for TCP/IP, moved from common speeds of kilobits to tens of megabits per second, to gigabits per second.

- High speed Internet and wider coverage of data connections, at lower prices, allowing larger traffic rates, more reliable simpler traffic, and traffic from more locations,

- The gradually accelerating perception of the ability of computers to create new means and approaches to communication, the emergence of social media and websites such as Twitter and Facebook to their later prominence, and global collaborations (which existed before but gained prominence as a result),

and shortly after (approximately 2007–2008 onward):

- The mobile revolution, which provided access to the Internet to much of human society of all ages, in their daily lives, and allowed them to share, discuss, and continually update, inquire, and respond.

- Non-volatile RAM rapidly grew in size and reliability, and decreased in price, becoming a commodity capable of enabling high levels of computing activity on these small handheld devices as well as solid-state drives (SSD).

- An emphasis on power efficient processor and device design, rather than purely high processing power; one of the beneficiaries of this was ARM, a British company which had focused since the 1980s on powerful but low cost simple microprocessors. ARM rapidly gained dominance in the market for mobile and embedded devices.

With the call to Web 2.0, the period up to around 2004–2005 was retrospectively named and described by some as Web 1.0.

Web 2.0

The term "Web 2.0" describes websites that emphasize user-generated content (including user-to-user interaction), usability, and interoperability. It first appeared in a January 1999 article called "Fragmented Future" written by Darcy DiNucci, a consultant on electronic information design, where she wrote:

> "The Web we know now, which loads into a browser window in essentially static screenfuls, is only an embryo of the Web to come. The first glimmerings of Web 2.0 are beginning to appear, and we are just starting to see how that embryo might develop. The Web will be understood not as screenfuls of text and graphics but as a transport mechanism, the ether through which interactivity happens. It will [...] appear on your computer screen, [...] on your TV set [...] your car dashboard [...] your cell phone [...] hand-held game machines [...] maybe even your microwave oven."

The term resurfaced during 2002 – 2004, and gained prominence in late 2004 following presentations by Tim O'Reilly and Dale Dougherty at the first Web 2.0 Conference. In their opening remarks, John Battelle and Tim O'Reilly outlined their definition of the "Web as Platform", where software applications are built upon the Web as opposed to upon the desktop. The unique aspect of this migration, they argued, is that "customers are building your business for you". They argued that the activities of users generating content (in the form of ideas, text, videos, or pictures) could be "harnessed" to create value.

Web 2.0 does not refer to an update to any technical specification, but rather to cumulative changes in the way Web pages are made and used. Web 2.0 describes an approach, in which sites focus substantially upon allowing users to interact and collaborate with each other in a social media dialogue as creators of user-generated content in a virtual community, in contrast to Web sites where people are limited to the passive viewing of content. Examples of Web 2.0 include social networking sites, blogs, wikis, folksonomies, video sharing sites, hosted services, Web applications, and mashups. Terry Flew, in his 3rd Edition of *New Media* described what he believed to characterize the differences between Web 1.0 and Web 2.0:

> "[The] move from personal websites to blogs and blog site aggregation, from publishing to participation, from web content as the outcome of large up-front investment to an ongoing and interactive process, and from content management systems to links based on tagging (folksonomy)".

This era saw several household names gain prominence through their community-oriented operation – YouTube, Twitter, Facebook, Reddit and Wikipedia being some examples.

The Mobile Revolution

The process of change generally described as "Web 2.0" was itself greatly accelerated and transformed only a short time later by the increasing growth in mobile devices. This mobile revolution meant that computers in the form of smartphones became something many people used, took with them everywhere, communicated with, used for photographs and videos they instantly shared or to shop or seek information "on the move" – and used socially, as opposed to items on a desk at home or just used for work.

Location-based services, services using location and other sensor information, and crowdsourcing (frequently but not always location based), became common, with posts tagged by location, or websites and services becoming location aware. Mobile-targeted websites (such as "m.website.com") became common, designed especially for the new devices used. Netbooks, ultrabooks, widespread 4G and Wi-Fi, and mobile chips capable or running at nearly the power of desktops from not many years before on far lower power usage, became enablers of this stage of Internet development, and the term "App" emerged (short for "Application program" or "Program") as did the "App store".

Networking in Outer Space

The first Internet link into low earth orbit was established on January 22, 2010 when astronaut T. J. Creamer posted the first unassisted update to his Twitter account from the International Space Station, marking the extension of the Internet into space. (Astronauts at the ISS had used email and Twitter before, but these messages had been relayed to the ground through a NASA data link before being posted by a human proxy.) This personal Web access, which NASA calls the Crew Support LAN, uses the space station's high-speed Ku band microwave link. To surf the Web, astronauts can use a station laptop computer to control a desktop computer on Earth, and they can talk to their families and friends on Earth using Voice over IP equipment.

Communication with spacecraft beyond earth orbit has traditionally been over point-to-point links through the Deep Space Network. Each such data link must be manually scheduled and configured. In the late 1990s NASA and Google began working on a new network protocol, Delay-tolerant networking (DTN) which automates this process, allows networking of spaceborne transmission nodes, and takes the fact into account that spacecraft can temporarily lose contact because they move behind the Moon or planets, or because space weather disrupts the connection. Under such conditions, DTN retransmits data packages instead of dropping them, as the standard TCP/IP Internet Protocol does. NASA conducted the first field test of what it calls the "deep space internet" in November 2008. Testing of DTN-based communications between the International Space Station and Earth (now termed Disruption-Tolerant Networking) has been ongoing since March 2009, and is scheduled to continue until March 2014.

This network technology is supposed to ultimately enable missions that involve multiple spacecraft where reliable inter-vessel communication might take precedence over vessel-to-earth downlinks. According to a February 2011 statement by Google's Vint Cerf, the so-called "Bundle protocols" have been uploaded to NASA's EPOXI mission spacecraft (which is in orbit around the Sun) and communication with Earth has been tested at a distance of approximately 80 light seconds.

Internet Governance

As a globally distributed network of voluntarily interconnected autonomous networks, the Internet operates without a central governing body. It has no centralized governance for either technology or policies, and each constituent network chooses what technologies and protocols it will deploy from the voluntary technical standards that are developed by the Internet Engineering Task Force (IETF). However, throughout its entire history, the Internet system has had an "Internet Assigned Numbers Authority" (IANA) for the allocation and assignment of various technical identifiers needed for the operation of the Internet. The Internet Corporation for Assigned Names and Numbers (ICANN) provides oversight and coordination for two principal name spaces in the Internet, the Internet Protocol address space and the Domain Name System.

NIC, InterNIC, IANA and ICANN

The IANA function was originally performed by USC Information Sciences Institute

(ISI), and it delegated portions of this responsibility with respect to numeric network and autonomous system identifiers to the Network Information Center (NIC) at Stanford Research Institute (SRI International) in Menlo Park, California. ISI's Jonathan Postel managed the IANA, served as RFC Editor and performed other key roles until his premature death in 1998.

As the early ARPANET grew, hosts were referred to by names, and a HOSTS.TXT file would be distributed from SRI International to each host on the network. As the network grew, this became cumbersome. A technical solution came in the form of the Domain Name System, created by ISI's Paul Mockapetris in 1983. The Defense Data Network—Network Information Center (DDN-NIC) at SRI handled all registration services, including the top-level domains (TLDs) of .mil, .gov, .edu, .org, .net, .com and .us, root nameserver administration and Internet number assignments under a United States Department of Defense contract. In 1991, the Defense Information Systems Agency (DISA) awarded the administration and maintenance of DDN-NIC (managed by SRI up until this point) to Government Systems, Inc., who subcontracted it to the small private-sector Network Solutions, Inc.

The increasing cultural diversity of the Internet also posed administrative challenges for centralized management of the IP addresses. In October 1992, the Internet Engineering Task Force (IETF) published RFC 1366, which described the "growth of the Internet and its increasing globalization" and set out the basis for an evolution of the IP registry process, based on a regionally distributed registry model. This document stressed the need for a single Internet number registry to exist in each geographical region of the world (which would be of "continental dimensions"). Registries would be "unbiased and widely recognized by network providers and subscribers" within their region. The RIPE Network Coordination Centre (RIPE NCC) was established as the first RIR in May 1992. The second RIR, the Asia Pacific Network Information Centre (APNIC), was established in Tokyo in 1993, as a pilot project of the Asia Pacific Networking Group.

Since at this point in history most of the growth on the Internet was coming from non-military sources, it was decided that the Department of Defense would no longer fund registration services outside of the .mil TLD. In 1993 the U.S. National Science Foundation, after a competitive bidding process in 1992, created the InterNIC to manage the allocations of addresses and management of the address databases, and awarded the contract to three organizations. Registration Services would be provided by Network Solutions; Directory and Database Services would be provided by AT&T; and Information Services would be provided by General Atomics.

Over time, after consultation with the IANA, the IETF, RIPE NCC, APNIC, and the Federal Networking Council (FNC), the decision was made to separate the management of domain names from the management of IP numbers. Following the examples of RIPE NCC and APNIC, it was recommended that management of IP address space then administered by the InterNIC should be under the control of those that use it, specifically the ISPs, end-user organizations, corporate entities, universities, and individuals. As a result, the American Registry for Internet Numbers (ARIN) was established as in December 1997, as an independent, not-for-profit corporation by direction of the National Science Foundation and became the third Regional Internet Registry.

In 1998, both the IANA and remaining DNS-related InterNIC functions were reorganized under the control of ICANN, a California non-profit corporation contracted by the United States Department of Commerce to manage a number of Internet-related tasks. As these tasks involved technical coordination for two principal Internet name spaces (DNS names and IP addresses) created by the IETF, ICANN also signed a memorandum of understanding with the IAB to define the technical work to be carried out by the Internet Assigned Numbers Authority. The management of Internet address space remained with the regional Internet registries, which collectively were defined as a supporting organization within the ICANN structure. ICANN provides central coordination for the DNS system, including policy coordination for the split registry / registrar system, with competition among registry service providers to serve each top-level-domain and multiple competing registrars offering DNS services to end-users.

Internet Engineering Task Force

The Internet Engineering Task Force (IETF) is the largest and most visible of several loosely related ad-hoc groups that provide technical direction for the Internet, including the Internet Architecture Board (IAB), the Internet Engineering Steering Group (IESG), and the Internet Research Task Force (IRTF).

The IETF is a loosely self-organized group of international volunteers who contribute to the engineering and evolution of Internet technologies. It is the principal body engaged in the development of new Internet standard specifications. Much of the work of the IETF is organized into *Working Groups*. Standardization efforts of the Working Groups are often adopted by the Internet community, but the IETF does not control or patrol the Internet.

The IETF grew out of quarterly meeting of U.S. government-funded researchers, starting in January 1986. Non-government representatives were invited by the fourth IETF meeting in October 1986. The concept of Working Groups was introduced at the fifth meeting in February 1987. The seventh meeting in July 1987 was the first meeting with more than one hundred attendees. In 1992, the Internet Society, a professional membership society, was formed and IETF began to operate under it as an independent international standards body. The first IETF meeting outside of the United States was held in Amsterdam, The Netherlands, in July 1993. Today, the IETF meets three times per year and attendance has been as high as ca. 2,000 participants. Typically one in three IETF meetings are held in Europe or Asia. The number of non-US attendees is typically ca. 50%, even at meetings held in the United States.

The IETF is not a legal entity, has no governing board, no members, and no dues. The closest status resembling membership is being on an IETF or Working Group mailing list. IETF volunteers come from all over the world and from many different parts of the Internet community. The IETF works closely with and under the supervision of the Internet Engineering Steering Group (IESG) and the Internet Architecture Board (IAB). The Internet Research Task Force (IRTF) and the Internet Research Steering Group (IRSG), peer activities to the IETF and IESG under the general supervision of the IAB, focus on longer term research issues.

Request for Comments

Request for Comments (RFCs) are the main documentation for the work of the IAB, IESG, IETF, and IRTF. RFC 1, "Host Software", was written by Steve Crocker at UCLA in April 1969, well before the IETF was created. Originally they were technical memos documenting aspects of ARPANET development and were edited by Jon Postel, the first RFC Editor.

RFCs cover a wide range of information from proposed standards, draft standards, full standards, best practices, experimental protocols, history, and other informational topics. RFCs can be written by individuals or informal groups of individuals, but many are the product of a more formal Working Group. Drafts are submitted to the IESG either by individuals or by the Working Group Chair. An RFC Editor, appointed by the IAB, separate from IANA, and working in conjunction with the IESG, receives drafts from the IESG and edits, formats, and publishes them. Once an RFC is published, it is never revised. If the standard it describes changes or its information becomes obsolete, the revised standard or updated information will be re-published as a new RFC that "obsoletes" the original.

The Internet Society

The Internet Society (ISOC) is an international, nonprofit organization founded during 1992 "to assure the open development, evolution and use of the Internet for the benefit of all people throughout the world". With offices near Washington, DC, USA, and in Geneva, Switzerland, ISOC has a membership base comprising more than 80 organizational and more than 50,000 individual members. Members also form "chapters" based on either common geographical location or special interests. There are currently more than 90 chapters around the world.

ISOC provides financial and organizational support to and promotes the work of the standards settings bodies for which it is the organizational home: the Internet Engineering Task Force (IETF), the Internet Architecture Board (IAB), the Internet Engineering Steering Group (IESG), and the Internet Research Task Force (IRTF). ISOC also promotes understanding and appreciation of the Internet model of open, transparent processes and consensus-based decision-making.

Globalization and Internet Governance in the 21st Century

Since the 1990s, the Internet's governance and organization has been of global importance to governments, commerce, civil society, and individuals. The organizations which held control of certain technical aspects of the Internet were the successors of the old ARPANET oversight and the current decision-makers in the day-to-day technical aspects of the network. While recognized as the administrators of certain aspects of the Internet, their roles and their decision-making authority are limited and subject to increasing international scrutiny and increasing objections. These objections have led to the ICANN removing themselves from relationships with first the University of Southern California in 2000, and finally in September 2009, gaining autonomy from the US government by the ending of its longstanding agreements, although some contractual obligations with the U.S. Department of Commerce continued.

The IETF, with financial and organizational support from the Internet Society, continues to serve as the Internet's ad-hoc standards body and issues Request for Comments.

In November 2005, the World Summit on the Information Society, held in Tunis, called for an Internet Governance Forum (IGF) to be convened by United Nations Secretary General. The IGF opened an ongoing, non-binding conversation among stakeholders representing governments, the private sector, civil society, and the technical and academic communities about the future of Internet governance. The first IGF meeting was held in October/November 2006 with follow up meetings annually thereafter. Since WSIS, the term "Internet governance" has been broadened beyond narrow technical concerns to include a wider range of Internet-related policy issues.

Politicization of the Internet

Due to its prominence and immediacy as an effective means of mass communication, the Internet has also become more politicized as it has grown. This has led in turn, to discourses and activities that would once have taken place in other ways, migrating to being mediated by internet.

Examples include political activities such as public protest and canvassing of support and votes, but also –

- The spreading of ideas and opinions;

- Recruitment of followers, and "coming together" of members of the public, for ideas, products, and causes;

- Providing and widely distributing and sharing information that might be deemed sensitive or relates to whistleblowing (and efforts by specific countries to prevent this by censorship);

- Criminal activity and terrorism (and resulting law enforcement use, to-gether with its facilitation by mass surveillance).

Net Neutrality

On April 23, 2014, the Federal Communications Commission (FCC) was reported to be considering a new rule that would permit Internet service providers to offer content providers a faster track to send content, thus reversing their earlier net neutrality position. A possible solution to net neutrality concerns may be municipal broadband, according to Professor Susan Crawford, a legal and technology expert at Harvard Law School. On May 15, 2014, the FCC decided to consider two options regarding Internet services: first, permit fast and slow broadband lanes, thereby compromising net neutrality; and second, reclassify broadband as a telecommunication service, thereby preserving net neutrality. On November 10, 2014, President Obama recommended the FCC reclassify broadband Internet service as a telecommunications service in order to preserve net neutrality. On January 16, 2015, Republicans presented legislation, in the form of a U.S. Congress H. R. discussion draft bill, that makes concessions to net neutrality but prohibits the FCC from accomplishing the goal or enacting any further regulation affecting Internet service providers (ISPs). On January 31, 2015, AP News reported that the FCC will present the notion of applying ("with some caveats") Title II (common carrier) of the Communications Act of 1934 to the internet in a vote expected on February 26, 2015. Adoption of this notion would reclassify internet service from one of information to one of telecommunications and, according to Tom Wheeler, chairman of the FCC, ensure net neutrality. The FCC is expected to enforce net neutrality in its vote, according to the New York Times.

On February 26, 2015, the FCC ruled in favor of net neutrality by applying Title II (common carrier) of the Communications Act of 1934 and Section 706 of the Telecommunications act of 1996 to the Internet. The FCC Chairman, Tom Wheeler, commented, "This is no more a plan to regulate the Internet than the First Amendment is a plan to regulate free speech. They both stand for the same concept."

On March 12, 2015, the FCC released the specific details of the net neutrality rules. On April 13, 2015, the FCC published the final rule on its new "Net Neutrality" regulations.

Use and Culture

Email and Usenet

E-mail has often been called the killer application of the Internet. It predates the Internet, and was a crucial tool in creating it. Email started in 1965 as a way for multiple users of a time-sharing mainframe computer to communicate. Although the history is undocumented, among the first systems to have such a facility were the System Development Corporation (SDC) Q32 and the Compatible Time-Sharing System (CTSS) at MIT.

The ARPANET computer network made a large contribution to the evolution of electronic mail. An experimental inter-system transferred mail on the ARPANET shortly after its creation. In 1971 Ray Tomlinson created what was to become the standard Internet electronic mail addressing format, using the @ sign to separate mailbox names from host names.

A number of protocols were developed to deliver messages among groups of time-sharing computers over alternative transmission systems, such as UUCP and IBM's VNET email system. Email could be passed this way between a number of networks, including ARPANET, BITNET and NSFNET, as well as to hosts connected directly to other sites via UUCP.

In addition, UUCP allowed the publication of text files that could be read by many others. The News software developed by Steve Daniel and Tom Truscott in 1979 was used to distribute news and bulletin board-like messages. This quickly grew into discussion groups, known as newsgroups, on a wide range of topics. On ARPANET and NSFNET similar discussion groups would form via mailing lists, discussing both technical issues and more culturally focused topics (such as science fiction, discussed on the sflovers mailing list).

During the early years of the Internet, email and similar mechanisms were also fundamental to allow people to access resources that were not available due to the absence of online connectivity. UUCP was often used to distribute files using the 'alt.binary' groups. Also, FTP e-mail gateways allowed people that lived outside the US and Europe to download files using ftp commands written inside email messages. The file was encoded, broken in pieces and sent by email; the receiver had to reassemble and decode it later, and it was the only way for people living overseas to download items such as the earlier Linux versions using the slow dial-up connections available at the time. After the popularization of the Web and the HTTP protocol such tools were slowly abandoned.

From Gopher to the WWW

As the Internet grew through the 1980s and early 1990s, many people realized the increasing need to be able to find and organize files and information. Projects such as Archie, Gopher, WAIS, and the FTP Archive list attempted to create ways to organize distributed data. In the early 1990s, Gopher, invented by Mark P. McCahill offered a viable alternative to the World Wide Web. However, in 1993 the World Wide Web saw many advances to indexing and ease of access through search engines, which often neglected Gopher and Gopherspace. As popularity increased through ease of use, investment incentives also grew until in the middle of 1994 the WWW's popularity gained the upper hand. Then it became clear that Gopher and the other projects were doomed fall short.

One of the most promising user interface paradigms during this period was hypertext. The technology had been inspired by Vannevar Bush's "Memex" and developed through Ted Nelson's research on Project Xanadu and Douglas Engelbart's research on NLS. Many small self-contained hypertext systems had been created before, such as Apple Computer's HyperCard (1987). Gopher became the first commonly used hypertext interface to the Internet. While Gopher menu items were examples of hypertext, they were not commonly perceived in that way.

This NeXT Computer was used by Sir Tim Berners-Lee at CERN and became the world's first Web server.

In 1989, while working at CERN, Tim Berners-Lee invented a network-based implementation of the hypertext concept. By releasing his invention to public use, he ensured the technology would become widespread. For his work in developing the World Wide Web, Berners-Lee received the Millennium technology prize in 2004. One early popular web browser, modeled after HyperCard, was ViolaWWW.

A turning point for the World Wide Web began with the introduction of the Mosaic web browser in 1993, a graphical browser developed by a team at the National Center for Supercomputing Applications at the University of Illinois at Urbana-Champaign (NCSA-UIUC), led by Marc Andreessen. Funding for Mosaic came from the *High-Performance Computing and Communications Initiative*, a funding program initiated by the *High Performance Computing and Communication Act of 1991* also known as the *Gore Bill*. Mosaic's graphical interface soon became more popular than Gopher, which at the time was primarily text-based, and the WWW became the preferred interface for accessing the Internet. (Gore's reference to his role in "creating the Internet", however, was ridiculed in his presidential election campaign.

Mosaic was superseded in 1994 by Andreessen's Netscape Navigator, which replaced Mosaic as the world's most popular browser. While it held this title for some time, eventually competition from Internet Explorer and a variety of other browsers almost completely displaced it. Another important event held on January 11, 1994, was *The Superhighway Summit* at UCLA's Royce Hall. This was the "first public conference bringing together all of the major industry, government and academic leaders in the field [and] also began the national dialogue about the *Information Superhighway* and its implications."

24 Hours in Cyberspace, "the largest one-day online event" (February 8, 1996) up to that date, took place on the then-active website, *cyber24.com*. It was headed by photographer Rick Smolan. A photographic exhibition was unveiled at the Smithsonian Institution's National Museum of American History on January 23, 1997, featuring 70 photos from the project.

Search Engines

Even before the World Wide Web, there were search engines that attempted to organize the Internet. The first of these was the Archie search engine from McGill University in 1990, followed in 1991 by WAIS and Gopher. All three of those systems predated the invention of the World Wide Web but all continued to index the Web and the rest of the Internet for several years after the Web appeared. There are still Gopher servers as of 2006, although there are a great many more web servers.

As the Web grew, search engines and Web directories were created to track pages on the Web and allow people to find things. The first full-text Web search engine was Web-Crawler in 1994. Before WebCrawler, only Web page titles were searched. Another early search engine, Lycos, was created in 1993 as a university project, and was the first to achieve commercial success. During the late 1990s, both Web directories and Web search engines were popular—Yahoo! (founded 1994) and Altavista (founded 1995) were the respective industry leaders. By August 2001, the directory model had begun to give way to search engines, tracking the rise of Google (founded 1998), which had developed new approaches to relevancy ranking. Directory features, while still commonly available, became after-thoughts to search engines.

Database size, which had been a significant marketing feature through the early 2000s, was similarly displaced by emphasis on relevancy ranking, the methods by which search engines attempt to sort the best results first. Relevancy ranking first became a major issue circa 1996, when it became apparent that it was impractical to review full lists of results. Consequently, algorithms for relevancy ranking have continuously improved. Google's PageRank method for ordering the results has received the most press, but all major search engines continually refine their ranking methodologies with a view toward improving the ordering of results. As of 2006, search engine rankings are more important than ever, so much so that an industry has developed ("search engine optimizers", or "SEO") to help web-developers improve their search ranking, and an entire body of case law has developed around matters that affect search engine rankings, such as use of trademarks in metatags. The sale of search rankings by some search engines has also created controversy among librarians and consumer advocates.

On June 3, 2009, Microsoft launched its new search engine, Bing. The following month Microsoft and Yahoo! announced a deal in which Bing would power Yahoo! Search.

File Sharing

Resource or file sharing has been an important activity on computer networks from well before the Internet was established and was supported in a variety of ways including bulletin board systems (1978), Usenet (1980), Kermit (1981), and many others. The File Transfer Protocol (FTP) for use on the Internet was standardized in 1985 and is still in use today. A variety of tools were developed to aid the use of FTP by helping users discover files they might want to transfer, including the Wide Area Information Server (WAIS) in 1991, Gopher in 1991, Archie in 1991, Veronica in 1992, Jughead in 1993, Internet Relay Chat (IRC) in 1988, and eventually the World Wide Web (WWW) in 1991 with Web directories and Web search engines.

In 1999, Napster became the first peer-to-peer file sharing system. Napster used a central server for indexing and peer discovery, but the storage and transfer of files was decentralized. A variety of peer-to-peer file sharing programs and services with different levels of decentralization and anonymity followed, including: Gnutella, eDonkey2000, and Freenet in 2000, FastTrack, Kazaa, Limewire, and BitTorrent in 2001, and Poisoned in 2003.

All of these tools are general purpose and can be used to share a wide variety of content, but sharing of music files, software, and later movies and videos are major uses. And while some of this sharing is legal, large portions are not. Lawsuits and other legal actions caused Napster in 2001, eDonkey2000 in 2005, Kazaa in 2006, and Limewire in 2010 to shut down or refocus their efforts. The Pirate Bay, founded in Sweden in 2003, continues despite a trial and appeal in 2009 and 2010 that resulted in jail terms and large fines for several of its founders. File sharing remains contentious and controversial with charges of theft of intellectual property on the one hand and charges of censorship on the other.

Dot-com Bubble

Suddenly the low price of reaching millions worldwide, and the possibility of selling to or hearing from those people at the same moment when they were reached, promised to overturn established business dogma in advertising, mail-order sales, customer relationship management, and many more areas. The web was a new killer app—it could bring together unrelated buyers and sellers in seamless and low-cost ways. Entrepreneurs around the world developed new business models, and ran to their nearest venture capitalist. While some of the new entrepreneurs had experience in business and economics, the majority were simply people with ideas, and did not manage the capital influx prudently. Additionally, many dot-com business plans were predicated on the assumption that by using the Internet, they would bypass the distribution channels of existing businesses and therefore not have to compete with them; when the established businesses with strong existing brands developed their own Internet presence, these hopes were shattered, and the newcomers were left attempting to break into markets dominated by larger, more established businesses. Many did not have the ability to do so.

The dot-com bubble burst in March 2000, with the technology heavy NASDAQ Composite index peaking at 5,048.62 on March 10 (5,132.52 intraday), more than double its value just a year before. By 2001, the bubble's deflation was running full speed. A majority of the dot-coms had ceased trading, after having burnt through their venture capital and IPO capital, often without ever making a profit. But despite this, the Internet continues to grow, driven by commerce, ever greater amounts of online information and knowledge and social networking.

Mobile Phones and the Internet

The first mobile phone with Internet connectivity was the Nokia 9000 Communicator, launched in Finland in 1996. The viability of Internet services access on mobile phones was limited until prices came down from that model, and network providers started to develop systems and services conveniently accessible on phones. NTT DoCoMo in Japan launched the first mobile Internet service, i-mode, in 1999 and this is considered the birth of the mobile phone Internet services. In 2001, the mobile phone email system by Research in Motion for their BlackBerry product was launched in America. To make efficient use of the small screen and tiny keypad and one-handed operation typical of mobile phones, a specific document and networking model was created for mobile devices, the Wireless Application Protocol (WAP). Most mobile device Internet services operate using WAP. The growth of mobile phone services was initially a primarily Asian phenomenon with Japan, South Korea and Taiwan all soon finding the majority of their Internet users accessing resources by phone rather than by PC. Developing countries followed, with India, South Africa, Kenya, Philippines, and Pakistan all reporting that the majority of their domestic users accessed the Internet from a mobile phone rather than a PC. The European and North American use of the Internet was influenced by a large installed base of personal computers, and the growth of mobile phone Internet access was more gradual, but had reached national penetration levels of 20–30% in most Western countries. The cross-over occurred in 2008, when more Internet access devices were mobile phones than personal computers. In many parts of the developing world, the ratio is as much as 10 mobile phone users to one PC user.

Web Technologies

Web pages were initially conceived as structured documents based upon Hypertext Markup Language (HTML) which can allow access to images, video, and other content. Hyperlinks in the page permit users to navigate to other pages. In the earliest browsers, images opened in a separate "helper" application. Marc Andreessen's 1993 Mosaic and 1994 Netscape introduced mixed text and images for non-technical users. HTML evolved during the 1990s, leading to HTML 4 which introduced large elements of CSS styling and, later, extensions to allow browser code to make calls and ask for content from servers in a structured way (AJAX).

Historiography

There are nearly insurmountable problems in supplying a historiography of the Internet's development. The process of digitization represents a twofold challenge both for historiography in general and, in particular, for historical communication research. A sense of the difficulty in documenting early developments that led to the internet can be gathered from the quote:

"The Arpanet period is somewhat well documented because the corporation in charge – BBN – left a physical record. Moving into the NSFNET era, it became an extraordinarily decentralized process. The record exists in people's basements, in closets. ... So much of what happened was done verbally and on the basis of individual trust."

—Doug Gale (2007)

References

- Kim, Byung-Keun (2005). Internationalising the Internet the Co-evolution of Influence and Technology. Edward Elgar. pp. 51–55. ISBN 1845426754.

- "Turing's Legacy: A History of Computing at the National Physical Laboratory 1945–1995", David M. Yates, National Museum of Science and Industry, 1997, pages 126–146, ISBN 0901805947. Retrieved 19 May 2015.

- Hafner, Katie (1998). Where Wizards Stay Up Late: The Origins Of The Internet. Simon & Schuster. ISBN 0-684-83267-4.

- Mueller, Milton L. (2010). Networks and States: The Global Politics of Internet Governance. MIT Press. p. 67. ISBN 978-0-262-01459-5.

- Mueller, Milton L. (2010). Networks and States: The Global Politics of Internet Governance. MIT Press. pp. 79–80. ISBN 978-0-262-01459-5.

- Stross, Randall (22 September 2009). Planet Google: One Company's Audacious Plan to Organize Everything We Know. Simon and Schuster. ISBN 978-1-4165-4696-2. Retrieved 9 December 2012.

- Kenneth P. Birman (2005-03-25). Reliable Distributed Systems: Technologies, Web Services, and Applications. Springer-Verlag New York Incorporated. ISBN 9780387215099. Retrieved 2012-01-20.

- Hillebrand, Friedhelm (2002). Hillebrand, Friedhelm, ed. GSM and UMTS, The Creation of Global Mobile Communications. John Wiley & Sons. ISBN 0-470-84322-5.

- "The First ISP". Indra.com. August 13, 1992. Archived from the original on March 5, 2016. Retrieved 2015-10-17.

- Ruthfield, Scott (September 1995). "The Internet's History and Development From Wartime Tool to the Fish-Cam". Crossroads. 2 (1). pp. 2–4. doi:10.1145/332198.332202. Archived from the original on October 18, 2007. Retrieved April 1, 2016.

- Dewey, Caitlin (12 March 2014). "36 Ways The Web Has Changed Us". The Washington Post. Retrieved 1 August 2015.

- "What is the difference between the Web and the Internet?". W3C Help and FAQ. W3C. 2009. Retrieved 16 July 2015.

- Strickland, Jonathan (2007-12-28). "How Web 2.0 Works". computer.howstuffworks.com. Retrieved 2015-02-28.

- Sepulveda, Ambassador Daniel A. (January 21, 2015). "The World Is Watching Our Net Neutrality Debate, So Let's Get It Right". Wired (website). Retrieved January 20, 2015.

- Weisman, Jonathan (January 19, 2015). "Shifting Politics of Net Neutrality Debate Ahead of F.C.C. Vote". New York Times. Retrieved January 20, 2015.

- Staff (January 16, 2015). "H. R. _ 114th Congress, 1st Session [Discussion Draft] – To amend the Communications Act of 1934 to ensure Internet openness..." (PDF). U. S. Congress. Retrieved January 20, 2015.

- Lohr, Steve (February 2, 2015). "In Net Neutrality Push, F.C.C. Is Expected to Propose Regulating Internet Service as a Utility". New York Times. Retrieved February 2, 2015.

- Flaherty, Anne (January 31, 2015). "Just whose Internet is it? New federal rules may answer that". Associated Press. Retrieved January 31, 2015.

- Fung, Brian (January 2, 2015). "Get ready: The FCC says it will vote on net neutrality in February". Washington Post. Retrieved January 2, 2015.

Permissions

Index

www.ingramcontent.com/pod-product-compliance
Lightning Source LLC
Jackson TN
JSHW052153130125
77033JS00004B/175